A HISTORY OF THE WORLD IN 100 WEAPONS

A HISTORY OF THE WORLD IN 100 WEAPONS

CHRIS MCNAB

FOREWORD BY ANDREW ROBERTS

OSPREY
PUBLISHING

First published in Great Britain in 2011 by Osprey Publishing,
This revised edition published 2012 by Osprey Publishing,
PO Box 883, Oxford, OX1 9PL, UK
PO Box 3985, New York, NY 10185-3985, USA
Email: info@ospreypublishing.com

Osprey Publishing is part of the Osprey Group.

ISBN: 978 1 7820 0370 0

Editing and picture research by Kate Moore and Emily Holmes
Page layout by Myriam Bell Design, France
Index by Alison Worthington
Typeset in Optima and Minion Pro
Originated by PDQ Media, Bungay, UK
Printed in China through World Print Ltd.

14 15 16 17 18   11 10 9 8 7 6 5 4 3 2

IMPERIAL WAR MUSEUM COLLECTIONS
Many of the photos in this book come from the Imperial War Museum's huge collections
which cover all aspects of conflict involving Britain and the Commonwealth since the start
of the twentieth century. These rich resources are available online to search, browse and buy
at www.iwmcollections.org.uk. In addition to Collections Online, you can visit the Visitor
Rooms where you can explore over eight million photographs, thousands of hours of moving
images, the largest sound archive of its kind in the world, thousands of diaries and letters
written by people in wartime, and a huge reference library.
    To make an appointment, call (020) 7416 5320, or e-mail mail@iwm.org.uk.
Imperial War Museum www.iwm.org.uk

www.ospreypublishing.com

FRONT COVER: An 1851 US Navy Colt. (The Bridgeman Art Library © Civil War Archive);
The Soviet T-34/76 Model 1943. (Artwork by Jim Laurier © Osprey Publishing Ltd.);
An ornately decorated halberd made for the Trabanten Guard in the 16th century.
(© Wallace Collection, London/The Bridgeman Art Library).
BACK COVER: Capture of Evreux, 1487 from *Chroniques de France ou de Saint Denis.*
(akg-images); F-15 Eagle (USAF).

EDITOR'S NOTE:
In the compilation of this volume we relied on the extensive Osprey library of previous
military history publications. Works of particular relevance were *Besieged* by Dr Duncan
Campbell, *Infantry Tactics of World War II* by Dr Stephen Bull, *Nuclear Dawn* by James
Delgano, *F-15 Eagle Engaged* by Steve Davies, *The Katana* by Dr Stephen Turnbull, *B-52
Stratofortress Units in Combat 1955–73* by Jon Lake, *Confederate Ironclad vs Union Ironclad*
by Ron Field, *Nimitiz-Class Aircraft Carriers* by Brad Elward, *SPAD XIII vs Fokker D VII* by
Jon Guttman, *Fw 190 vs B-17* by Robert Forsyth, *M1 Abrams vs T-72, V-2 Ballistic Missile,*
and *Unmanned Aerial Vehicles* by Steven J. Zaloga.

CONTENTS

FOREWORD by Andrew Roberts   6

INTRODUCTION   9

THE ANCIENT WORLD   12
5000 BC–AD 500

THE MEDIEVAL WORLD   44
500–1500

THE EARLY MODERN WORLD   88
1500–1800

IMPERIAL WARS   118
1800–1914

WORLD WAR I   160
1914–18

WORLD WAR II   208
1939–45

MODERN WARFARE   278
1945–PRESENT

ACKNOWLEDGMENTS   378

ENDNOTES   378

INDEX   379

FOREWORD

THE IDEA OF WRITING A HISTORY OF THE WORLD IN ONE hundred weapons is a truly inspired one, for warfare has been the driving force of history, and we cannot really consider the story of mankind without inevitably looking at how wars have shaped our cultures and societies. That might be a disconcerting comment upon the human condition, but it's nonetheless true.

Certainly, no-one could be better qualified than Dr Chris McNab to write such a definitive book about the interaction between world history and individual weapons. His expertise straddles the centuries and all the weapon types, as witnessed by the eclectic nature of the books that he has either written, edited, or contributed to, such as *Tools of Violence: Guns, Tanks and Dirty Bombs, Firearms, Fighting Techniques of the Oriental World, Guns: A Visual History, The AK47, Gunfighters: The Outlaws and Their Weapons, The Machine Gun Story,* and *Deadly Force: Firearms and American Law Enforcement,* as well as many others. This tremendous body of scholarship means that his readers are in safe hands when he tells us about the weapons themselves, how they were deployed, how battlefield tactics evolved to accommodate their lethal power, and what it was like both to wield and try to defend against them.

The best weaponry affords defensive as well as offensive capability, principally through affording the maximum possible physical distance between the attacker and his opponent. From the day that the first cave dweller threw a rock at his enemy or prey rather than grappling hand-to-hand, this principle has governed the development of weaponry, right the way up to the stealth bombers and drones of the present day. To strike yet still remain out of reach of immediate counterattack: that has always been the key.

Magnificently diverse though the hundred weapons presented in this superbly illustrated book undoubtedly are, I believe that all weapons of war can be divided into only eight categories. These "families" of weapons comprise:

Artillery – including cannon, howitzers, shells, and
   anti-aircraft guns
Handheld Weapons – axes, swords, pikes, halberds, bayonets,
   and suicide vests
Handheld Projectiles – longbows and crossbows, muskets
   and rifles, flamethrowers, machine-guns, hand and
   rocket-propelled grenades, and bazookas
Missiles – Roman *ballistae*, Greek Fire, torpedoes, V-weapons,
   SCUDs, Sidewinders, Exocets, Tomahawks, Cruise and
   intercontinental ballistic missiles
Land Armor – siege-trains, heavy-armored cavalry,
   and tracked vehicles (primarily tanks)
Seaborne – triremes, ships of the line, submarines,
   dreadnoughts, cruisers, and aircraft carriers
Airborne – zeppelins, fighter planes, poison gas, bombers,
   helicopters, jet fighters, stealth bombers, and Unmanned
   Aerial Vehicles (UAVs)

Bombs: landmines, depth charges, atomic bombs,
    and Improvised Explosive Devices (IEDs)

The fascination of this book lies in how human ingenuity – and inventors of the caliber of Messrs Mauser, Browning, Thompson, Baker, Gatling, Maxim, Vickers, Lewis, Colt, Kalashnikov, Schmeisser, Messerschmitt, and so on – has learnt from past achievements going back centuries to deliver ever more efficiently destructive power. Great commanders have therefore constantly had to innovate new tactics, and on occasion entirely new strategies, in order to make the best use of new weaponry.

Historically, people have been quick to learn how to copy, improve, and perfect weapons that have been used against them. The very nature of warfare, where enemy weapons can be captured on the battlefield and instantly analyzed, facilitates this important phenomenon. Although in 1720 BC the Hysos invasion of Egypt was immeasurably aided by the use of composite bows and chariots, for example, it did not take long for the defeated Egyptians to learn from them and use both to devastating effect themselves. Similarly, many weapons intended in an offensive capacity can be quickly adapted to defense. Perhaps the supreme example of this came in March 1799 when the British admiral, Sir Sidney Smith, captured seven French vessels on their way to Acre, which carried the siege train with which Napoleon Bonaparte had hoped to destroy the city's walls. Once mounted on those self same walls in defense, the heavy guns meant that Smith was able to deny the French the city, and thus halt Napoleon's march on the Orient.

Very few weapons have been invented and not used, and no weapon can be dis-invented, as the world has discovered with the atom bomb. Although Ronald Reagan was routinely denounced as a warmonger, it was he who decreed in 1986 that the neutron bomb – which was capable of killing people but leaving buildings intact – should no longer be produced, much to the chagrin of its inventor, Samuel T. Cohen. But such examples are rare in history.

In the course of writing my history of the Second World War, *The Storm of War*, Lieutenant-Colonel Alexandr Anatolyevich Kulikov, formerly of the Red Army, showed me around the Museum of Tank Construction at Kubinka, about 40 miles outside Moscow. With no fewer than four hundred different types of tank it is the largest museum of its kind in the world, and I heartily recommend it to any reader of this book. What I saw there entirely supports Dr McNab in his contention that sheer numbers of mass-produced but inferior weapons – such as the T-34 that took on and defeated the better but fewer German tanks – can overwhelm superior weaponry, and that simplicity of production and use is vital.

Of course many factors other than numbers can lead to victory or defeat in battle – courage, leadership, morale, Intelligence, speed of movement, lie of the land, and so on – but none is more important than the amount and quality of weaponry deployed. In the calendar year 1944, for example, when Britain produced 28,000 warplanes and the Russians and Germans each produced 40,000, the United States churned off their production lines no fewer than 98,000 warplanes (several marks of which are included in this book). It was an incredible achievement, and an unmistakable pointer to which side would ultimately prevail. This book is full of amazing facts; I didn't know, for example, that Sam Colt created the industrial production line some 60 years before Henry Ford, but it serves to remind us that the desire for military victory, even more than the desire for financial profit, is the true mainspring of industrial development.

Some weapons can be useful far outside their allotted hour in history. Dr McNab reminds us that the ancient order to "Fix bayonets!" was heard as recently as 2004, when a detachment of the Argyll and Sutherland Highlanders had to use cold steel after they were pinned down by Iraqi insurgents and started to run out of ammunition. The attack was wholly successful, and the circumstances will thrill the heart of any reader. As for other supposedly "obsolete" weapons, there are some military historians who argue that the British Army's accuracy, stopping power, and rate of fire would have been higher at the battle of Waterloo had it used longbows instead of Brown Bess muskets.

The sheer aesthetic of some of the 16th, 17th and 18th century weapons, including the beautiful workmanship of the rapiers, halberds, and arquebuses, is beautifully depicted in this sumptuous Osprey edition, making this book something of a collector's item in itself. Yet however attractive some of these weapons might look, we must not blind ourselves to the terrible uses to which they were designed to be put. In his magisterial Nobel Prize Lecture of 1986, the great Jewish novelist Elie Wiesel pointed out that:

> Of course some wars may have been necessary or inevitable, but none was ever regarded as holy. For us, a holy war is a contradiction in terms. War dehumanizes, war diminishes, war debases all those who wage it. The Talmud says *"Talmidei hukhamim shemarbin shalom baolam"* (It is the wise men who will bring about peace). Perhaps, because wise men remember best.

So what of the future? Technological advances seem to have been developing exponentially in recent decades, bringing with them ever-deadlier weapons, yet conflicts are becoming less likely to be state-on-state affairs so much as the kind of guerilla and insurgency warfare seen around the world since 1945, and most notably recently in the Global War Against Terror. Dr McNab reminds us that IEDs – such as a roadside bomb made out of Plaster of Paris and painted over to look like a kerbstone – have led to over half of all British and American casualties in Iraq.

Overall for the past half-millennium, the West has had the edge, especially when it comes to retaining control of the air, which proved to be so important in the Second World War and other postwar conflicts. Yet with the Chinese now making decisive strides in weapon technology – especially in the field of drones, lasers, nuclear-powered aircraft carriers, and space – perhaps the West's days of primacy are now numbered. It might even be that whichever country can neutralize its enemies' space satellites first might decide the future hegemony of the world, almost without any fighting needing to be done terrestrially. Whatever the future holds, we know that it is vital to be on the cutting edge of weapons technology, and this book tells us how this has been achieved over the past millennia.

I therefore take great pleasure in introducing this fine book to you.

Andrew Roberts
December 2010

INTRODUCTION

TECHNOLOGY IS ONE OF THE MOTIVE POWERS OF history. Inventions great and small, from fire-making wooden drills to Global Positioning Satellite (GPS), not only reshape individual human existence but, to varying degrees, human consciousness itself. Think, for example, how mobile phones have altered inter-human relations, language, and culture. At the same time, technology can act as an engine of wider social and political revolution. We need only reflect on the invention of the wheel in Mesopotamia in the 4th millennium BC, or on the application of steam power to transport and manufacturing during the Industrial Revolution, to comprehend what it can achieve. Seminal technologies such as these can also transform the nature of state power and international relations, and in so doing lead either to cooperation or – the subject of this book – conflict.

TRANSFORMATIVE WEAPONS

Warfare is, sadly for humankind, one of the most technologically and intellectually productive social conditions. Ever since prehistoric man first grabbed a rock as a "force-multiplier" for his fist, war has been fundamentally bound up with the attempt to achieve technological superiority over the enemy. The incentives to design decisive weaponry are powerful. The 19th-century inventor Hiram Maxim was experimenting with domestic inventions relating to gas and electricity, until one day a friend recommended: "Hang your electricity. If you want to make your fortune, invent something to help these fool Europeans kill each other more quickly!" True to the advice, Maxim went away and invented the machine-gun, which has been scything down all nationalities, not just Europeans, ever since. Maxim's motivation to invent new weaponry was primarily commercial, but warfare also adds further grinding compulsions, such as patriotism, curiosity, and, most important, fear.

This book attempts to view history through the prism of military invention. Any claim to define the "Top 100" of history's most influential weapons is contentious, and doubtless will inspire much debate and disagreement. Broadly speaking, the weapons here have either helped to shape history itself (military or otherwise), or they act as important snapshots of military technology and tactical thinking at a particular moment in time. Examples of the former include the flintlock musket, which became the dominant tool of infantry warfare for three centuries, and the intercontinental ballistic missile (ICBM), the weapon system that defined the politics of the Cold War. The latter include the German Me 262 fighter jet and the SCUD missile, weapons that were salient in their field and time, if only by laying foundations for future developments.

A persistent question underpins this book. Why do some weapons technologies succeed, while others fail, or at least disappoint? The answer is not straightforward, and can't be resolved simply by pointing to technological excellence. In the armored battles of World War II, the Germans on many occasions fielded armor, artillery, and aircraft that were superior to anything the Allies presented, yet they still lost the *Materialschlacht* (material warfare), overwhelmed by the superior numbers of often, although not always, inferior weapons.

That example alone, however, gives us one important quality of many influential weapons – widespread distribution. Regardless of its sophistication, if a weapon is not delivered prolifically, its battlefield effect will be limited. Distribution is itself dependent upon a whole host of factors, including manufacturing processes, production and purchasing budgets, availability of raw materials, market conditions, and so on. From such complexity, the message seems to emerge that in tactical scenarios at least, it is far better to have a simpler weapon in the hands of many than an advanced weapon in the hands of few. The AK47 assault rifle, for example, is actually a fairly rudimentary firearm, yet the fact that 80 million AK-type weapons have been distributed since 1947 has literally reshaped the nature of post-World War II global conflict. The same could not be said for, say, excellent weapons such as the Heckler & Koch HK33 or the Beretta AR70/90.

FUNCTIONALITY AND SUPERIORITY

The AK47 perfectly illustrates another quality that sets a weapon apart – functionality. Technology and functionality don't always meet happily in the middle, as the goals of inventors and the expectations of soldiers are not always the same. While a scientist might strive to invent a weapon that breaks new boundaries, a soldier wants a robust tool that will simply work well and keep on working *in extremis* – any weapon that fails mechanically threatens a warrior's very survival. Similarly, the weapon must also be easy to use, as complex procedures tend to be forgotten in the midst of battle. During the ancient, medieval, and Early Modern periods, simple weapons tended not to be too much of a problem at the infantry and cavalry levels, which were dominated by blades, staff weapons, and later, muzzle-loading firearms and cannon. (Siege warfare admittedly produced plenty of impractical engines that consumed more time, effort, and materials than warranted.) Yet from the 19th century, the pace of technological

change produced legions of overworked and impractical designs, as engineers crafted weapons they felt could achieve superiority on the battlefield largely by technological virtues. For example, during the 1960s the US Army developed the M551 Sheridan Armored Reconnaissance/Airborne Assault Vehicle, armed with a dual-purpose M81E1 152mm gun/launcher system. The gun/ launcher was designed to fire both conventional high-explosive anti-tank (HEAT) shells and MGM-51 Shillelagh missiles from the same tube, to cover both medium- and long-range gunnery requirements. In reality, the system was over-complex and inefficient, and the tank's neglected armor requirements meant that the vehicle suffered high losses from RPGs and mines during its service in Vietnam. The later Abrams tank, by contrast, combined a straightforward, high-velocity smoothbore cannon with excellent fire control, ease of operation, and resilient armor to become arguably the best postwar main battle tank (MBT) in the world.

To emphasize simplicity of *use*, however, is not to say that the weapon itself cannot be of state-of-the-art technology. Warfare produces the curious situation in which both the brilliance and brutality of humankind are revealed in the same inventive activities. (Think of the development of the V-2 rocket system during World War II, for which an estimated 20,000 slave laborers died.) Whatever their purpose, it is undeniable that machine-guns, atomic weapons, air-to-air missiles, and helicopter gunships are all astonishing works of engineering and science. Furthermore, since 1945 we have entered a world in which technology truly can be king of the battlefield, in the right conditions and as long as it is allied with good tactics and training. In the utterly one-sided 1991 Gulf War, the US-led coalition was quite effortlessly dominant over the technologically inferior Iraqi forces. Its major warfighting systems were computer linked through aerial and satellite surveillance platforms that cast an all-seeing electronic eye over occupied Kuwait and Iraq. The result was that thousands of Iraqi armored vehicles, artillery pieces, command posts, bunkers, and other facilities were wiped out by air-launched weapons before their crews were even aware they were under attack, and in armored engagements US M1A1 Abrams and British Challenger MBTs destroyed their opponents at thousands of yards without experiencing significant return fire. At least in terms of conventional wars, it does seem that technological advantage, as long as it is of sufficient scale, can be a war-winning element.

CONTEXTUAL WAR

Having argued the case for technology, we need to pull back a little. A weapon system may well be available, easy to use, reliable, and technologically advanced, but such status still, ironically, doesn't guarantee that it will be battle-winning. The fact remains that however good the weapon system, it is still operated by people, with all their fallibilities. The way weapons are applied tactically, above everything, is critical to what they achieve. The Soviet T-34 tank, for example, is rightly included in this book, but its achievements would have been that much greater had thousands not been wasted through amateurish Soviet tactics and training – only its huge volumes and exceptional qualities saved it from complete annihilation at the hands of skilled German tank and anti-tank gun crews. Looking further back in time, the pike was little more than a long wooden pole with a spike on one end, but used in intelligent fashion by Swiss pikemen or Landsknecht mercenaries during the 15th and 16th centuries, it became a weapon that unnerved an entire continent. In modern times, professional soldiers often rightly claim that training will more than compensate for even mediocre equipment. (For many years, the US Marine Corps virtually wore outdated weapons and equipment as badges of honor.) Following the 1991 Gulf War, many US Army tank crews even suggested that the outcome of their armored battles would still have been the same if they had been riding in Iraqi T-72s and the Iraqis had their M1A1 Abrams.

One other contextual point to remember is that the technology doesn't necessarily have to be of the fighting variety to dictate the terms of conflict. In fact, although outside the scope of this book, there are numerous non-martial technologies that have helped mold the face of warfare. The scale and human cost of wars, for example, were magnified enormously by the introduction of the railways during the 19th century. Railways enabled the effective deployment and sustenance of mass armies in the field, increasing both the regularity and size of battles, and driving up the death tolls commensurately. It is noteworthy that the US Civil War (1861–65) was the first major conflict to rely on rail supply, and it cost the United States 600,000 dead – more than the death toll of all subsequent US conflicts combined – with battles at an average frequency of one every four days.

Other technologies boast similar authority over history. The telegraph, radio, ship's rudder, nuclear powerplants, artificial lighting, lasers, GPS, steam engines, internal combustion engines – such inventions have plugged easily into warfare as much as they have altered civilian lifestyles. Many were, in fact, first developed within a military context, only later to prove valuable for wider, more equable living. Historians, for instance, often credit Henry Ford with establishing production line assembly, but in actual fact Samuel Colt was using such processes 60 years earlier to manufacture his revolvers. The boundaries between civilian and military technology are therefore more blurred than we care to admit. It often doesn't take much to "weaponize" a civilian technology, or turn the core technology of a weapon to more gentle purposes.

PAST, PRESENT, AND FUTURE

Going back to our earlier question about why some weapons succeed and others fail, our analysis hasn't entirely led us to a definitive answer. Essentially, the viability and performance of a weapon system depends on myriad mechanical, industrial, personal, and tactical factors all coming together in a single device, and at an advantageous time and place. Furthermore, in one context a weapon system can excel, while in others it becomes a positive burden – a 50-ton MBT is a force to be reckoned with in open landscape, but stick it in narrow, rubble-strewn streets without adequate infantry cover, then it suddenly becomes as awkward and vulnerable as a wounded dinosaur.

What we have here, nevertheless, are 100 weapons that seem to punch through this complexity to take a deserved place in history. The technological journey we shall make from the ancient past to the computerized present is huge, and leads us from fire-hardened wooden spears through to sea-skimming guided anti-ship missiles. Such a journey is technologically fascinating, but we should always remind ourselves that the end result is endlessly, terribly, the same – people die or suffer a lifetime of debilitating injury. That same result will unfortunately be played out thousands, perhaps millions, of times in the future, when weaponry promises to achieve levels of sophistication that make science fiction appear nostalgic. We must therefore approach the study of fighting technology with fascination, but also with humility and a certain trepidation.

THE ANCIENT WORLD
5000 BC–AD 500

FLINT AXE

THE SPECIFIC ORIGINS OF HUMANKIND'S FIRST WEAPONS are lost in time. At some point in prehistory, human beings picked up sticks or rocks with violent intent, and smashed them into other people, awakening a world of dark possibilities. Thus, unfortunately, were the beginnings of a technological evolution that would eventually lead to Stealth fighters and GPS-guided bombs.

WEAPONS OF OPPORTUNITY

During the Stone Age, which roughly takes history up to about 3000 BC, primitive weaponry gradually became more practical. While the first combat tools would have been objects of opportunity picked from a tree or from the ground, over time the available materials were shaped and crafted specifically for the purpose of killing or inflicting injury. Sticks, for example, were crudely sharpened, and their points fire-hardened to make spears. In due course, these spears received separate heads made from splinters of stone or bone, increasing both penetration and the severity of the injury inflicted. Indeed, some early spears were specifically designed to leave their spearhead inside the victim when the spear was withdrawn, maximizing the wounding effect.

In terms of bladed weapons, evidence from across Asia and Africa indicates that basic stone cutting implements were in

BELOW: An early example of a simple flint axe head discovered in rural England and now housed in the Devizes Museum. (The Art Archive)

ABOVE: A beautiful example of an axe-head from the Neolithic period and discovered in Wiltshire, England – the same county where Stonehenge is found. The Neolithic period is characterized by the advent of ground and polished axe heads. Originally flint was the material of choice but it was increasingly replaced with harder-wearing metals. (akg-images/Erich Lessing)

use up to 2.5 million years ago. Over time, the techniques of lithic reduction refined the rudimentary blades – by chipping away flakes of rock with a hammerstone, a single rock could acquire a relatively practical cutting edge. Thus prehistoric man was able to produce a basic range of knives, which would serve as both hunting and cooking implements. It wouldn't take much of a leap of imagination to realize that a blade that could kill an animal, could do the same to a human.

At some point during this vast period of time, two critical changes occurred. First, fixing a bladed weapon to a hilt or grip significantly improved its power through principles of leverage, while also providing a protective distance, albeit a small one, between user and prey/victim. Second, techniques of lithic reduction were significantly improved, including the use of "pressure flaking" – using antler or bone to chip off very small pieces of rock, producing a more refined edge. Flint was particularly responsive to

these techniques, hence flint weaponry – be it arrowheads, speartips, knives, or the flint axe featured here – reached considerable levels of sophistication. In areas with a volcanic geology, obsidian was another stone ideally suited to creating pressure-flaked blades, which had edges often rivaling those of modern blades in terms of sharpness, although not in durability. Blades could either be straight edged or serrated, the latter useful for cutting through bone or gristle when preparing meat.

LEVERAGE AND POWER

Bringing together improved blades with the principles of leverage, battle axes were developed that were easily capable of inflicting a fatal head injury or shattering a limb bone. Stone axes would be amongst the most highly prized of prehistoric weapons. Examples from the Neolithic period typically feature a cutting head (or a more rounded club head) fitted into a partially split or bored-through hardwood haft, and lashed firmly into place with animal sinew. Greater adhesion between head and shaft was achieved by using birch-tar, one of history's earliest glues. Some designs were even more elaborate, fitting the axe head into a sleeve of antler or horn, which was in turn bound to the shaft. The sleeve served to lessen the impact on the stone when the axe was being used, which in turn reduced the

risk of splitting the haft. Axe head shape varied from very broad, rounded configurations to long, thin blades that created a basic adze.

The hafts from Stone Age axes have not survived to the present day. Yet based on later examples, haft length was likely to have been a factor in separating war axes from general-purpose hand axes. Battle axes typically have a haft about the length of an adult human's arm, providing maximum practical leverage and fighting distance. Such devices laid the foundations of the very idea of weaponry itself, which once metal-working arrived would reach new heights of lethality.

LEFT: Two examples of flint axes dating from 1 million BC or the Paleolithic period, discovered by archaeologists in France. (akg-images/Album/Oronoz)

BOW

The bow was a true game-changer in the history of weapons development. Its origins, as with so many ancient weapons, are uncertain. Stone arrowheads have been discovered in Africa that date back to 40000–25000 BC, and it is believed that flighted arrows probably appeared before 18000 BC. By the Mesolithic (20000–7500 BC) and Neolithic periods, (7500–3500 BC), we have cave artworks specifically depicting hunters killing antelope, bear, and other large creatures with bow and arrows.

OPPOSITE: A beautiful Assyrian relief showing King Ashubanipal on his chariot from the ancient palace of Nineveh, which was located on the banks of the Tigris now in modern-day Iraq. The relief dates from *c.* 650 BC and clearly shows the use of a composite bow by the king while on a hunting trip. (The Art Archive)

SELF BOWS

These early weapons would have been rudimentary self bows (or simple bows), made from a single piece of wood, horn, or bone and stringed with either tough plant material or animal sinew. At first the bow wood was likely to have been unseasoned and green, a type that was easily available but had limited durability and power. The eventual switch to seasoned woods provided far greater properties of compression and release, increasing the range and the force (and hence the penetration) of the weapon. Classic bow woods are ash, oak, elm, and yew, which in their seasoned forms, and properly cut,

ABOVE: The first surviving representation of the composite bow is that carried by Naram-Sîn, an ancient king of Mesopotamia who reigned in the 3rd century BC. This is a section of his victory monument which is now held in the Louvre Museum and his attendants are shown carrying composite bows. (Musée National du Louvre, Paris, SB4. Fields-Carré Collection)

specimens from Denmark measure up to 5ft 6in (1.7m) in length. Yet archery truly came of age in the Middle East and Asia during the Bronze Age (about 3500–700 BC), alongside the introduction of worked metals. Metal arrowheads offered better penetration compared to most stone types, and could be crafted into shapes that delivered more serious injuries, such as backward-facing barbs that were harder to extract from the body. Metal tools also made the process of bowmaking much more controllable, leading to a fascinating variety of bow shapes and sizes. Bows became curved, recurved, double curved, asymmetric, triangular, or B-shaped, each delivering different power characteristics.

COMPOSITE BOWS

Material construction also moved forward. "Backed" bows appeared, these multiplying the elastic properties of the self bow by gluing strips of bone or animal sinew to the back of the stave. More sophisticated yet was the composite bow, typically made of three layers of material – a wooden core with animal horn glued to the face of the stave and sinew to the back. Composite bows were typically shorter than self bows, but they gave exceptional power – their pull weights could reach 150lb (68kg) – making them ideal for both foot

BELOW: Two Turkish composite bows and one set of arrows. Despite its small size, the composite bow could pull weights up to 150lb (68kg). (akg-images/Erich Lessing)

provide both the strength and the elasticity needed for a good bow. Power was improved by cutting the bow so that the sapwood sat on the bowface while the heartwood was on the inside – the sapwood was more flexible, meaning the bow could be drawn back further, while the heartwood gave good properties of compression, both these features adding to the strength of the bow release.

Some of the earliest extant examples of bows come from northern Europe (particularly Denmark and northern Germany), and date back as far as 9000 BC. In their unstrung form they have either a straight or slightly curved shape, and

ABOVE: An artistic recreation of Parthian horsemen from the 3rd century AD. Parthian horse-archers relied on the composite bow as their main weapon of attack for over five centuries. (Artwork by Angus McBride © Osprey Publishing Ltd.)

soldiers and mounted warriors. Composite bows had superior range compared to the self bow, despite the reduction in length. When the people of Hyksos invaded Egypt, for example, around 1720 BC, the Egyptians found that their rivals' composite bows outranged their self bows by up to 200yds (182m). The gradual 50-year takeover of Egypt by the Hyksos was not only a military affair, but the use of composite bows, amongst other technologies (such as the penetrating axe and the chariot), was a root cause of their success.

Composite bows were first used with militarily significant effect by chariot-borne Sumerian, Hittite, Egyptian, and Assyrian warriors from the 3rd millennium BC (see next entry). They revolutionized the art of missile warfare, giving the range and penetration that made bows lethally practical battlefield weapons. Archers could work dismounted, operating in units to deliver volley fire, while others such as the Scythians and Parthians could fight from horseback, using double-arched composite bows on the move with astounding precision.

By the time of the rise of ancient Greece and Rome in the 1st millennium BC, therefore, archery had established itself as a key component of both cavalry and infantry warfare, although the skill required to be a good archer meant bowmen still largely formed the secondary portions of the ranks. Bows gave soldiers a lethality that wasn't dependant on sheer muscle, auguring the "democratization" of the battlefield eventually brought by firearms.

CHARIOT

THE WAR CHARIOT EMERGED OUT OF THE FUSION OF two fundamental social developments. First was the invention of the wheel – evidence for wheeled vehicles, mainly unwieldy carts, dates back to the Middle East of the 4th millennium BC. At roughly the same time, horses became domesticated rather than wild food, although these animals would have been generally small and weak compared to many of today's creatures.

MOBILE WARFARE

The synergy between horse and wheeled cart therefore began its journey. By the 3rd millennium BC, horse-powered carts were familiar, although the hefty nature of early carts meant that oxen were preferred for pulling heavy loads. Yet during this millennium the military also saw the potential of the new transportation. Evidence suggests that the Sumerians produced the predecessor of the war chariot, the "battle wagon." These were essentially boxy wooden carts set on four solid wooden wheels and drawn by a pair of onagers. Within the cart stood a javelin-armed soldier, next to the driver. Both speed and maneuverability were unimpressive – the cart probably delivered little more than a human running pace and the four-wheel design meant it would have been hard to turn out of a straight line. But change was on the horizon...

True war chariots emerged around 2000 BC, possibly in Central Asia. The four wheels were replaced by only two, these supporting a small two-man platform made of a lighter wood frame, typically cedar, with a floor made from leather straps.

OPPOSITE: A unit of Egyptian chariots deploy for battle, as displayed on the Qadesh relief, at the temple of Rameses II, cut into the rock at Abydos. Note the line of spear-armed troops, who could be runners operating in support of the chariots. (Fields-Carré Collection)

OPPOSITE PAGE, TOP: The Battle Standard of Ur is a Sumerian artifact discovered in the 1920s during an archaeological dig in the ancient city of Ur located in modern-day Iraq (south of Baghdad). The scene, which would have once adorned the royal cemetery, shows four-wheeled battlewagons equipped with quivers containing short spears. (British Museum, London, WA121201. Fields-Carré Collection)

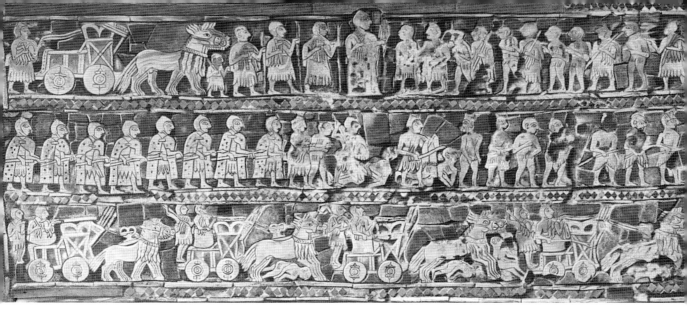

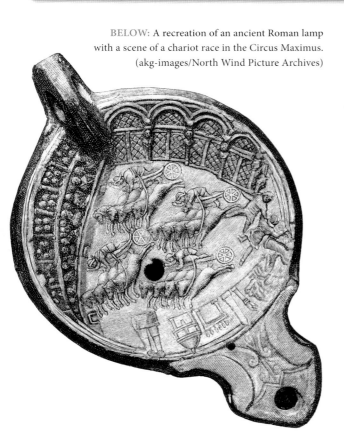

BELOW: A recreation of an ancient Roman lamp with a scene of a chariot race in the Circus Maximus. (akg-images/North Wind Picture Archives)

A two-man crew fulfilled the same roles – driver and fighter. The soldiers also wore armor, usually made from thick layers of animal skin protected by scales of bronze or copper. Pulled by the best horses the state could find, these chariots were fast – top speed was about 24mph (39km/h) – and nimble.

The chariot's appearance on the battlefield had the same disruptive effect on tactics, at least on regions with conducive flatlands, as tanks would have in the 20th century. Their use spread rapidly, rippling outwards from Central Asia into the Middle East, India and East Asia, and upwards through the Mediterranean into Europe. In doing so, the design was perfected, particularly by the Egyptians, whose takeover by the Hyksos from 1720 BC had first introduced them to chariot warfare. The Egyptians replaced the two solid wheels with far lighter spoked wheels, and moved the chariot axle from the front or middle of the platform to the rear, producing a much-improved turning circle. The Egyptians also largely replaced the javelin with the composite bow (see previous entry) as the primary chariot weapon. Indeed, the composite bow/chariot became the defining pairing, the chariot providing fast deployment, while the bow gave long-range killing capability.

CHARIOTS IN ACTION DURING THE ROMAN INVASION OF BRITAIN, 55 BC

" Their [the Britons'] mode of fighting with their chariots is this: firstly, they drive about in all directions and throw their weapons and generally break the ranks of the enemy with the very dread of their horses and the noise of their wheels; and when they have worked themselves in between the troops of horse, leap from their chariots and engage on foot. The charioteers in the meantime withdraw some little distance from the battle, and so place themselves with the chariots that, if their masters are overpowered by the number of the enemy, they may have a ready retreat to their own troops. Thus they display in battle the speed of horse, [together with] the firmness of infantry; and by daily practice and exercise attain to such expertness that they are accustomed, even on a declining and steep place, to check their horses at full speed, and manage and turn them in an instant and run along the pole, and stand on the yoke, and thence betake themselves with the greatest celerity to their chariots again. "

– Julius Caesar[1]

ABOVE: The famous statue of Boudicca, queen of the Iceni, a Celtic tribe, who led an uprising against the occupying forces of the Roman Empire. Despite their use of war chariots, the Celts were eventually overpowered by the better-organized Roman forces. (i-Stock)

LEFT: The battle of Kadesh in 1274 BC is one of the most famous battles of the ancient world. It was a colossal encounter between the two-man Egyptian chariot and the three-man Hittite chariot. The latter displayed a major advance in chariot technology as they were the first to use a spear in conjunction with a chariot. The battle was a stalemate. (Artwork by Adam Hook © Osprey Publishing Ltd.)

CHARIOT TACTICS

Tactically, chariots provided a means to assault infantry ranks at range, inflicting attrition and disrupting formations. They did so by zipping across the battlefield at speed, closing to within bow range – but staying outside that of the self bows used by many enemy foot-archers – and loosing showers of arrows into the unfortunate soldiery. If the enemy charged, the charioteers could about turn and disappear at speed, but if the enemy spread out, they would provide more isolated targets for the charioteers to pick off. In chariot versus chariot encounters, the opposing forces would thunder at each another, fire their arrows on the fly, then mutually about turn (maintaining fire on the turn) – no one wanted to risk wrecking an expensive chariot through crashing into each other. The Egyptians also pioneered chariots as a defensive shield for the infantry. The infantry would advance behind the chariots, the chariots fighting off enemy chariots and bringing their infantry up close for a rapid assault on the enemy lines.

In time, chariots became a visible representation of military wealth, and chariot battles grew to epic proportions – at the battle of Kadesh in 1274 BC, an estimated 5,000 chariots were involved. Yet by the end of the 1st millennium BC, chariots had largely disappeared from warfare. Several factors were involved in their vanishing, including chariots' unsuitability for use on complex terrain, the increasing use of improved archery within the infantry and more powerful cavalry forces – individual mounts could outpace the chariot. Yet they were used effectively as far afield as Britain as late as the 1st century BC, and in many places they lingered on into the new millennium. What chariots demonstrated was that firepower could be transformed by mobility, a lesson that remains true to this day.

BRONZE AGE SWORD

The Bronze Age was a revolutionary era in many respects, not least in the creation of the first metal weaponry. Stone weapons had been serving humanity respectably throughout prehistory, but their development was always limited by material constraints. Stone was prone to fracturing from impact, particularly when sharpened to an edge. It was also virtually impossible to produce uniform items of weaponry for entire groups; each individual weapon was unique to the warrior who wielded it. Then there was the weight issue. A stone dagger was perfectly manageable, but a weapon approaching sword length would be unwieldy and impractical.

METALLIC BLADES

The metal revolution changed everything. Copper was humankind's first worked metal, originating in the Middle East perhaps as far back as 9000 BC, and weapons made from unalloyed copper first appeared around the 3rd millennium BC. They originally took the form of simple flat daggers, but other forms soon developed, including sickle-like slashing weapons used throughout much of Asia. The Egyptian *khopesh* was a classic example of this type. Measuring around 23¾in (60cm), the *khopesh* design sat somewhere between a battle-axe and a sword. It was essentially a slashing weapon, used both as a tool of execution and in the fury of infantry warfare.

By the 2nd millennium BC, copper was being worked into swords proper – typically double-edged short swords of lozenge-shaped or curved cross-section, sometimes with a thin fuller cut into the metal both to lighten and strengthen the blade. This lengthening of weapons from daggers to swords could be explained by the increasing use of horses for mounted warfare,

OPPOSITE: A collection of four Bronze Age swords, all of varying lengths, but dating from the same period (*c.* 1000 BC). (akg-images/Erich Lessing)

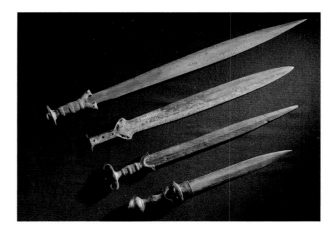

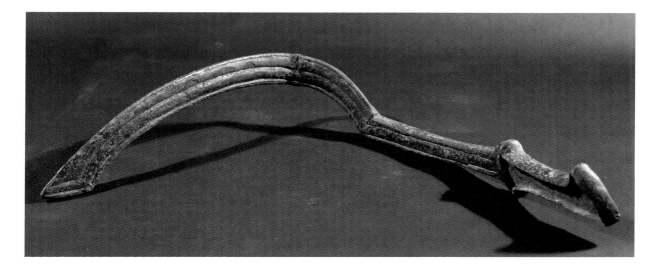

ABOVE: A *khopesh* sword, also known as a sickle-word, from New Kingdom Egypt (*c.* 14th century BC). This sword was discovered in a tomb and may have been deliberately spoiled and bent prior to burial with the dead person. (akg-images)

RIGHT: A collection of Bronze Age weapons from *c.* 1000 BC including a sword, shield, and spear head. (akg-images)

which required a weapon of greater length to deliver a blow from horseback. Some of these swords were true works of art, featuring ornate pommel designs and gold filigree scabbards.

Such weapons were visually impressive, and many were doubtless used for ceremonial rather than combat purposes. However, copper had fundamental problems for use in edged weapons, not least that it was not ideally suited to take, and hold, a good edge, copper being a soft metal and one easily damaged by impacts. Yet around 3000 BC, a critical metallurgical step was taken, probably in Iran or Sumeria, when copper was alloyed with tin to produce bronze. Previously, a form of bronze had been created by alloying copper with arsenic, but tin-bronze supplanted it, being stronger and more malleable.

BRONZE WEAPONRY

It was really the invention of bronze that ushered in the age of the sword. Bronze was easier to cast, and could be hammered into more complex shapes. It was a harder metal, holding a better, more resilient edge. From the 2nd millennium BC, therefore, we begin to see bronze swords appearing throughout the Mediterranean countries, the Middle East, Asia,

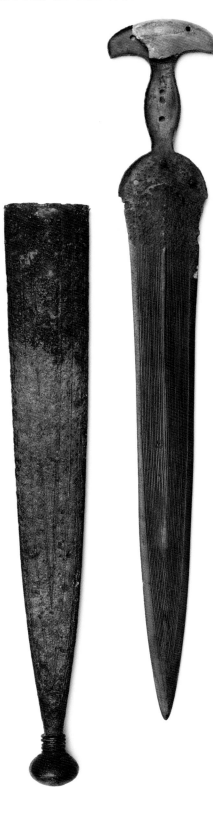

and Europe. A leap forward in design came through casting the blade and the hilt as one, creating a unitary weapon of great strength and martial utility. In European and Mediterranean swords in particular, a wide disk pommel was often hammered out at the base of hilt, while broad blade shoulders gave moderate protection to the user's grip hand. With progressively improved skill in casting, the blades also lengthened. Typical northern European "grip-tongue swords," for example (so called because the grip has the appearance of a tongue), could measure up to 33.5in (85cm), and like many swords was fitted with hilt plates of bone or wood. The grip-tongue sword was a cut-and-thrust weapon, used for both slashing and stabbing attacks, the typical configuration of many Bronze Age blades.

Bronze swords were in time replaced by iron and steel versions, the former because they were cheaper and the latter because they were superior. Yet the Bronze Age sword laid the groundwork for the transformation of warfare. Although in many cultures, particularly in the Middle East and Mediterranean, the bow and spear remained dominant for many centuries, bronze swords established the template for the personalized, close-quarters edged weapon.

> " The spear then he [Lycaon] let go, and sat him down,
>   Outspreading both his arms: whereat Achilles
>   Drew his keen sword, and at the collar-bone
>   Smote him beside his neck: and into him
>   The double-edge sword all plunged: and headlong
>   Outstretched upon the ground he lay; and forth
>   The cloudy blood did stream and drenched the ground. "
>
> – Homer[2]

SIEGE TOWER

FROM AS EARLY AS THE 8TH MILLENNIUM BC, civilizations were building fortifications to protect them from the dangers outside. Prior to the medieval age, protection largely came from defensive walls and earthworks, the former more common in the Middle East and Asia, while the latter are still seen contorting the hilltop landscapes of Europe. Defenders would fight from atop the walls, repelling those who attempted to get inside.

GETTING INSIDE

For the attackers attempting to break into a fortified town or city, there were several options. Siege was an obvious choice, with the aim of starving or isolating the enemy into submission, but such could be as costly to the attackers as to the besieged – starvation and disease would prey on both sides

OPPOSITE: The siege towers of the ancient world have captured the imagination of historians and engineers throughout the ages. This is a 19th-century recreation of the siege of Gaza in 332 BC, when the use of siege towers was crucial to Alexander the Great's successful assault on the walled city. (akg-images/North Wind Picture Archives)

ABOVE: Epimachus of Athens was a famous Athenian engineer and architect who coordinated the construction of the *Helepolis*, a massive siege machine, designed to be used in the siege of Rhodes in 305 BC. According to the ancient chronicler Diodorus, 3,400 of the strongest men were employed to propel the machine, but there can only have been room for, at most, 800 of them to push against the joists of the undercarriage at any one time. The *Helepolis* itself was divided into nine storeys, each of which had two stairways, one for men moving upwards through the tower, the other for men climbing down, to avoid congestion. Even 800 men may not have been enough to move this immense machine, and it is possible that draught animals were used, in conjunction with pulleys anchored in the ground beneath the front of the *Helepolis*. (Artwork by Brian Delf © Osprey Publishing Ltd.)

equally. An alternative, therefore, was mining – digging under the foundations of the defensive wall in order to promote its collapse. Mining was in use from at least the 5th century BC, with documented instances in China,

the Middle East, and Greece. Another option was literally to attack the fabric of the wall, or entrances, with various missile weapons, smashing through at a key point. While doing so, the attackers would have to endure reciprocal barrages of arrows and other airborne perils, so such a tactic was not without cost.

Yet another possibility was not to undermine or go through the walls, but to go over them. The most rudimentary method of surmounting defensive walls was escalade – placing ladders against the walls and climbing up them. While ascending the ladders, the doubtless weak-kneed attackers were exposed to all manner of horrors, including arrows, boiling oil or other incendiaries, rumbling barrages of rocks, or the ladders being simply pushed away from the wall. The siege tower, by contrast, offered far more protection to those engaged in an over-the-top assault. Speaking generally, siege towers consisted of a wooden tower structure mounted on four or

Plan de la Tour

ABOVE: A French 18th-century reconstruction of the *Helepolis* of Epimachus incorporates several errors, such as the number of wheels (there were in fact eight, although it is not known if they were in two rows, each with four wheels or vice versa), the number of storeys, and the provision of gigantic drawbridges. But it demonstrates the inventive use of block-and-tackle for winching the machine forwards. No ancient author indicates the methods by which these ancient machines were moved, so a definitive answer continues to allude historians to this day. (Collection of Dr Duncan Campbell)

That the greatest tower that is constructed may be one hundred and twenty cubits high, and twenty-three and a half wide, diminishing at the top one fifth of its base; the upright piece one foot at bottom, and half a foot at top. The large tower is made with twenty floors, and to each floor there is a parapet of three cubits, covered with raw hides to protect it from the arrows... The construction of the tortoise ram is similar: it was thirty cubits wide, and, exclusive of the roof, sixteen high. The height of the roof from the eaves to the ridge, seven cubits. On the top thereof in the centre rose a small tower, not less than twelve cubits wide: it was raised with four stories, on the upper of which the scorpions and catapultæ were placed, and in those below was kept a large store of water, to extinguish the flames in case it should be fired. In it was placed the machine for the ram, which the Greeks called kriodovkh, wherein was the round smooth roller on which the ram worked backwards and forwards by means of ropes, and produced great effect. This, like the tower, was covered with raw hides.

– Marcus Vitruvius Pollio[3]

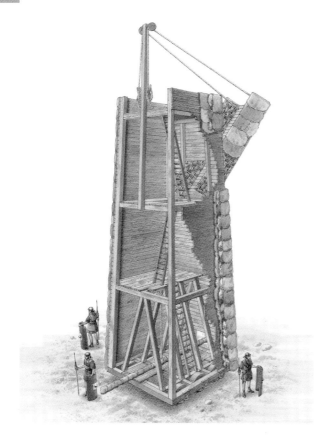

ABOVE: From around 200 BC, Roman armies made increasing use of siege towers. As a defense against fire, the entire structure was clad in rawhide and layers of rags as shown here. During Rome's Jewish Wars (AD 66–74), the siege towers were hung with iron plates; the additional weight penalty presumably offset by the increased protection. However, Roman engineers were not always mindful of the extra stress caused by the heavy cladding and some towers did spontaneously collapse. (Artwork by Brian Delf © Osprey Publishing Ltd.)

TECHNICAL SPECIFICATIONS OF THE *HELEPOLIS* OF EPIMACHUS (as recorded by the chronicler Diodorus):

Number of wheels	8
Wheel width	3ft (0.92m)
Side width	72ft (21m)
Height	300ft (40m)

more wheels. The wheeled design meant that the tower could be pushed up close to the defensive wall or fortification, the occupants partially protected from enemy missiles by the tower walls. Once the tower was in position, a gangplank could be dropped between tower and wall, over which the attackers would then flood across.

MASSIVE STRUCTURES

Siege towers were one of several types of siege engine, but were arguably the most impressive. In use from early in the 1st millennium BC, they were not simply passive armored structures, but contained all manner of weaponry to keep the defenders busy while the tower closed the gap. An Assyrian relief from the palace of Nimrud, dated to the 9th century BC, shows what appears to be a six-wheeled siege tower rolling into action with archers firing from a central tower and a battering ram projecting from the front of the structure. Siege towers also reached majestic proportions. The famous *Helepolis* ("Taker of Cities"), used during the Antigonid siege of Rhodes in 305 BC, was about 130ft (41m) high, 65ft (20.6m) wide and was manned by some 200 men on nine different levels, the levels connected by two staircases. Three sides of the tower were covered by iron plates to make it fireproof, and shuttered firing ports allowed the tower's occupants to lay down a fearsome barrage, with on-board weapons including large *ballistae* and catapults.

Not all siege towers would have been as bold as the *Helepolis*, but their general size meant that they would typically be constructed on-site, almost literally beneath the noses of the defenders, the engineers relying on archers to suppress enemy fire while they toiled. They were most intensively used during the sieges of the medieval period, but this era also saw their downfall. The growing use of cannon from the 14th century meant that suddenly flimsy wooden siege towers became increasingly vulnerable to gunpowder-based return fire, and the labour involved in their construction ceased to pay convincing dividends. Yet these epic fighting platforms still impress us today as ungainly motifs of counterfortress warfare.

ROMAN BOLT ARTILLERY

The Romans, for all their undoubted inventive genius, were never above borrowing good technologies when they saw them. During the Punic Wars of the 3rd century BC, Roman soldiers became acquainted with Greek torsion-powered artillery, used either for hurling stones or for launching large, destructive bolts. Roman engineers took up these designs and reworked them, and in so doing created weapons that not only prefigured gunpowder artillery, but even, albeit obliquely, the advent of the machine-gun and heavy suppressive fire.

HEAVY WEAPONS

There were several different types of arrow-firing Roman weapon, and we start by looking at the biggest – the *ballista*. To modern eyes, the *ballista* looks largely like a huge crew-served crossbow. Republican and early imperial Roman *ballistae* were made of wood, the parts secured by iron plates, although later imperial versions became iron framed and were thus more durable and consistent in performance, especially in poor weather. They were torsion-powered devices, the power to the bow coming from two torsion springs made of twisted animal sinew, into which the bow arm was inserted. The bowstring was drawn back by means of lever power, and was held in place by a ratchet. When the string was released, the torsion springs released their tension and the bow arm whipped forward, launching either a stone or a heavy dart.

Ballistae were serious weapons. A typical example could throw a 2.5lb (1.1kg) bolt to an effective range of 300yds

OPPOSITE: A 17th-century interpretation of a Roman *scorpio*, with a two-man crew preparing to fire a salvo of arrows. (akg-images/IAM/World History Archive)

ABOVE: Invading Roman armies did not allow difficult terrain to stop them deploying their siege machinery. This photograph shows the remains of the ancient fort of Gamala in modern-day Israel, which was successfully captured by the Romans. In recent years archaeologists have discovered *ballista* balls in the ground, definitively proving that *ballistae* would have been transported to the site of the siege. (Collection of Dr Duncan Anderson)

LEFT: A modern recreation of a large-scale Roman *ballista*, a one-talent stone projector built in 2002 for the BBC under the direction of Alan Wilkins, following the Roman engineer Vitruvius' specification as laid out in his work for the Emperor Augustus entitled *The Ten Books of Architecture*. The 57lb (26kg) stone missile can be seen behind the machine. (Courtesy of Alan Wilkins)

(274m). Estimates for the largest examples theorize that a 10lb (4.5kg) bolt could be whipped out to 450yds (420m). They were also accurate, with historical accounts testifying to individuals deliberately picked off at extended ranges. The skeleton of an Iron Age Briton, killed in battle against the Romans at Maiden Castle, Dorset, in AD 43, has a *ballista* bolt lodged neatly in its spine.

ROMAN REACH

Torsion artillery obviously proved its worth in battle for the Romans, as they went on to develop several different variations. The *scorpio* was a particularly interesting offshoot. It remained a torsion catapult, but on a smaller scale than the *ballista* – it could be fired by one man, as opposed to the six men often required by the *ballista* – and had tactical distinctions. While the *ballista* was essentially a siege device, the *scorpio* was a battlefield weapon, ideal for delivering mobile, long-range suppressive fire. Each Roman legion would take about 60 *scorpio* into battle, often using them in concentrated batteries on high ground. From there, the *scorpio* of a single legion could fire up to 240 bolts per minute, accurately and to ranges of between 90 and 360yds (100 and 400m). They had power enough to punch through enemy shields and crude body armor, and they show how the concept of infantry support fire is not necessarily an invention of later times.

Beyond the *ballista* and *scorpio*, the Romans invented other types of crossbow-like weapons. These include the hand-held

> ❝ *Ballistae* are constructed on varying principles to produce the same results. Some are operated by handcranks and windlasses, others by the means of capstans, and yet others by means of drums. No *ballista*, however, is made without due consideration for the weight of the stone that the engine is intended to throw. Hence their principle is not easy for everybody, but only for those who possess the knowledge of geometrical principles used in calculation and multiplication. ❞
>
> – Vitruvius[4]

cheiroballistra and the cart-mounted *carroballista*, the latter which could be wheeled about the battlefield in the manner of light field artillery. There is even evidence for a magazine-fed "repeating" crossbow called the *polybolos*, which could load, cock, and fire bolts mechanically. A BBC documentary team studying this weapon reconstructed such a device, and found that it was capable of firing up to 11 bolts every minute, possibly giving history's earliest example of automatic fire.

At many levels, therefore, the Roman bolt-firers were at the forefront of weapons technology for their day. They show that the many Roman victories were not simply a matter of muscle, blade, and spear, but were also supported by the intelligent use of mechanical firepower.

LEFT: Roman reenactors with a recreated small-scale Roman *ballista* able to launch stones weighing 4 Roman pounds (1.3kg). (Courtesy of the Ermine Street Guard)

TRIREME

War galleys – fighting ships powered primarily by oars (although most also had sail assistance when not in combat) – were plying Mediterranean waters by about 3000 BC. Although sail power was equally ancient and available, in the days before the invention of the rudder (as opposed to the earlier steering oar) sail ships had limited capacity for both speed and maneuverability, particularly when cutting close to the wind. It must also be remembered that maritime conflict in the Mediterranean was largely a matter of coastal engagements, often precipitated when an invasion fleet met a defensive flotilla along a city-state's coastline. For this reason, ships had to be able to turn quickly in a physically complicated environment. Oared galleys offered this facility, plus could develop impressive turns of speed even when sailing directly into the wind.

OPPOSITE: Marble relief found on the Acropolis in the 19th century and dated to the end of the 5th century BC. This is a key piece of evidence in the reconstruction of the trireme oar system and, in particular, the outriggers for the top, *thranites* tier. (From the Acropolis Museum, Athens, courtesy of William Shepherd)

OPPOSITE PAGE: A trireme under sail in the Aegean Sea. (Hellenic Navy)

OAR POWER

The first galleys were developed by the Greeks and the Phoenicians. They initially had a single bank of oars on each side, and were known as *pentecoter*. The bireme followed, having two banks of oars, each set on a different level, and with each oar powered by multiple rowers. Triremes emerged around the 8th century BC, probably from Phoenicia, and were simply a logical development of the idea that more oars provided more power.

In combat, the trireme had two main weapons – ramming and boarding – although the emphasis varied according to the nationality of the combatants. A typical Athenian trireme ram was a bronze-sheathed wooden projection jutting out from the bows at the waterline. Weighing some 440lb (200kg), it was easily capable of punching through a ship's hull when thumped home at full speed. Tactically, fleet commanders would get their ships to attack in either line astern or as a line abreast, the objective being to punch through or outflank the enemy, and so attack his rear. Triremes often mounted small units of archers and marines, the former to inflict attrition on the enemy ship at distance, while the latter could conduct boarding actions if the opposing vessels were close enough.

Naval warfare depends on skill... Our citizen helmsmen and deck crews are our most powerful asset, and we have more of them, and of better quality than the whole of the rest of Greece.

Pericles, 1.142 – 43

ENDURING DESIGN

Triremes, and war galleys in general, were a feature of maritime warfare for more than a thousand years. They defined some of the great naval battles of the ancient world, such as Salamis in 480 BC, when some 30–40 Greek triremes crushed a larger Persian invasion fleet after luring it into the narrow Salamis Channel, where the triremes had the advantage of maneuver. The Romans, Byzantines, and many other civilizations also used triremes for centuries, the Romans adding heavier weaponry such as on-board *ballistae* and catapults. As time went on, triremes expanded into larger craft such as *quadriremes* and *quinqueremes* (these didn't have more banks of oars, but were wider and had increased numbers of rowers per oar). Indeed, the success of the galley design meant that galleys remained a feature of warfare as late as the 18th century, the battle of Lepanto between the Christian states and Ottoman

TRIREME DIMENSIONS

Taking a Greek trireme as a representative type, the typical vessel would have been about 130ft (40m) long, 19ft (5.8m) in the beam, and with a height above the waterline (to the top of the hull) of about 6ft 6in (2m). The draught was just 3ft 3in (1m), ideal for moving around frequently shallow coastal waters, and the flat hull profile meant that the trireme could be beached easily for amphibious landings. Around 170 individual oars projected from the sides, and these could take the trireme up to a speed of about 8 knots, although cruising speed was more in the region of 4–6 knots.

Muslims in 1571 being the last major clash of galley warships. By this time, it was becoming evident that galleys were not ideally suited to serving as platforms for cannon, and the invention of the rudder and improved sails had taken away their maneuverability advantages. Combined with the fact that sailing ships were now capable of the oceanic voyages demanded by the "Age of Exploration" (galleys did not perform well in rough, deep-water seas), the galley was relegated to the history it had dominated for so long.

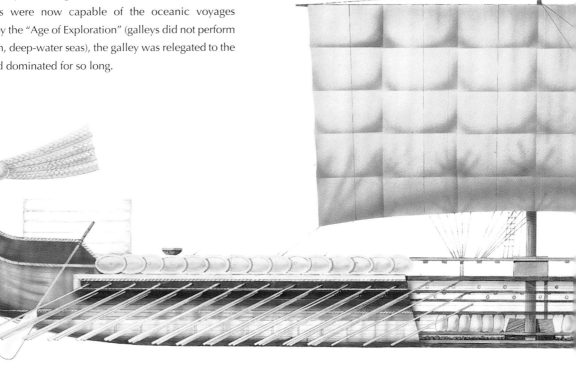

LEFT: *Thranites* and *zygios* "rowing benches" on the modern recreation of a trireme christened the *Olympias*. Note the mast stowed in the central companionway, demonstrating the desirability of having it on shore and out of the way in battle. (Courtesy of William Shepherd)

RIGHT: Attic black-figure kylix from the Etruscan burial site at Vulci, dated *c.* 540 BC. On the inside of this cup, the Greek god Dionysos is shown reclining on the deck of a warship armed with a ram. (Fields-Carré Collection)

BELOW: An illustration of a Roman trireme with cut-away detail showing the interior of the vessel where the rowers would have sat. (Getty Images)

GLADIUS

For more than 250 years, the Roman legionary went into battle armed principally with three elements: the *pilum* javelin, the *scutum* shield, and the *gladius* sword. These three weapons, combined with the formidable discipline, training, and ruthlessness of the men who wielded them, were in large part responsible for the creation of one of the largest empires the world has ever seen. The *gladius* takes our focus here because it represents a perfect general-purpose infantry weapon of the ancient world, thrust in battle from the forests of Europe to the gladiatorial arenas of Rome itself. Yet it has to be noted that we are not dealing with a single type of sword here, but an evolutionary weapon, which changed in configuration during the great years of republican then imperial Rome.

OPPOSITE: The Roman *gladius* was not only used by legionaries but also by gladiators, who fought to the death in Roman circuses throughout the length and breadth of the Roman Empire. This mosaic once formed part of the decoration of a Roman townhouse and dates from *c.* AD 200. (akg-images/Bidlarchiv Steffens)

SWORD TYPES

Its first incarnation is known as the *gladius Hispaniensis* (Spanish sword), and it came into use during the 2nd century BC. The name alludes to Spanish origins, although the actual ancestry is uncertain. It was the largest of the *gladius* family, with a blade length of between 25 and 27in (64 and 69cm) and with a width of some 1.5–2in (4–5.5cm). The blade edges ran parallel, or were slightly waisted, for most of the blade length, before narrowing steeply to a sharp point. A large pommel at the end of the hilt acted as a counterweight.

The *gladius Hispaniensis* was a true infantryman's weapon, nicely balanced and useful in either the cut or the thrust. The sharp point indicated that it was primarily intended for the latter

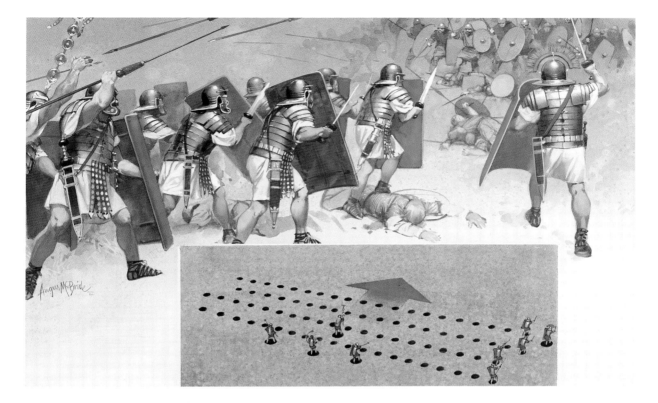

ABOVE: A typical attacking formation of Roman legionaries. The *prior* who carries the battle standard leads the attack followed by *gladius*-wielding legionaries who are supported in turn by the spearmen. The inset illustration shows the perfect "chessboard" battle formation of legionaries. (Artwork by Angus McBride © Osprey Publishing Ltd.)

– the point would have been ideal for splitting light mail armor or pushing between an opponent's ribs. From the time of Augustus (r. 27 BC–AD 14), however, the Spanish sword was challenged by another variant. Known as the Mainz/Fulham type *gladius* (after locations in which examples have been found), this sword was shorter and stockier, with a blade measuring about 20–24in (50–60cm) in length and 2–2.5in (5–6cm) wide. It was a highly maneuverable and powerful close-quarters weapon, which retained the sharp point for dealing with armored enemies.

The *gladius Hispaniensis* has been described as the "sword that had conquered the world," and the Mainz/Fulham type blade continued this tradition through Augustus' great years of expansion. Yet around the middle of the 1st century AD, both these types were ousted by a new design, called the Pompeian type after specimens found in the ash-encrusted ruins of that city. The blade length was further reduced to *c.* 16.5–21.6in (42–55cm), giving a lighter, faster weapon (it weighed about 2.2lb/1kg), and there is some suggestion that the Pompeii sword was derived from those used by gladiators in the arena, the undeniable masters of sword craft in ancient Rome.

ABOVE: A *gladius* with the remains of its beautiful scabbard, from the late Roman Republic. (© Board of the Trustees of the Armouries, object no. IX 5583)

The Pompeii *gladius* would serve the Romans until the mid 2nd century AD, before it finally gave way to the longer *spatha*.

IN ACTION

All of the *gladius* swords were excellent combat weapons, particularly when wielded in combination with the legionary's shield and spear. In action, the Roman would typically wear his sword on his right hip, not his left. (Performing a cross-draw from the left would have endangered the man standing to the legionary's immediate left.) The shield would be in his left hand, and his spear in the right. Advancing alongside his comrades, once within throwing distance the legionary would launch his javelin at the enemy, then draw his sword and move into close-quarters combat. With his torso protected by the shield, the legionary would hack, slash, and jab, systematically cutting down the ranks or man before him.

Thus wielded, the *gladius* sword became a force for building an empire. We must not over-emphasize its qualities – in many ways, it was a fairly humble sword, suited to equipping the ranks of a mass army. Yet it did its intended job superbly well, augmenting the martial talents of the formidable Roman Army.

BELOW: The Roman *gladius* continued to serve as the primary weapon for the legionary well into the 2nd century. Indeed, Roman swordsmiths began to develop pattern-welded swords, formed around a core of multiple iron bars with differing carbon contents to produce different tones, twisted into a screw then hammered and folded countless times, providing a strong yet flexible core. Cutting edges were then welded into the sword ensuring that each blade was entirely unique. (Artwork by Angus McBride © Osprey Publishing Ltd.)

❝ ...a sword never kills anybody, it is a tool in the killer's hand. ❞

Lucius Annaeus Seneca, *Ad Lucilium Epistulae Morales*, Letter 87, c.63–65

HOPLITE *DORY*

SPEARS WERE UNDOUBTEDLY AMONGST HUMANITY'S earliest weapons, if only in the form of a simple sharpened stick with a fire-hardened point. Over time, and in the context of human combat, they separated into two basic types – throwing spears and stabbing spears. The former were used to inflict casualties at a distance, hopefully wearing down enemy numbers before close-quarters battle, at which point the stabbing spear would come into play. Noting the distinction, there is nonetheless a natural limitation to the design of a spear – regardless of material sophistication, all spears consist of little more than a shaft and a head. Yet at certain times in history, even the most basic weapons were harmonized so perfectly with infantry tactics that they helped entire states either become great or fend off great enemies. Such is the case with the hoplite *dory*.

OPPOSITE: A remarkably preserved ancient Greek marble clearly showing a Hoplite warrior armed with his *dory*. (akg-images/Nimatallah)

HOPLITE WARRIORS

Hoplites were citizen-soldiers of the ancient Greek city-states, and from the 7th to the 4th centuries BC they were amongst the most proficient warriors on earth. They were essentially amateur soldiers, obliged to present themselves for military service to their state when needed. Their ranks tended to consist of the social elite of the day, largely because they were themselves responsible for meeting the costs of body armor, shield, sword,

and spear. The state would provide some military training, although being an amateur force meant that much reliance was placed on the natural toughness, athleticism, and motivation of the hoplites, rather than high levels of martial skill (with the exception of warrior states such as Sparta).

What made the Greek hoplite such a daunting warrior was a combination of formation and weaponry. The principal weapon of the hoplite was the *dory* spear. It was unusually long

– it could measure up to 10ft (3m) in length, and weighed about 4.4lb (2kg). At the business end was a broad, leaf-pattern spearhead, while at the other end was a corresponding metal butt spike called a *sarouter*. The purpose of the spike is much debated. It almost certainly acted as a counterbalance, to make the spear easy to hold and wield. Yet it would have also had some combat utility – it could have been used as an improvised spear point if the leaf point was broken off, or for making

ABOVE: Hoplites shown in formation across a vase of the 7th century BC. (The Art Archive/Museo di Villa Giulia Rome/Gianni Dagli Orti)

RIGHT: This well-trained sub-unit, a half-file of eight men, marching in step with spears over their right shoulders, are most likely a mercenary contingent. The fifth officer from the left turns his head as he is about to give orders. (Courtesy of Nicolas Sekunda)

downward attacks on the enemy's exposed feet if the *dory* was pushed up vertical on the enemy's shields. It might even have been embedded in the ground to keep the spear in place against enemy charges.

The *dory*'s qualities can only be seen in the context of the phalanx formation in which the hoplites fought. The phalanx consisted of dense ranks of soldiers standing shoulder to shoulder, typically around eight ranks deep and with a face of up to several hundred yards across. In action, the opposing phalanxes would march at each other with their spears presented, merging into a bloody, surging mass as they came to blows. The length of the *dory* created an initial, limited, protective distance between the ranks, but it also meant that ranks further behind could stab through or over those in front, and still reach their opponents. The spears were thrust repeatedly between the opposing wall of shields, inflicting horrifying, deep injuries on those with whom they connected. The phalanxes would eventually merge into a violent, compressed scrum, the ranks further back maintaining forward pressure with their shields to keep those in front pressing forward. This clash was known as *othismos* – a "shoving match" – perfectly encapsulating this form of warfare.

PHALANX VICTORIES

Life inside the phalanx was claustrophobic and brutal, but in the hands of a skilled commander the formation was also extremely effective. Between 334 and 323 BC, for example, Alexander of Macedon, following in his father Philip's footsteps, used the phalanx to conquer much of Eastern Europe and central Asia. His phalanx, however, could be between 16 and 32 ranks deep, and they utilized the longer *sarissa* spear, which could reach up to an arm-breaking 23ft

GREEK WARRIOR EQUIPMENT

As well as his *dory* spear, the Greek warrior also took into battle several other important items of kit and equipment. In terms of additional weaponry he would have a double-edged *xiphos* sword or possibly a scythe-like *kopis* single-edged blade, both being one-handed weapons. He would also wear basic body armor. In the 5th century BC, this would consist of the *linothorax* – multiple thick layers of hemp, linen, and leather – or interlinked bronze scales. Metal greaves would protect the lower legs, while a beaten metal helmet provided protection for the skull, neck, and face. The most important piece of protective gear, however, would be the *hoplon* shield, made of wood but sometimes with a sheet of bronze on the face.

(7m) long. Alexander's troops were also professional soldiers, properly drilled and trained. In the 2nd century BC, the phalanx showed its limitations against the Romans, who utilized maneuver, firepower, and rough terrain to break up the phalanx's tight formation, which then left it vulnerable to sword-wielding Romans. Yet the *dory* and the *sarissa* had demonstrated what could be achieved through a bristling wall of spears, and that lesson would continue on in modified form until the Middle Ages.

BELOW: Reconstruction drawings based on positions detailed on ancient Greek vases to illustrate weaponry training for a Hoplite soldier with his *dory*. (© Peter Connolly courtesy of akg-images)

THE MEDIEVAL WORLD
500–1500

GREEK FIRE

GREEK FIRE WAS NOT THE WORLD'S FIRST INCENDIARY weapon. Simple fire alone had potential to be "weaponized," if only in the form of burning an enemy's crops, fortifications, or houses as part of a "scorched earth" policy. Arrows wrapped in burning pitch-soaked cloth were in flight by the 8th century BC, with records of their use by Assyrians and Judeans at the siege of Lachish in 701 BC, and as early as the 5th century BC there are mysterious accounts of flamethrower-type devices and sulfur-based incendiaries. In *c.* 672, however, an engineer called Kallanicus from Heliopolis, but then living in Constantinople, reputedly created a substance far more destructive.

DESTRUCTIVE MIX

The composition of "Greek Fire" is uncertain – it most likely consisted of petroleum-based substances mixed with elements such as quicklime or saltpeter – but it was essentially a viscous, flammable liquid capable of transforming an enemy ship or structure into a conflagration in virtually a matter of seconds. Moreover, it appeared to be inextinguishable by dousing with water, some contemporaries stating that such an action simply incited the flames. It was primarily developed as a naval weapon for mounting aboard *dromons* (Byzantine galleys), and was deployed in two main ways. First, the composition was held in clay grenades, which were wrapped in burning cloths and fired from an on-deck catapult. (These grenades also contained caltrops as an early form of shrapnel.) The jars broke apart when they hit the enemy vessel, and the contents ignited. Second, and more creatively, Greek Fire was ejected in a horrifying plume of flame from a bronze tube, known as a *siphōn*, at the bows of the ship, the tube often held in an intimidating carving of a dragon or lion's head. In essence, here was one of the earliest flamethrowers. How it worked is educated conjecture, but the substance was probably heated in a metal tank, raising its pressure before the *siphōn* valve was opened to release and ignite the fluid. Effective range could have been as much as 49ft (15m).

OPPOSITE: Greek Fire was widely adopted by all combatant armies throughout the medieval period, including Saracen forces. This image shows a reported divine intervention when a change of wind saves Crusader soldiers and blows back the Greek Fire on the Saracen army. (British Library 041845 Royal 15 E. I, f.266)

ABOVE: Greek Fire was not only a naval weapon. It could also be used effectively to protect or seize fortresses, as shown here. (Taken from *Codex Vaticanus Graecus, c.* 1605)

BELOW: The Byzantine Empire successfully used Greek Fire to dominate huge swathes of the Mediterranean world in the early medieval period. Using a flammable composition consisting of sulfur, naphta, and quicklime, jets of liquid fire were sprayed out of bronze tubes mounted on their own galleys, as shown in this original manuscript image. On at least two occasions entire fleets of Saracen warriors were destroyed by Greek Fire from Byzantine vessels. (The Bridgeman Art Library)

BATTLE TESTED

For five centuries the Byzantine Empire utilized Greek Fire in combat. In this period, it helped the Byzantines rise to become one of the most powerful maritime nations upon earth. Greek Fire helped secure critical victories against Arab siege fleets around Constantinople in the 7th and 8th centuries, and subsequently helped defeat various Middle Eastern and Eastern European enemies during Byzantium's imperial expansion. It also became a land warfare weapon – the *cheirosiphōn* hand-operated launcher was mounted on siege towers for spraying the flame over enemy fortifications and defenses.

Yet by the 13th century, Greek Fire had largely disappeared from the records, and did not return. Why this occurred is uncertain. It was doubtless effective in ideal conditions, but at anything like extended range, or in windy conditions, its practicality would have been limited. Certainly, the advent of cannon in the 14th century would have rendered it obsolete.

Yet Greek Fire illustrates that the incendiary weapons of the 20th century had some very ancient ancestors.

EXPERIENCING GREEK FIRE

Jean de Joinville, a French nobleman of the 13th century, here recounts facing Greek Fire during the Seventh Crusade, as wielded by the Saracens:

> " This was the fashion of the Greek fire: it came on as broad in front as a vinegar cask, and the tail of fire that trailed behind it was as big as a great spear; and it made such a noise as it came, that it sounded like the thunder of heaven. It looked like a dragon flying through the air. Such a bright light did it cast, that one could see all over the camp as though it were day, by reason of the great mass of fire, and the brilliance of the light that it shed. Thrice that night they hurled the Greek fire at us, and four times shot it from the tourniquet crossbow. "

ABOVE: Greek Fire could also be used in siege warfare, as can be seen in this English 13th century illustration. (Ancient Art and Architecture Collection)

MEDIEVAL LONGSWORD

IT IS IMPOSSIBLE TO TALK ABOUT A SINGLE TYPE OF sword defining an entire period. Throughout the medieval period, our focus here, swords took a huge variety of designs, from lengthy two-handed longswords to dagger-like baselards. Yet there were some dominant general designs, weapons that would define the martial classes of the European battlefields for centuries.

OPPOSITE RIGHT: A German manuscript image shows the brutal effectiveness of the broadsword as it slices through a rival knight's helmet. (akg-images)

OPPOSITE: The great seal of Edward III depicts the king holding a chained broadsword in his right hand, and a shield in his left. The sword was a clear status symbol in the medieval world due to the sheer cost of produce one. (British Library Egerton Charter 2132)

FIGHTING BLADES

The classic Western fighting swords dating from the 6th–9th centuries were typically between 35 and 42in (90 and 102cm) long, with straight, broad double-edged blades that terminated in rounded points. Fullers ran along the flat of the blade, and hilts featured bulky pommels in shapes ranging from squares to triangles, these acting as both decoration and counterbalances. Simple straight crossguards provided some protection to the user's hand from enemy blades. Pattern-welding – a process of combining steels with different carbon contents – gave blades greater strength and also attractive swirling coloration in the steel. The Vikings in particular produced many refined examples of this type of sword, often with hilts decorated in silver, brass, or gold geometric designs.

ABOVE: The battle of Wakefield, December 30, 1460. Richard, Duke of York, can be seen wearing Italian armor with a tabard over it, and was killed during the battle. Fought as part of the English Wars of the Roses, the brutal killing and subsequent executions marked the beginning of a less chivalrous form of warfare that lasted until the the end of the wars. The knight to the left of center is wielding a longsword with both hands. (Artwork by Graham Turner © Osprey Publishing Ltd.)

Tactical realities shaped and reshaped the design of the medieval sword. The classic "arming sword," in use from about 1000 to 1300, was a lighter cut-and-thrust weapon designed to be wielded with a single hand. The other hand could, therefore, be occupied with a small, round "buckler" shield, this combination allowing for the nimble fighting techniques depicted in many medieval instructional manuscripts. Over time, body armor became increasingly heavy, and consequently arming sword blades tended to become longer and heavier, to increase the momentum of the swing and hence its impact on the opponent. Thus by the early 14th century, a blade would measure about 50in (125cm), the hilt also lengthening both as a counterbalance to the blade and also to allow hand-and-a-half or two-handed grips.

Such weapons are known as longswords, and weighing about 3.3lb (1.5kg) they were capable of delivering massive injury in one stroke.

PLATE ARMOR

The greatest challenge for the traditional European sword came during the 13th and 14th centuries, when plate armor became increasingly prevalent on the battlefield. Plate armor was generally dismissive of slashing blows, and therefore blade design steadily came to adopt a more rigid diamond-

ABOVE: Example of the medieval longsword. (© Board of the Trustees of the Armouries, object no. IX 1169)

shaped cross-section and sharper point. The redesign focused much of the blade's strength in the thrust rather than the cut, with the aim of puncturing through thinner sections of plate or gliding between plate joints. Often mounted knights hedged their bets by riding into battle with a cut-and-thrust sword on the hip and a thrusting sword kept at the ready on their saddles. (More about the switch to thrusting swords will be discussed on pp.94–96.)

When discussing the medieval sword, we must acknowledge that it was largely relegated to use by those higher classes that could afford it. Consequently, the battlefield was dominated, at least in sheer numbers, by the staff weapons, bows, and crude blades of the lower orders. Yet the sword was undoubtedly the most versatile weapon on the battlefield, requiring skill and courage to wield properly. Only once firearms established themselves during the Early Renaissance was the value of the sword thrown into question.

LONGSWORD GRIP

In combat, the length of the longsword's grip provided for some subtlety in how power was applied. The sword could, of course, be gripped and swung like a bat, but the hand near the pommel could also apply pressure to a thrust, or sit above the crossguard on the ricasso to guide slicing actions. Manuscripts such as that by Fiori de Liberi, dated to *c.* 1410, also show longswords being wielded with just one hand. Note that the blade was not the only offensive feature of the arming sword and the longsword. The wide crossguard could be used to hook an opponent's limbs or sword to create an opening for attack, and the pommel was a crude tool for inflicting blunt trauma on a skull or chest.

DANE AXE

On the Bayeaux Tapestry, that most famous of visual military records depicting the Norman conquest of Britain in 1066, one weapon stands out with unnerving power. A scene depicts a housecarl of King Harold's army smashing a broad-headed axe into the skull of a Norman horse, the fatal effects of such a blow being seen in other tumbling mounts. The weapon was the Dane axe, and for several centuries it was one of the most devastating hand-held weapons available.

VIKING ORIGINS

As its name denotes, the Dane axe was a Viking brand of battle-axe, first developed during the 8th century AD and used thereafter by various armies until about the 14th century. The Vikings actually had several types of fighting axe. The smallest was the skeg axe, which had a long metal "beard" dropping down beneath the cutting edge; the beard was used to hook over the rim of an enemy's shield, pulling the shield down to expose the man behind to a strike from a spear or sword. General-purpose battle axes, by contrast, had no such beard, but featured a sharp steel cutting blade about 6in (15cm) deep mounted on a shaft some 24in (60cm) long. These were not only good close-quarters weapons, light enough to be wielded with one hand while gripping a rawhide and wooden shield with the other, but they were also thrown as missiles.

OPPOSITE: The triangular iron axe blade discovered during excavation work at London Bridge during the 1920s. As the name implies, the Dane axe was Viking in origin, and a number of battles were fought along the River Thames as various Scandinavian rulers tried to gain control of England throughout the 9th and 10th centuries. (The Art Archive)

ABOVE AND RIGHT: The famous Bayeaux Tapestry, created in the late 11th century to document the 1066 Norman invasion of England. Axe-wielding Saxons stand as the front line of defense against charging Norman cavalry during the battle of Hastings. (akg-images/Erich Lessing)

The Dane axe, however, took the battle-axe principle to its ultimate expression. It was exclusively a two-handed weapon, the grip being a necessity in a weapon with a haft measuring up to 5ft (1.5m) long. Its iron or steel blade flared out broadly at both the top and the bottom, producing a total cutting edge that could measure up to 18in (46cm). In overall configuration, the edge slanted downwards and backwards to maximize the slicing effect of the blow, probably reflecting an ancestry in animal slaughtering tools. The bit of the blade was usually made from a steel with a higher carbon content than other parts of the head, forming a more durable, harder edge.

The lethality of the Dane axe is unquestionable. When swung with force, it was easily capable of shattering open a helmet, splitting mail links, or removing a head or limb. It was

ABOVE: A 19th-century artwork shows a range of Celtic axeheads, with considerable variation in blade width and profile. (akg-images/North Wind Picture Archives)

probably swung either straight down in a cleaving blow against the opponent's skull, or at a 45-degree angle, aiming for the neck, shoulders, and upper arms. Nor are the Bayeaux Tapestry's depictions of horse-killing unfounded. In fact, this may have been the Dane axe's most useful application, as the axe man would have been more disadvantaged in combat against a dismounted warrior more nimbly armed with a sword (see below).

DECLINE

The Dane axe was certainly effective in action, and over the centuries it was adopted by several other peoples beyond Scandinavian shores. Saxon adoption led, in turn, to its spreading to England and Ireland, and it was also used by Norman forces, hence its regular appearance on the Bayeaux

Tapestry. It appears to have remained in use as late as the 14th century in mainland Europe and England, but endured for a further two centuries in parts of Ireland and Scotland.

Several factors influenced its eventual disappearance. First, steady improvements in sword design meant that an axe-wielding soldier was unable to match the subtle movements of a swordsman. If the axe warrior missed with his first blow, the sword-armed soldier could quickly maneuver inside the axe's swing radius; with both hands on the axe haft, the axe-man would be exposed to a quick sword thrust or slash. Second, polearms such as the poleaxe and halberd became more practical options for arming mass soldiery, being able to deliver a more versatile range of offensive and defensive techniques on the battlefield. Yet for the duration of its useful life, the Dane axe was, in terms of sheer power, the ultimate edged weapon, and its effect on the enemy must have been as much psychological as physical.

BELOW: The battle of Brunanburh was fought at an unknown date in the 9th century between an Anglo-Saxon army and a combined Scots/Viking force. Both sides wielded Dane axes as shown here. (Artwork by Gerry Embleton © Osprey Publishing Ltd.)

HALBERD

Although the halberd, as we shall see, was a revolutionary weapon on the battlefields of the High Middle Ages, in many ways it was simply another variation in the ancient history of pole-arms. Pole-arms made good sense as infantry weapons for massed-rank battles. By combining a long haft with a fearsome head – varieties of which included blades, spikes, forks, tridents, axes, and hammers – the foot soldier could inflict injury and death while retaining some degree of protective distance between him and his opponent.

OPPOSITE: An ornately decorated halberd made for the Trabanten Guard of the Electors of Saxony in the 16th century. (© Wallace Collection, London/The Bridgeman Art Library).

POLE-ARMS IN BATTLE

The most elementary pole-arm was the thrusting spear, although in the forms of the lance and the infantry pike this was actually one of the most durable types. Yet as the medieval period progressed, we see an increased elaboration in pole-arm varieties, largely to meet the challenges of dealing with both enemy infantry and cavalry. The "partisan," for example, featured a powerful central spearhead flanked by two outward curving projections, these being useful for deflecting sword blows from a mounted or dismounted knight. Glaives, by contrast, featured a head comprising a hefty cleaver-like cutting blade, and over time the rear, blunt edge of the blade acquired various protrusions for trapping blades or hooking riders. Similarly, the bill – an agriculturally derived weapon popularly wielded by the lower classes – featured a hooked blade on the end of a haft measuring from 5ft (1.5m) to 9ft (2.7m) long. It could be swung like an powerful axe, or the bill's hook could be used to snare riders or puncture their armor. War-hammers were another option, these being

ABOVE: Detail from the tomb of King Francois I of France showing halberdiers of the French Army. (Giraudon/The Bridgeman Art Library)

RIGHT: Knights shown competing at a tournament *c.* 1513 with halberds. (INTERFOTO/Sammlung Rach/Mary Evans Picture Library)

OPPOSITE: Capture of Evreux, 1487 from *Chroniques de France ou de Saint Denis*. (akg-images/British Library)

pole-arms fitted with blunt smashing heads, perfectly capable of crushing a helmet or smashing a limb.

The halberd emerged into this complex picture during the 13th and 14th centuries. Here was a time in which plate armor, worn by mounted knights, was altering the dynamics of medieval warfare. Plate armor, if well made, could largely

resist the blows of sword, spear, and many other edged weapons. If there was a vulnerability, it was to narrow, strong spikes (such as a stiletto dagger), and in the way that the armor could make the wearer physically cumbersome.

MULTIPURPOSE WEAPON

The halberd was such a formidable weapon because it combined multiple weapons in one multipurpose pole-arm that was equally dangerous to foot soldiers as mounted knights. A basic combat halberd (as opposed to the decorative versions, with their many ornate flourishes) consisted of a hardwood haft 5–6ft (1.5–1.8m) long and a head that featured three components. At the front was a large axe blade, which was surmounted by a long, thin spike or blade (double-edged if the latter). At the back side of the head was a substantial hook or "thorn." Used in trained hands, the head of the halberd was therefore a weapon of versatility and power. The axe blade could chop down on men or horses with lethal slicing blows, while the thin spike was used to puncture plate or mail armor, or simply

hold back or control a horseman at a convenient distance. By using the hook, the halberdier could also snag swords, reins, limbs, and armor, using it even to drag a knight off his horse, where he could be finished off by the stiletto knives and hammers of other soldiers. Charles the Bold of Burgundy, for example, was reputedly killed by a Swiss halberd at the battle of Nancy in 1477, his head cleaved in two by the power of the strike.

It is undoubted that the halberd was one of the most effective weapons on the medieval battlefield, especially if they were wielded by a coordinated mass of infantry, pushing and cutting as one body. Indeed, the halberd's strength really lay in unified tactics, although the full range of the weapon's techniques could be somewhat limited by the halberdier's comrades standing close on each side. The halberd gradually fell out of use, outlasted by the longer pike. They, like many other weapons, became increasingly impractical in the age of gunpowder, although they lingered on as ceremonial weapons for many centuries.

LEFT: An English knight from the late 15th century shown carrying a glaive together with his broadsword and dagger. (Artwork by Graham Turner © Osprey Publishing Ltd.)

PIKE

IN MUCH THE SAME WAY AS THE GREEK *DORY* OR *sarissa*, the strength of the medieval pike was its length. With a haft measuring some 10–20ft (3–6m), the pike provided a defensive reach that surpassed all other pole-arms on the battlefield. Yet unlike many other pole-arms, the pike endured well into the Early Modern period, only falling out of use altogether in the early 18th century. Why it did so was as much about tactical innovation as it was about simple technology.

PIKE MASS

Pikes were a well-established feature of medieval warfare by the 14th century. As with other pole-arms, they only made tactical sense when deployed in massed ranks. The Scottish, for example, wielded the pike in the *schiltron*, a dense rectilinear or circular formation of men all presenting their pike towards the enemy. The banks of pike – those of the ranks further back hung over the heads of the front rank – presented a virtually impenetrable wall for enemy cavalry. Pike *schiltron* formations were thus central to many notable Scottish victories, such as at the battle of Bannockburn in 1314. The Flemish were also skillful exponents of the pike. At the battle of Golden Spurs in 1302, for example, the Flemish successfully used the long *geldon* spear to resist thunderous French cavalry charges.

Pike formations were undoubtedly formidable. In trained ranks the pike could be presented in any direction from a single command, and squares of pike could turn in unison to face emerging threats. But the pikemen were not invulnerable. When used defensively, they became easy targets for enemy archers, crossbowmen, and, in time, arquebusiers, who used their projectiles to thin down the ranks and create gaps that the cavalry

OPPOSITE: The Swiss were famed for their use of skilfully trained pikemen who wielded an 18ft (5.5m) long pike. Here they are shown in a marble relief at the battle of Marignano in 1515, fighting against the armies of Francois I of France. (Getty Images)

could then exploit. Yet ironically, in the early decades of the gunpowder age the pike actually became one of the most feared battlefield weapons of its day. The "pike renaissance" was largely due to the Swiss, who from the 15th century took pike warfare to new levels of influence.

SWISS PIKEMEN

The Swiss had used pike for many years, but had often relied more on the shorter halberd, paying the price for this imbalance in defeats such as the battle of Arbedo in 1422, when Milanese crossbows and lancers broke up the Swiss ranks. In response to such defeats, the Swiss adopted an 18ft (5.5m) long pike, but refined the training of pikemen to make them much more offensively oriented. At the given command (the Swiss also pioneered the use of drums to command the infantry squares), the pikemen could move at unexpected speed across the battlefield, counterattacking cavalry charges or slamming into less-disciplined enemy ranks. Archers and

arquebusiers worked on their flanks to provide counterfire against enemy soldiers' missiles.

At battles such as Grandson (1476), Morat (1476), and Nancy (1477), the pikemen proved their worth in great victories. Others also mastered the pike along similar lines, including the European (mainly German) Landsknecht, mercenaries who on occasions fought the Swiss in huge crushes of pike. In the 16th century, the Spanish developed the *tercio*, a mixed-arms formation of about 3,000 men that formed pike-, firearm-, and sword-equipped men into mutually supporting squares, each element aiming to compensate for the weakness of the other. Victory at the battle of Pavia in 1525 showed that the tactic could pay real dividends.

BELOW: Pikemen were used alongside troops armed with early medieval handgonnes during the era of so-called "Pike and Shot" tactics. This manuscript image shows the typical formations of the late 16th century; the pikemen form the bulk of the attacking party, with arquebusiers on the wings. (Courtesy of Keith Roberts)

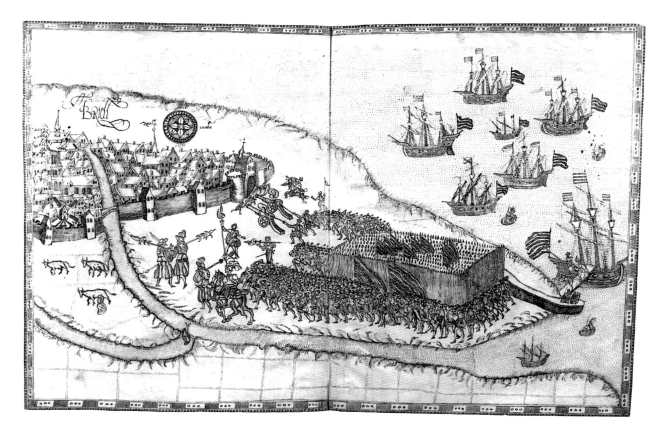

The pike square ultimately died out around 1700, when refinements in artillery and the use of flintlock weapons meant that pike formations became horribly exposed to gunfire. The heavy pike became an anachronism, but its longevity and battlefield success illustrate how the simplest weapon can be decisive if wielded intelligently.

ABOVE: Scottish pikemen opposing the English cavalry at the battle of Bannockburn in 1314. (Artwork by Graham Turner © Osprey Publishing Ltd.)

BELOW: Formed infantry with pikes could withstand a cavalry assault as they could keep the riders at bay. The length of the cavalryman's lance is exaggerated in comparison with that of the pike. (Courtesy of Keith Roberts)

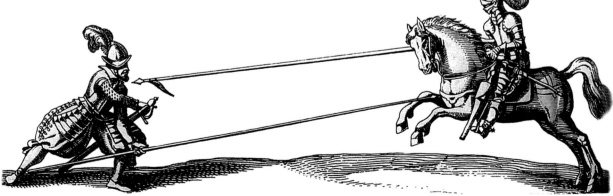

TREBUCHET

FROM THE 12TH CENTURY UNTIL THE 16TH CENTURY, the trebuchet was the medieval world's most powerful siege engine. Torsion-powered weapons such as catapults and *ballistae* had, in their most formidable forms, superior range, but the trebuchet was the only device truly capable of throwing fortress-threatening missiles. For this reason, trebuchets are arguably history's first convincing example of heavy artillery.

OPPOSITE PAGE: A historic engraving of the use of a trebuchet by a Crusader army. Trebuchets were widely used throughout the Middle East, most famously by the Ottoman Empire when they attempted to seize the island of Rhodes from the Knights Templars. (iStock)

OPPOSITE: A 16th-century illustration showing the use of a trebuchet siege engine to hurl flaming Greek Fire. Apparently on occasion even dead bodies were thrown in a medieval form of biological warfare, although most commonly large rocks were the projectile of choice. (Mary Evans Picture Library/The Tann Collection)

OPERATION

Torsion- and spring-powered siege engines were always limited by the ability of natural materials to endure the loading forces applied to them. The trebuchet, however, worked on very different principles, ones that allowed for far greater missile weights. Trebuchets were counterweight-powered engines that used simple principles of leverage to hurl a rock or other missile. In its basic configuration, the trebuchet consisted of a long, pivoted arm mounted on a frame, the pivot fixed about one-quarter of its length from the bottom of the arm. To this end of the arm was fitted a huge counterweight (or counterpoise), typically manufactured from a wooden box filled with earth and stones. At the other end of the arm was either a cavity or scoop-like structure or a separately attached sling, these being used for holding the missile (see feature box).

When left for physics to take its course, the trebuchet arm naturally wanted to adopt a vertical position, with the counterpoise at the bottom. To fire the trebuchet, therefore,

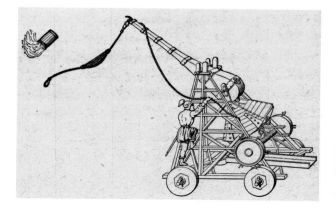

TREBUCHET MISSILES

Trebuchets had limited range, but their missiles gave much cause for fear. For example, it is estimated that a trebuchet with a 50ft (15m) arm and a counterpoise of 20,000lb (9,070kg), could throw a 300lb (136kg) rock to a distance of 300yds (274m). Examples from history show that some trebuchets were capable of launching stones up to 3,300lb (1,500kg) in weight, which must have had crushing effects on whatever they hit. Such monstrous loads, however, were utterly exceptional, and missiles of around 220lb (100kg) were typical. Even these rocks delivered a powerful punch. Trebuchet operators often aimed such missiles at the battlements of fortifications, smashing the masonry, and killing defenders until the time was right for escalade or the deployment of a siege tower. Alternative missiles included dead horses and men, designed to spread disease within the enemy fortress.

the sling end was drawn down low to the ground using a system of ropes, pulleys, and windlasses, hoisting the counterpoise into the air. When the mechanism was released, the counterpoise dropped back down towards the earth, propelling the opposite end of the arm upwards at speed, which in turn flung the missile towards the target with a howitzer-like trajectory.

POWER AND LIMITATIONS

Trebuchets were used in siege warfare throughout medieval Europe and the Middle East, and also, from the 13th century at least, by the Chinese and the Mongols. They developed into several different types; variations in the positioning and number of the counterpoise, for example, gave the user

BELOW: A modern-day reconstruction of a trebuchet built in France. The origins of the word are French; loosely translated it meant something like "to fall over" or "rotate about the middle," but came to mean any large-scale catapult used in siege warfare. (Chris Hellier/Ancient Art and Architecture Collection)

ABOVE: An artistic representation of a trebuchet at work against a medieval castle. (© *Look and Learn*/The Bridgeman Art Library)

greater or lesser degrees of control over accuracy, range, and rates of fire. They were monstrous pieces of equipment to construct, however, a process that had to be done at the site of the siege. "Warwolf" – King Edward I's mighty trebuchet constructed for the siege of Stirling Castle in 1304 – took 54 people three months to complete. "Warwolf" was believed to have destroyed the castle's gatehouse, by which time the castle's garrison had surrendered anyway.

As with so many other medieval weapons, the trebuchet was rendered obsolete by the invention of gunpowder weaponry. Cannon, when they arrived in the 14th century, were more portable and, once casting techniques and gunpowder had improved, delivered a harder punch than trebuchet rocks. As an example of mechanical ingenuity, however, the trebuchet remains an impressive weapon.

ENGLISH LONGBOW

THE LONGBOW'S ORIGINS ARE DISPUTED – POPULARLY it is held to have come from the Welsh Marches, but the exact provenance is uncertain. Certainly, Welsh longbowmen were an important component of many English armies. In material construction the stave was ideally cut from a yew tree, although ash and elm were also used. The cut of the wood was critical, the outer surface of the stave being of the tree's sapwood, while the belly of the stave was from the heartwood, this combination giving the ideal pairing of compression and powerful release.

OPPOSITE: An English archer *c.* 1500. This archer is considerably better armed with other weapons than those of a previous generation at the height of the Hundred Years' War. By this stage the golden age of the English archer was coming to an end. (Hulton Archive/Getty Images)

PULL WEIGHT

The distinctive properties of the longbow were its length and its pull weight. Longbows recovered from the *Mary Rose*, the Tudor warship that sank in 1545, were between 6ft 1in and 6ft 10in (1.87 and 2.11m) long, making them longer than most

ABOVE: Almost six decades prior to Agincourt, the English forces of Edward the Black Prince, son of King Edward III, defeated heavily armored French troops at the battle of Crécy in 1346. (akg-images/Erich Lessing)

of the men who used them. Pull weight on the same bows was put at 150–160lbf (667–712N). Such enormous draw weights required herculean strength from the longbowman, and skeletons of longbowmen are recognizable from deformities to arms, wrists, shoulders, and fingers. The longbow was also a difficult weapon to master, hence English monarchs often put in place various ordinances encouraging or commanding the lower orders to practice the arts of archery. (Longbowmen were almost all from middle or lower orders of society, the knightly class believing that killing from a distance was somehow ignoble.) Longbowmen would typically begin training in their early teens, and only reach a state of combat proficiency in their twenties.

LONG-RANGE WEAPON

The upshot of the training and the bow's power was a lethal range of hundreds of yards. A reconstruction of a *Mary Rose*

Stiffen the sinews, summon up the blood,
Disguise fair nature with hard-favoured rage;
Then lend the eye a terrible aspect.

Shakespeare, *Henry V*, 3.1.1

AGINCOURT

During the Hundred Years' War (1337–1453), the longbow was integral to English victories at Crécy (1346), Poitiers (1356), and, most famously, Agincourt (1415). In the latter battle, approximately 6,000 English soldiers – the majority of whom were longbowmen – faced a French army of up to 30,000. When the French knights finally attacked, on October 25, their ranks were horribly thinned by a sky-darkening hail of arrows that began to kill and injure men and mounts well before they could close to fighting distance. Trained archers could release about six aimed shots each minute, or 12 unaimed, meaning that the archers at Agincourt probably fired more than 30,000 arrows at the French in the first minute.

The devastation caused by the longbow barrage weakened the French attack, and left dismounted warriors vulnerable to an English counterattack that took the battlefield.

bow fired a relatively lightweight arrow out to 360yds (328m), but a more typical effective range would be in the region of 247yds (230m). A clue to range capabilities came in 1542, when Henry VIII ordered that no archer of 24 years old or more was to shoot his bow at a target of less than 220yds (201m), such was his concern over declining longbow skills.

OPPOSITE: Agincourt is one of the great English victories, in Shakespeare's words, "a small band of brothers" achieving success against a far larger force thanks in part to the skill of their archers. (Artwork by Gerry Embleton © Osprey Publishing Ltd)

ABOVE: An artistic re-creation of a pair of archers from the mid-14th to early 15th century. Each demonstrates the two medieval methods of "stringing" the bows, the one on the right the more common of the two. Modern archery places a leg between the bow and string, resting the lower bow tip on the other foot and "bending" the bow around the back of the thigh. This is due to the fact that modern archers do not have the physical strength for the medieval technique. (Artwork by Gerry Embleton © Osprey Publishing Ltd)

On the battlefield, the longbow was a weapon of long-range attrition. Not only could it reach the enemy at great distances, the arrows also delivered impressive penetration, puncturing (with the heavy bodkin point) some types of thin plate armor and mail. The longbow was, in many ways, superior to firearms for many centuries. Ironically, however, the longbow disappeared at just about the same time as the matchlock musket appeared on the battlefield, about the 15th century. For all their deficiencies, arquebus and muskets offered remote lethality, just like the longbow, but without the years of intensive training. Moreover, periods of peace resulted in an irrevocable decline in longbow training. Combined with an increasing shortage of yew wood, and the longbow gradually slipped from supremacy into obsolescence.

CROSSBOW

Crossbows were an eastern invention, extant examples dating back to the 6th century BC, and they endured in various forms throughout the eras of Greece and Rome. The heyday of the individual, hand-held crossbow, however, was the medieval period in Europe.

COMPACT POWER

The principle of the crossbow was simple enough. A short bow, or "prod," was fitted on the front of a stock that featured a running groove along its top. To load the crossbow, the bowstring, made from a rigid twisted cord (usually hemp), was pulled back until it engaged with a restraining mechanism further back up the stock. Unlike the bow, which fired a long, light arrow, the crossbow propelled a stocky, heavy bolt. The bolt was simply placed in the stock groove, the base of the bolt up against the cocked bowstring, and when the trigger was pulled the prod tension was released and the crossbow bolt fired.

Set side-by-side, the standard infantry crossbow had a more limited range and a lower rate of fire than a longbow. There were also issues with power. The short prods of crossbows were actually capable of holding more draw weight than a bow. Yet converting that power into velocity proved something of a problem. Heavy bolts and thick bowstrings (necessarily substantial to cope with the immense pull weights) all sapped away the power of the release. The crossbow designers responded, however, with impressive increases in draw weights, riding on the back of improved material

OPPOSITE: A 15th century Bavarian crossbow with a steel bow and unusually decorated with red painted flowers. Crossbows were common throughout continental Europe during this period. (© Wallace Collection/The Bridgeman Art Library)

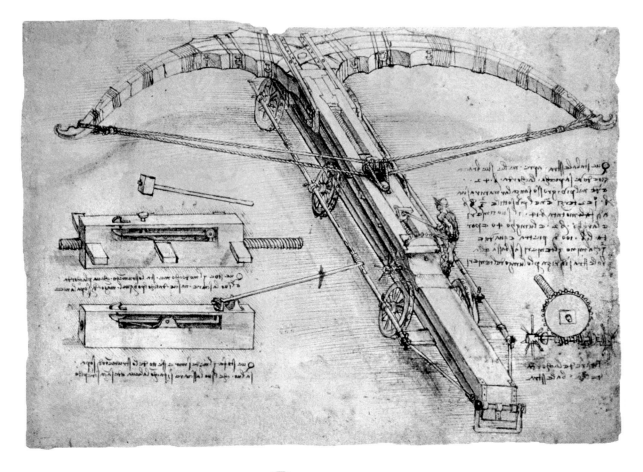

ABOVE: At the end of the 15th century, Leonardo da Vinci even envisaged the creation of a giant crossbow as an effective siege device as well as a psychological weapon. (akg-images/Oronoz)

LEFT: A Flemish medieval illustration of Mordred, a figure in Arthurian legend, attacking the Tower of London, which is defended by crossbowmen. (© British Library/The Bridgeman Art Library)

construction. At first crossbows had simple wooden prods, but during the 11th century stronger composite prods made of wood, horn, and sinew became the norm. These in turn were superseded by mild steel prods in the 13th century, as the crossbow sought to defeat the challenge of plate armor. The result was a prodigious climb in draw weights, from about 150lb (68kg) to more than 700lb (318kg). Ranges of such weapons could exceed 400yds (366m).

Naturally, there came a point at which simply cocking such weapons went beyond normal physical capabilities. The simple wooden or composite bows were mainly cocked by hand action alone – the crossbowman would put his foot in a stirrup at the front of the stock, then span (cock) the crossbow to the trigger catch using both hands and much upper body strength. For the most resistant bows, the crossbowman might also use an assisting hook fitted to his belt – the hook was attached to the bowstring, and the crossbowman could therefore use his whole upper body weight to cock the bow. When prods became too powerful for even these procedures, mechanical cocking devices were introduced in the form of windlasses and cranequins (rack-and-pinion winding mechanisms). Using these meant the crossbow had a very sluggish rate of fire – crossbowmen would crouch behind large convex shields called *pavises* during their vulnerable reloading phase. Yet they meant that crossbows could reach velocities equal to those of the longbow, with greater penetrative power on account of the momentum carried in the heavy bolt.

BELOW: A 15th-century depiction of a soldier firing his crossbow while two companions take shelter behind a large shield. (Mary Evans Picture Library)

BATTLEFIELD ADVANTAGES

The crossbow's popularity was also based on reasons other than brute physics. Crucially, while it took years to train an archer to a convincing level of skill, a crossbowman could reach proficiency with about a week of instruction. As we shall see frequently in this book, the equations of force often prefer simpler, less effective weapons in more hands than complex, sophisticated weapons in fewer hands. For this reasons, crossbows were often viewed as threatening the social order, giving the ability for a commoner with little training to kill a venerated knight. The British Magna Carta document pledged to banish crossbowmen from the kingdom "once peace is restored," and in 1139 Pope Innocent II even banned the use of crossbows against Christians, calling the crossbowman "hated of God." Eventually, the rise of firearms and the crossbow's slow rates of fire – which left its user particularly exposed to cavalry attacks – meant it fell out of use in combat by the late 15th century. By this time, however, it had made a signal contribution to what has been called the "infantry revolution," the steady shift of battlefield power from mounted knights to footsoldiers.

LANCE

By the beginning of the medieval period, particularly in Europe, much warfare was conducted on foot. Yet around the 6th and 7th centuries, Europe received an importation from Asia that was to reshape mounted combat. The invention was the stirrup, and for a cavalryman it was a transforming piece of technology.

OPPOSITE: An engraving depicting the battle of Crécy in 1346, one of the most significant English victories during the Hundred Years' War against France. The English won thanks to a brilliant use of combined arms including the lance and the English longbow, as well as early cannon. (The Bridgeman Art Library)

STABLE MOUNT

Before the stirrup, the horseman relied mainly on the grip of knees and thighs to keep him on his horse, which could create problems with balance during the impact between lance and target. We must not overstate these problems – the ancient world produced many battle-winning lance-wielding cavalry formations, such as Alexander the Great's Companion Cavalry during the 4th century BC, who delivered mass lance charges with perfect conviction and effect. Yet the stirrup certainly provided a greater degree of stability on the saddle. Saddles themselves also improved; in fact, the developments in saddles could actually be more significant to cavalry than those involving stirrups. Higher pommels and cantles braced the rider more firmly, providing a decent platform from which to fight. The Franks led the way. During the 8th century, the elite of the Frankish army moved from being a primarily dismounted force to being a true cavalry, and the age of the European knight was born.

haftyng

Dgard

Knights fought with many weapons, but the classic battlefield combination was the lance and sword. Unlike spears, lances were heavier, more robust weapons that were unsuited to throwing. Made from woods such as ash and, later, cypress, the typical war lance was about 12ft (3.6m) in length, and featured a metal or iron spear head (unlike the blunt coronal used for tournament jousting). The weapon would swell out at the grip end, and a small, round metal shield called a vamplate was sometimes fitted just in front of the grip hand, to protect it against the enemy's weapons.

The emergence of the stirrup and improved saddle meant that the mode of employing the lance changed significantly. Images from the Bayeaux Tapestry depict many Norman knights riding into battle with their lances held aloft above their heads, or gripping them in an underhand fashion. Yet a few knights have the lance in the "couched" position – tucked beneath their armpits in a very solid grip that allowed for heavy impacts delivered at speed. Actually, earlier 9th-century Frankish images also show Carolingian cavalry holding lances in the couched position. Yet whenever the practice began, it appears that the couched lance technique had become standard by the 12th century.

SHOCK TROOPS

The combination of couched lance, stirrup, and high saddle welded the horse, rider, and weapon into a single, durable unit. Now the knight could deliver shock charges and ride out the heavy impact of lance and enemy. The grip also allowed lances to lengthen, meaning that the knight could strike his enemy out of the range of other pole-arms. Once combat closed into a cavalry melee, the knight would discard his lance and fight with his sword.

Against infantry ranks the charge of couched-lance cavalrymen could be devastating. The cavalry became the main striking force of the medieval army, the maneuver element that

ABOVE: A modern reenactor charges with a couched lance. The knight would have to commit his entire body weight to the thrust to avoid being unseated by the blow on his opponent. (iStock)

could decide a battle. Such was the significance of the lance, that it endured through the introduction of firearms (although with much-diminished authority) and remained in use in the 19th century, in dedicated lancer formations. Couched-lance charges were even conducted by German, Russian, and Austro-Hungarian units on the Eastern Front during World War I (1914–18). By that time, the lance had become grossly anachronistic, but its persistence says much about the combined power of a galloping horse and a leveled lance.

> **He should frequent tourneys and joust for his Lady Love.**
>
> **Eustace Deschamps**

CHINESE ROCKETS

ROCKETS, OF COURSE, REQUIRE PROPELLANT TO WORK. The Chinese had been experimenting with pyrotechnic compounds probably since the 1st century AD, and by the 7th century they seem to have progressed to manufacturing ceremonial fireworks. A century later, they had created what we today know as black powder.

FIRE WEAPONS

Black powder was formed from a mixture of ground potassium nitrate (saltpeter), charcoal, and sulfur, mixed in proportions of roughly 75:15:10 by weight. While the Chinese initially used many of their combustible substances ceremonially, the military applications gradually became apparent. The first recorded military use of black powder appears to have occurred in 904, at a siege during the Tang dynasty in which lumps of smoldering black powder were catapulted over a defenders' walls. During the 12th century, more advanced black-powder based weapons emerged, including rudimentary bombs and "fire lances" (see feature box). Rockets were far more sophisticated weapons, and thus took a little longer to emerge. They required, for example, a far more sustaining propellant than pure black powder. During the 11th century, black powder was mixed with oily hydrocarbons, forming a propellant that could be packed into a bamboo tube, which was in turn strapped to a long arrow.

FROM FIRE ARROWS TO ROCKETS

The result was the "fire arrow." In essence, the fire arrow was little more than a firework on a stick, with a similar range to a comparable domestic display firework. They were inaccurate

OPPOSITE: The oldest accurately dated handgun in the world is Chinese and dates from 1351. It shows a natural progression in the use of black powder. (© Stephen Turnbull)

ABOVE: The Chinese used rockets to repel Mongol invaders at the battle of Kai-fung-fun in 1232. According to one historic report: "When the rocket was lit, it made a noise that resembled thunder that could be heard for five leagues [*c.* 5 miles]…" (NASA/MSFC History office)

BELOW: A Chinese infantryman *c.* 1260 is shown firing on a Mongolian warrior. (Artwork by David Sque © Osprey Publishing Ltd.)

and of uncertain destructive force, but rather than launching them singly, the Chinese pioneered multiple rocket launchers, firing the missiles from wooden boxes or numerous rails, with barrages of possibly several hundred missiles at a time. The first use of rockets in battle appears to be in reference to the battle of Kai-fung-fun in 1232, when a Mongol attack was dispersed by heavy rocket fire. The multiple launchers seem to have taken hold during the 14th and 15th centuries, and the launcher units were even mounted on wheeled carts, giving the rocket weapon battlefield mobility. Smaller units could be carried by individual men, gripped underarm, although the tendency of rockets to explode immediately following ignition must have given such men constant anxiety.

Regardless of the actual power of the fire arrows, a whistling, sparking barrage of them must have at least psychologically shaken the ranks of the enemy. They also had enough value to spread across Asia to Europe via the Mongols and the Arabs – rockets appear in accounts of warfare in Spain and Italy as early as the 13th and 14th centuries. Valencia, for example,

ABOVE: A depiction of Chinese rocket launchers *c.* 1450. This illustration is itself based on a reconstructed scale model in the National Historical Museum in Peking. Reportedly hundreds of rockets could be fired in just a few seconds. (Artwork by David Sque © Osprey Publishing Ltd.)

BELOW: A Chinese soldier shown launching a fire rocket. (NASA/MSFC History office)

was reportedly bombarded by rockets in 1288. Of course, rocketry would not become a truly significant part of warfare until the 20th century. Yet during the 14th century, gunpowder became the propellant for another type of weapon, this time one that would shape both warfare and history.

BLACK POWDER WEAPONS

The Chinese produced some of the earliest bombs in history – clay, iron, bamboo or cloth casings packed with gunpowder and assorted shrapnel (typically pieces of metal or broken porcelain), fitted with a rudimentary fuse, and hurled against enemy buildings or personnel. While they would have been of relatively low power compared to modern devices, at close quarters they would still deliver lethal effects. Another invention was the *huo qiang* or fire lance, which may date back to the 10th century. It was essentially a hollow tube made from thick layers of paper, inside which was put a charge of gunpowder and shrapnel pieces. When the *huo qiang* was lit, it blasted out a jet of flame and projectiles, the flames having an endurance of several seconds and reaching out to a range of 9ft (3m). In a sense, here was the earliest hand-held flamethrower.

EARLY CANNON

REFERENCES TO CANNON CROP UP IN THE EARLY 1320s, but the earliest authenticated illustration is in an English treatise by Walter de Milemete dated to 1326. It depicts a vase-shaped gun, set on a four-legged wooden frame. A figure behind the gun touches a vent-hole with a burning match, and from the "barrel" – essentially the mouth of the vase – flies a large arrow. The ballistic properties of such a weapon would have been erratic at best, but significant improvements came quickly. The vase shape was dropped in favor of straight-sided barrels and dart ammunition was supplemented, and later entirely replaced, by balls of stone, lead, iron, and bronze. Mounts also improved, and ranged from static wooden blocks through to wheeled carts, the latter giving early cannon some degree of battlefield mobility.

IRON AND BRONZE

Until the 16th century, cannon barrels were made essentially by welding together longitudinally arranged hoops of iron. Scaled up the process could produce "bombards" of considerable power and scale. The famous wrought iron "Mons Meg," for example, was 13ft (4m) long, weighed 7.3 US tons (6.6 tonnes) and could fire a 19.5in (49.5cm), 549lb (250kg) stone shot to a distance of 2,800yds (2,560m), and a 1,125lb (511kg) iron shot to 1,400yds (1,280m). Yet wrought iron guns were hugely heavy and given to structural weaknesses, and it was nigh on impossible to manufacture multiple weapons of standardized bores. Cast bronze cannon, by contrast, could be lighter, stronger, and more suited to standardization (particularly once stone cannon balls were dropped in favor of iron shot by the end of the 16th century). Manufactured from the early 15th century, cast bronze cannon had largely replaced wrought iron varieties within 100 years, permitting artillery to become a far more widespread presence.

OPPOSITE: A man fires a large medieval "handgonne" in a manuscript image dating from 1405. The handgonne was a natural extension of cannon within Europe and would eventually result in the development of the matchlock musket. (akg-images/Erich Lessing)

URBAN'S GUNS

The fall of Constantinople in 1453 was a defining moment in the history of early artillery. The great city, with its seemingly impregnable defensive walls – the inner wall alone was 15ft 6in (4.7m) thick – was besieged by the forces of Mohammed II in the spring of that year. Mohammed commissioned a European gunmaker named Urban to create artillery pieces equal to the challenge. Urban responded by casting in bronze 18 guns of unprecedented size and power. Each measured 17ft (5.18m) in length, and weighed 19 US tons (17.27 tonnes). Caliber was around 25in (63.5cm), and each cannon could fire a granite ball weighing 1,500lb (680kg) to a range of more than a mile. Urban's guns opened fire on Constantinople on April 1, 1453. After some 4,000 shots had been fired, the walls were breached by May 29, and the city subsequently fell, casting a lengthening, ominous shadow over the age of fortification.

ABOVE: During the Hundred Years' War, the English use of cannon alongside traditional weapons such as the longbow helped to secure several victories. This slightly fanciful 19th-century depiction of an attack on a French castle does at least show both kinds of weaponry. (akg-images/IAM/World History Archive)

SOCIAL REVOLUTION

Over its first centuries of use, the cannon transformed the face of warfare, and of society in general. Castles – those visible bastions of medieval feudal power – began their slow, steady decline in authority under the wall-breaking power of cannon shot (see feature box), although it would take until the 17th century before the process was largely complete. Artillerymen, often of rough origins, became some of the most important individuals in warfare, unsettling the position of the knight and beginning the rise of widespread technological professionalism in military ranks. Furthermore, once cannon became lighter and more mobile, they demanded that the entire system of infantry tactics be revised, emphasizing firepower and mobility as much as, then more than, manpower and muscle. For example, at the battle of Marignano in 1515,

French artillerymen devastated the great Swiss pike phalanx, the balls carving through the close-packed ranks well before the pikemen could close to fighting distance. Early cannon were frequently crude, smoky, and smelly weapons, but they irrevocably changed the history of our planet.

LEFT: Gunpowder appears to have been invented in China in the 8th century AD. The first European recipes are found in the 13th century. By the 15th century it was in widespread use, as this French manuscript image from that period clearly shows. (Ancient Art and Architecture Collection)

BELOW: Thanks to the efforts of Urban, a Hungarian gun master, the Ottoman army could put into position giant cannon alongside smaller cannon to attack the huge walls of Constantinople. Without the cannon, the city walls would never have been breached and the history of this region of the world would have been very different indeed. (Artwork by Peter Dennis © Osprey Publishing Ltd.)

MATCHLOCK

The first firearms emerged in Europe during the second half of the 14th century, and are known collectively as "handgonnes." At its simplest, the handgonne consisted of little more than a thick metal tube, with a vent hole bored through at the chamber end. Firing the handgonne was a fiery, clumsy process. Powder and ball were rammed down into the chamber using a ramrod, and a small amount of powder was poured down into the vent hole. The handgonne was then leveled in the general direction of the enemy, and the vent hole powder ignited by a smoldering slow match held in a linstock, either by the gunner himself or by a third party.

OPPOSITE: A musketeer carrying a matchlock gun and rest, together with bandoleers of ammunition, *c.* 1640 (Getty Images)

MECHANICAL IGNITION

Handgonnes were the forerunners of all the firearms that we use today, yet as battlefield weapons they were heavy, awkward to handle, and had a very slow rate of fire. Practical range was probably in the region of 50yds (46m). Around 1411, however, handgonnes were transformed by a new technology, the matchlock. In essence, the matchlock was the first mechanical means for firing a gun. At its most basic, it consisted of an

S-shaped piece of metal known as a "serpentine," which pivoted in the middle – the hinge was either on the outside of the gun stock or set inside a slot cut into the stock. The upper end of the serpentine held the slow match. When the gunner, therefore, pulled on the lower end of the serpentine, the upper part pivoted forward to drop the match onto a pan that held the priming powder.

This invention was simple, but revolutionary. Its most salient benefit was that the gunner could now maintain a steady aim on the target while firing the gun, and it is notable that simple bladed sights became more common around this time. Further improvements accentuated the progress. During the last quarter of the 16th century, the matchlock became two separate components – a spring-powered cock and a separate but connected trigger mechanism, producing the "snapping matchlock." Now when the trigger was pulled, it took just a split second for the released cock spring to drive the match down into the pan, and hence further improve accuracy (there was less time to wobble off target) and ignition.

BELOW: At the battle of Pavia in 1525, the higher number of arquebusiers within the Hapsburg Imperial army helped to ensure victory over the French, who had far less matchlocks deployed. (The Art Archive/Museo di Capodimonte/Gianni Dagli Orti)

ARQUEBUS

Matchlock weapons ushered in a new age of warfare, albeit slowly. The arquebus – a long-barrelled matchlock firearm – became a standard feature of many European and Asian armies. They were still inaccurate, dirty, and heavy – they were typically fired with the front end supported on a forked rest – and in terms of performance they were outclassed by bows and crossbows on many levels. Yet they were simple to operate and it was easy to train someone in their use. In time, the arquebus gave way to the lighter, more portable musket, which had a barrel length of 4ft (1.2m), a smooth-bored barrel of caliber ranging between 0.5in and 1in, and an effective range of around 55yds (50m). As we will see in the study of the flintlock in the next chapter, the musket age was to last for nearly 400 years, and eventually placed firearms above any other type of infantry weapon.

BELOW: An engraving of a matchlock musket. The matchlock was essentially the first mechanical means of firing a gun – a giant step forward from medieval handgonnes. (akg-images/IAM/World History Archive)

COMMONER vs NOBLE

What was so important about the early firearms is that they leveled the playing field between the rough, common soldier and the noble, highly trained warrior. A knight with centuries of martial tradition behind him, could be unseated and killed by an individual who spent most of his life tilling fields, or at least serving in the lower branches of the armed forces. At the battle of Pavia in 1525, for example, 1,500 Spanish arquebusiers under Habsburg monarch Charles V scattered and destroyed a vaunted force of French cavalry. Similarly, at the battle of Nagashino, Japan, in 1575, some 1,500–3,000 arqubusiers, commanded by Oda Nobunaga and set behind protective stockades, decimated the cavalry charges of Takeda Katsuyori's samurai warriors. Once firearms became widely distributed, high social status became increasingly irrelevant in combat.

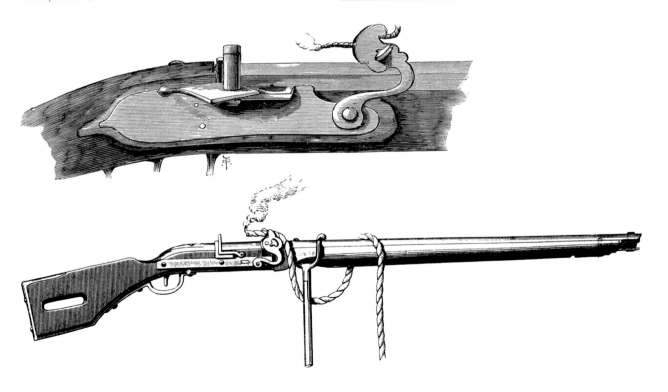

慶応三年(長五郎・四十七才)

荒神山

良吉田の仁吉に援を求む

兇仁吉の義侠に組し三十三人

伊勢荒神山に穴太徳

の徒と闘う浪人門之助を

政で囲み大政の槍に倒す

見法印大五郎・幸太郎

子仁吉も鏡創にて

す

THE EARLY MODERN
WORLD 1500–1800

FLINTLOCK

FOR ALL ITS EARLY INFLUENCE, THE MATCHLOCK remained a troublesome weapon to use convincingly. For example, by being reliant upon a length of smoldering slowmatch, the matchlock was next to useless in damp or wet weather. Furthermore, the need to have the slowmatch lit to fire the gun meant that the gun could not be held ready for action in an inert state. If firearms were going to have a genuine shaping effect on warfare, a different system of ignition was needed.

OPPOSITE: A close-up of the flintlock mechanism on an original flintlock gun held at Sutter's Fort, an early 19th-century settlement near Sacramento, California. (akg-images/North Wind Picture Archives)

WHEELLOCKS

During the early 16th century, one such system emerged. Known as the wheellock, its action consisted of a roughened metal wheel, which could be wound up under spring tension like a clockwork toy. Above it was a cock holding a piece of iron pyrites. When the trigger was pulled, the wheel was released and the cock fell and brought the iron pyrites into contact with the spinning wheel. The resulting flash of sparks ignited the powder in the pan and the gun fired. The wheellock worked well, and gave the world a firearm that no longer relied upon flame for ignition. Unfortunately, wheellock firearms were lavishly expensive to make, being akin to precision watch mechanisms. Therefore, while they caught on with affluent officers and citizens, and with the cavalry in particular, they were never going to be general issue weapons.

SNAPHANCE TO FLINTLOCK

A different approach came with the "snaphance" lock. Here the system for generating sparks was a piece of flint, again gripped by a spring-loaded cock. This time, the sparks were created by

the flint being propelled against an angular steel arm known as the frizzen, which sat over the pan. The snaphance lock also featured a hinged or sliding pan cover, meaning that the gun could be loaded but the powder kept dry and in place ready for later action.

ABOVE: An American soldier uses his powder horn to prime the pan of his flintlock musket. (The Bridgeman Art Library/Peter Newark American Pictures)

ABOVE: The development of the flintlock mechanism, allied with rifling, eventually led to far greater accuracy of shot. During the American Revolutionary War, sharpshooters were used to pick off high-level commanders such as General Simon Fraser, killed during the Saratoga campaign. (Painting by Hugh Charles McBarron, courtesy US Army Center of Military History)

The snaphance was a critical step forward in gun design, as it laid the foundations for the flintlock itself, which emerged about 1620. In the new lock, the mechanism had both half cock and full cock modes (half cock allowed loading, but the gun couldn't be fired from this position), but with greater simplicity than those snaphances that had the same feature. The flintlock also combined the frizzen and pan cover in one spring-loaded piece, making the gun simpler to manufacture while retaining all the advantages of the covered pan.

The flintlock was the true beginning of the firearms revolution. The flintlock musket became the standard firearm of virtually every modern army in the world, and remained

RIFLING

Rifling is the process of cutting helical grooves in the bore of a gun, in order to impart spin to a projectile as it is fired. A spinning projectile has a gyroscopic stability around its central axis, and therefore it flies more accurately and to a greater range. The origins of rifling are uncertain, but date back to the 15th and 16th centuries. Rifling required a tight fit between bullet and bore, which meant that rifled weapons were slower to load than smoothbores, but the accuracy advantages were profound. Standard military muskets were typically capable of hitting targets at no more than 100yds (91m), but there are accounts of 17th- and 18th-century marksmen with rifled guns hitting human-sized targets at up to 600yds (550m), even beyond.

so for more than 300 years. Its reliability, and predictable operation even in fairly poor weather, meant that synchronized fire (necessary to compensate for smoothbore inaccuracy) could be delivered in massive, coordinated volleys from ordered infantry ranks. More importantly, flintlocks were relatively cheap to produce, and became even more so once mass production was adopted, so here was the means for eventually equipping every combat soldier in an army with a firearm. Once the flintlock system was allied to rifled barrels, furthermore, accurate shots could be taken out to ranges of hundreds of yards, giving birth to the marksman or sniper. Flintlocks not only changed warfare, but by their influence and ubiquity, and their eventual role in deciding mankind's greatest battles, they also changed history itself.

RAPIER

As we saw in the last chapter, the emergence of plate armor in the 13th and 14th centuries had a fundamental effect on the nature of sword design. The classic double-edged slashing sword was largely replaced by cut-and-thrust arming swords and longswords. As armor developed in its sophistication – by the beginning of the 15th century fully articulated top-to-toe suits were being worn on the battlefield – so swordmakers sought to meet the challenge in various ways. One expression was the *estoc*, a longsword with a steeply pointed, rigid blade designed purely for thrusting attacks, and the blades of many hand-and-a-half swords became more compact and stiffer. At the mightiest end of the scale were enormous two-handed longswords, measuring up to 5ft 9in (1.75m) and weighing up to 8lb (3.6kg), and wielded with particular notoriety by German and Swiss infantrymen.

OPPOSITE: A German rapier with intricate carved details. The beauty of the weapon belied the deadly effect it could achieve. (akg-images)

CIVILIAN WEAPON

The rapier emerged into this picture fully during the 16th century, although in many ways its evolution began in the previous century. During the late 1400s, the hilts of some swords developed an increasingly elaborate format, which included ornate quillons, knuckle-guards, finger rings, and pommels. Such hilts became a defining characteristic of the

RAPIER WOUNDS

In skilled hands the rapier had both reach and speed, and built its techniques upon finding the shortest, quickest route to hit and penetrate the target. Target areas for the trained swordsman included the chest, abdomen, and throat. With their narrow blades, rapiers left slender internal injuries that were difficult to fix and heal, hence many rapier duels and confrontations ended initially in injury, only for the wounded party to die later of infection or slow blood loss. A straight pierce through the heart, however, would bring almost immediate death. Note, however, that in street combat rapiers were used brutally in combination with punches, kicks, trips and whatever other advantages the fighters could throw into the battle.

rapier, but in terms of blades the early rapiers tended to be very different from those they would become. The blades of the late 15th century are often broad, double-edged, and highly pointed, making them cut-and-thrust weapons suited to light infantry use.

The rapier proper, however, was a 16th-century creation, and corresponded with a time in which swords became important items of civilian dress, used for both social distinction and for self-defense in an age of dueling and violent robbery. The classic rapier blade was typically long, thin, and designed almost entirely for nimble swordplay and delivering fast, deep, thrust injuries with an extremely sharp

LEFT: The development of the rapier was a direct result of the huge advances made in armor design. This armor was designed for Henry VIII to be worn at the Field of Cloth of Gold tournament in 1520, although it was replaced with different armor at the final moment. There was no chink in its protection, which completely covered the body. (© Board of the Trustees of the Armouries, object no. II 6)

point. Pure military swords typically retained the cut-and-thrust characteristics required for the multiple targets of opportunity found on the battlefield. The rapier, by contrast, reflected the needs of one-to-one combat against unarmored opponents. A man fighting for his life in a narrow back alley would have limited opportunity to make broad swings with a blade, but with a rapier he could thrust and stab with astonishing repetitive speed – the blades were exquisitely balanced for rapid movements.

The rapier bred schools of swordsmanship throughout Europe, and helped create the sport of fencing that is still practiced to this day. During the 17th century, long, large-hilted rapiers gradually fell out of use. Firearms were taking away the rationale of the sword, and the shorter, lighter, and altogether more decorous "smallsword" came to be the preferred side-arm for the gentleman on the street. Fighting with the smallsword was more ritualistic and codified, and hence was largely the realm of the formal duel. For nearly

200 years, however, the rapier had embodied the reality of combat on the street – a tool to finish the fight decisively and quickly.

LEFT: A beautiful example of a rapier probably crafted in Italy but in English use. The hilt is gold with silver inlays and fine carving. (© Wallace Collection The Bridgeman Art Library)

KATANA

THE CLASSIC JAPANESE *KATANA* SWORD IS WIDELY HELD as the perfection of the swordmaker's art. Entering use during the Muromachi Period (1392–1477), the best examples are not only perfectly balanced, lethally sharp, and extremely resilient, they are also objects of exquisite beauty. It is little wonder, therefore, that they virtually came to represent the entire samurai class of warriors.

PERFECT CUT

Sword-making already had a long ancestry in Japan before the adoption of the *katana*. Until the 10th century, Japanese swords tended to be single-edged, straight weapons such as the *chokuto*, which often had more resemblance to Western swords than later samurai blades. Yet around the middle of the 900s,

OPPOSITE: A modern reworking of an original Japanese woodblock print showing a samurai armed with his *katana*. With one foot on the plinth of a Buddhist statue, he holds his sword in the raised position, in preparation for a downward slash. (Courtesy of Stephen Turnbull)

Japanese swords began to develop a definite curve, improving their abilities as slashing weapons. By the 13th century, these blades had reached a state of perfection both in terms of their cutting efficiency and their manufacture.

It is worth noting what is special about a traditionally constructed samurai sword. The challenge for the swordmaker was to produce a blade that was hard enough to retain its edge, but flexible enough to resist shattering. The former quality is associated with high-carbon steel, the latter with low-carbon steel, and the Japanese swordmaker sought to combine both types in one single-edged weapon. He achieved this by forming the centre of the sword – the *shigane*

BELOW: A depiction of the 1866 swordfight known as the "Spray of blood on Kojinyama," from the Shimizu Jirocho Memorial Museum, Shimizu City. (Courtesy of Stephen Turnbull)

– from a low-carbon billet, folded just a few times, and wrapping this with the high-carbon *hadagane* outer steel, which was heated and folded up to 15 times to adjust its carbon content appropriately. The finishing was performed through a complicated mix of heating and quenching (sudden cooling), the quenching process being that which actually gave the blades their curved shape. The skills of swordmaking and of sword polishing were hard-achieved, although it is worth reminding ourselves that there were always plenty of poor-quality swords in circulation in Japan. But when produced by a master, the result was formidable.

SAMURAI BLADES

By the 15th century there were three blade types that could be considered typically Japanese. The shortest, essentially large daggers, were the *tanto*. The next stage up in length were the

" *A sword should not be drawn from its scabbard unless it is to attack.* "
Traditional saying from the Jigen-ryu swordfighting school

wakizashi, which were short swords that extended to about 23.6in (60cm), where the *katana* roughly began. *Tanto* and *wakizashi* could be carried by the members of any social class entitled to be armed, including some women. The right to train with and carry a *katana*, however, was the exclusive reserve of the samurai class. (Note, however, that today the term *katana* is often used generically to describe all types of samurai sword, and some historians argue against the idea that the *katana* is associated with any particular length.) For the samurai, the *katana* and *wakizashi* were generally worn

SWORD FIGHTING POSITIONS

1   2   3   4   5   6

The six classic swordfighting positions when using a *katana*:

1. *Ukaketsuzen kennoisei*: a defensive position against an enemy who has his sword raised ready to cut downwards.
2. *Ukaho kennosei*: a similar defensive position but with a more relaxed or casual posture favoured by some of the more experienced swordsmen.
3. *Chudan*: a strong guard position with the sword held at medium height.

4. *Sachu senkennosei*: a threatening posture in which the swordpoint is aimed at the enemy's throat.
5. *Heijozen kennosei*: an unusual posture with the sword edge uppermost and supported by the left hand.
6. *Jordan no kamae*: a strong posture in which the sword is held ready to deliver a devastating downward strike.

THE *KATANA* FROM BLADE TO SCABBARD

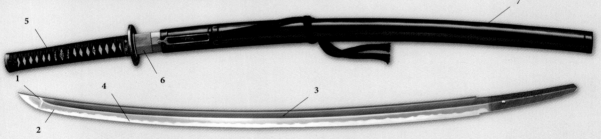

5   7   1   4   6   3   2

1. *kissaki*: the fan-shaped cutting tip of the blade
2. *boshi*: the wave-pattern of the tip
3. *shinogi-suji*: the ridge running the length of the blade
4. *hasaki*: the fiercely sharp cutting edge
5. *same-kawa*: the wrapping on the helm known as "shark-skin" but actually the skin of a giant ray

6. *menuki*: decorative metal fittings placed under the hilt wrapping
7. *saya*: the scabbard

toshin: the sword as a whole

as a matching pair, although the *katana* was the primary battlefield weapon. And a fearsome weapon it was. The *katana* was designed to deliver powerful slashing attacks – it was worn with the blade facing upwards to facilitate a quick draw and cut. The key targets were the head, neck, forearms, stomach, and lower abdomen, and a single clean hit on many of these areas could prove fatal. *Katana* swords had been developed specifically for speed, being lighter and shorter than the *tachi* sword previously favored, and perfectly balanced for both one- and two-handed use. It was easily capable of separating a head from a body with a single stroke, as depicted in numerous martial paintings or wood carvings from Japan's past.

All swords were eventually overshadowed by the development of firearms, which eventually subjugated swordsmanship to weight of lead. Yet the *katana* represents the perfect blending of sword and warrior, and as such these objects remain venerated amongst collectors to this day.

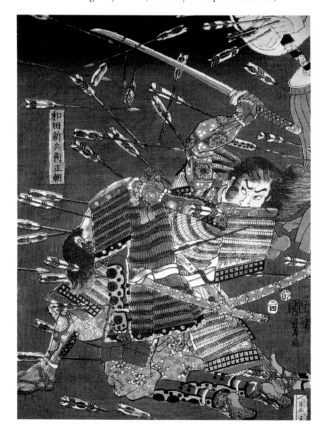

BELOW: Kusunoki Masatsura (1326–48) uses his slain cousin's body as a shield against a storm of arrows while he wields his sword during the battle of Shijo-Nawate in 1348. A key military commander during this period of civil instability in Japan, he was killed in the battle at the age of just 22. (Courtesy of Stephen Turnbull)

SWORD PLAY AND *BUSHIDO*

Over time, the use of the *katana* became deeply imbued with the spirituality of *bushido* – the "Way of the Warrior." *Bushido* is a slippery concept to define, not least because it took its firmest shape retrospectively from the 19th century onwards. Nor was there ever a single ethical or martial code for the samurai. Roughly speaking, *bushido* is rather like medieval chivalry, denoting a set of virtues such as respect, courage, and loyalty. The idea of swordsmanship as a way of expressing these qualities, particularly bravery and a disdain for death, took shape over time, through works such as Miyamoto Musashi's *Book of Five Rings* (c. 1645). Even once the samurai became more of an administrative class from the 17th century, the *katana* remained an emblem of status and martial spirit. The "soul of the sword" idea persisted well into the 20th century – during World War II, Japanese officers commonly donned cheap *katana* swords, using them for either prisoner dispatch or while making typically suicidal charges against Allied guns. Although such attacks were futile in an age of mechanized warfare, they nevertheless left a powerful impression on those who faced them.

SABER

When looking for the origins of the saber, three blades stand out as formative – the Ottoman *kilij*, the Indian *talwar*, and the Persian *shamshir*. The *kilij* is a useful starting point, as during the Early Modern period its influence spread out from Turkey throughout the Middle East and Asia (including India), courtesy of the Ottoman Empire, and eventually would either inform European saber design or be adopted by Westerners directly. In design, the *kilij* had a long, curved, single-edged blade measuring about 33.5in (85cm). For about two thirds of the blade's length, the sides kept fairly parallel, but in the final third the back edge flared out, creating a wider, heavier section that put extra weight (and therefore power) behind the cut.

The *talwar* and *shamshir*, by contrast, were more slender, but the curves of the blade could be even more pronounced. Indeed, in the case of the *shamshir* the curve was almost impractical, describing an angle of up to 15 degrees from hilt to tip. The *talwar* hilt typically had a pistol grip that swelled in the middle, framed by a disc pommel and quillons, sometimes with a knucklebow angling backwards. *Shamshir* hilts were generally plainer, with short quillons and a simple L-shaped configuration.

SLASHING WEAPON

All these swords, and variations such as the Arab *saif*, were serious battlefield weapons. They were particularly suited to making powerful "draw-cut" blows, striking the opponent near the lower end of the blade then widening the cut with a long slashing action. Sixteenth-century British records of warfare in India include accounts of *talwar* splitting helmet and head in two with single blows.

For European armies, curved swords were in use with cavalry by at least the 16th century. Indigenous designs included the cleaver-like falchion and the hefty hunting hangar, but it was warfare in India and against Ottoman and Arab Muslim forces that really brought the saber – as such curved swords became

OPPOSITE: A beautifully designed Russian saber, also known as a *shashka*, from the 19th century. (akg-images/RIA Nowosti)

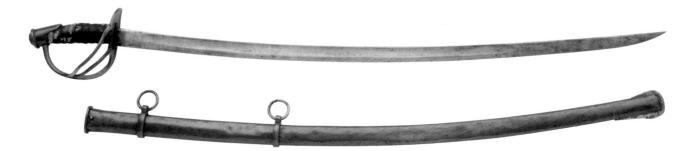

ABOVE: An American Civil War saber. (The Bridgeman Art Library © Civil War Archive)

BELOW: The road to Gettysburg began at Brandy Station on June 9, 1863, when Union cavalry commander General Alfred Pleasonton launched his cavalry corps against the Confederate forces of General J.E.B. Stuart. The Confederate force was almost defeated in 12 hours of bitter fighting, but reinforcements saved the day. It was the most hotly contested clash of sabers in the entire Civil War. Here the 35th Virginia Cavalry Battalion, later nicknamed "The Grey Comanches," is shown overrunning the 6th New York Independent Battery, clearly demonstrating the "shock and awe" effect a sabre charge could achieve. (*The Grey Comanches*, painting by Don Troiani, www.historicalimagebank.com)

generically known – to the West. During the 17th–19th centuries, battlefield body armor largely disappeared (apart from the breastplates of some cavalry) and firearms were dominant, so what light cavalry in particular needed was a fast, lethal cutting weapon for use in the melee.

REFORM

British Army officer John Gaspard Le Marchant recognized this fact while fighting in the French Revolutionary Wars, seeing that the lengthy, heavy, straight swords of many British cavalrymen were impractical – at close-quarters, hacking was more instinctive than the thrust. In response, he helped design the Pattern 1796 Light Cavalry Saber, modeled directly on Eastern blades. Light, fast, and capable of inflicting horrible wounds, it not only equipped many British light cavalry formations, but it was also used by the Prussians, Portuguese, and Spanish. Le Marchant also wrote a manual of instruction in sword fighting and training, which became part of the army's official regulations and helped thousands of cavalry officers achieve proficiency in the blade.

The Pattern 1796 was followed by several other British pattern sabers, while other countries adopted their own standards, such as the French An XI, the classic Russian *shashka* (whose origins stretched back to the 12th century) and the American Model 1860, to name but a few. (From the 17th century, sword manufacture was increasingly industrialized, producing many uniform, standardized patterns of hilt and blade suited to uniformly equipping large formations.) Indeed, even as late as the American Civil War (1861–65), saber-armed infantry were shaping the outcomes of battles, such as at the battle of Brandy Station in June 1863. It says much about the fighting qualities of the saber that they were still being swung in action even in the age of percussion firearms.

George Farmer of the 11th Light Dragoons, here recounts a battle between French and British cavalry in 1811, during the Peninsular War:

" Just then a French officer stooping over the body of one of his countrymen, who dropped the instant on his horse's neck, delivered a thrust at poor Harry Wilson's body; and delivered it effectually. I firmly believe that Wilson died on the instant yet, though he felt the sword in its progress, he, with characteristic self-command, kept his eye on the enemy in his front; and, raising himself in his stirrups, let fall upon the Frenchman's head such a blow, that brass and skull parted before it, and the man's head was cloven asunder to the chin. It was the most tremendous blow I ever beheld struck; and both he who gave, and his opponent who received it, dropped dead together. The brass helmet was afterwards examined by order of a French officer, who, as well as myself, was astonished at the exploit; and the cut was found to be as clean as if the sword had gone through a turnip, not so much as a dint being left on either side of it.[5] "

RIGHT: A member of the Bengal Irregular Cavalry parries a thrust from a lance with his *tulwar*, a curved sword design that would heavily influence the development of the European saber. (The Bridgeman Art Library/NAM)

BAYONET

For all that the flintlock musket changed the face of warfare, it had its problems. Its rates of fire, for example, were extremely low, and became worse as the bore of the gun became clogged up with powder residues from continuous firing – about 2–3 rounds per minute were typical from a fouled gun. Therefore, infantrymen were particularly vulnerable during the reloading phases, especially from a sudden cavalry assault or infantry charge. Furthermore, the musket was in no way a close-quarters weapon, and therefore had limited offensive potential.

OPPOSITE: Recruits at a British Army infantry training center bayonet sacks of straw on an assault course, c. 1942. Despite first being introduced in the 1600s, the bayonet saw extensive use during the two world wars and beyond. During the battle of Tumbledown in the Falklands War, the Royal Scots Greys fought at night with bayonets fixed. Major John Kiszely received a Military Cross after storming a Falklands trench, shooting two of the soldiers and bayoneting the third. (IWM H 18462)

PLUG AND SOCKET

For these reasons, the musketeer worked alongside pikemen for centuries, the latter providing both protection and the substance of a charge. Yet in the 17th century, everything changed. The revolution was the bayonet, a device that essentially fused the musketeer and the pikeman into one individual, capable of both delivering volleys of fire but also of charging into the enemy ranks with cold steel, or of protecting himself against enemy cavalry.

The first bayonets, invented about 1650, were of the crude "plug" variety, the blade (about 1ft/30cm long) literally projecting from the muzzle of the gun. (The blade was fitted with a slender wooden hilt that slipped down the bore.) Yet, obviously, when fitted the plug bayonet prevented the firearm from being discharged, so a better solution was sought. The critical breakthrough was the socket bayonet, developed within the French Army in the 1670s. In this case, the bayonet fitting consisted of an open-ended steel tube, which slipped around the muzzle and locked into place via a zig-zag slot engaging with studs. The slim, usually triangular bayonet projected out from the socket on an arm, sitting clear of the muzzle.

COMME A VALMY

La charge à la baïonnette au chant de la " Marseillaise "

The socket bayonet spread quickly throughout the armies of Europe, replacing the pike and giving infantry the rounded offensive and defensive capability they had previously lacked. In the defense, a standard tactic was for one rank of soldiers to present their bayonets while the next rank reloaded to fire, the ranks swapping roles frequently. On the attack, the "bayonet charge" became a decisive tactical moment, the point at which the soldiers closed with the enemy and sought the final victory.

SWORD AND KNIFE BAYONETS

Bayonet design, of course, did not stand still. In the 19th century, the sword bayonet took its place alongside the socket bayonet. The type was established by the British Pattern 1800 Baker Sword bayonet, which had a 24in (61cm) blade plus a hilt with a brass knuckle-guard. Sword bayonets made a strong appearance during the 19th century, but the impracticalities of weight and length meant that they became largely relegated to ceremonial or detached use. From the end of the century, therefore, much shorter "knife bayonets" made an appearance, these essentially being daggers with a secondary use as a bayonet.

ABOVE: An 18th-century instruction manual for bayonet use. (The Bridgeman Art Library)

LEFT: An engraving of the Napoleonic era showing French troops with bayonets. (akg-images)

BELOW: An American cavalry carbine from *c.* 1842 with separate bayonet. (The Bridgeman Art Library © Civil War Archive)

THE LAST BAYONET CHARGE?

In May 2004, soldiers of the Argyll & Sutherland Highlanders made the first bayonet charge since the Falklands War. Coming under insurgent ambush near the city of Amara, Iraq, the 20 British soldiers, traveling in Land Rovers, were pinned down by heavy mortar, rocket-propelled grenade (RPG), and small-arms fire. Running low on ammunition, the Highlanders then fixed bayonets to their SA80 rifles and charged the enemy, engaging in hand-to-hand fighting. The insurgents were defeated with up to 35 of their number killed (British reinforcements arrived during the fighting), for the cost of only three men wounded. The action proves that although the rationale for bayonet has largely gone, it still has a valid place in the soldier's equipment.

The first examples of knife bayonets included the US M1861 "Dahlgren" and the German 1871/84, but long sword-type bayonets persisted well into the 20th century – the British Pattern 1907 Sword bayonet, for example, had a 17in (43cm) blade, and accompanied Lee-Enfield rifles through World War I and into the next world war. Yet as the century progressed, the perfection of small-arms firepower largely made the bayonet charge redundant (with some famous exceptions), so although knife bayonets became the norm and are issued to this day, they largely serve as utility items, incorporating features such as wire cutters. Yet in their heyday, bayonets reshaped the nature of infantry combat.

LIGHT FIELD ARTILLERY

Up until the 17th century, artillery was largely of heavy caliber and limited mobility. In most battles, artillery tended to deliver its opening fire from static positions, and once the ranks of infantry started to move, repositioning the guns meaningfully was extremely difficult.

LIGHT GUNS

True mobile field artillery, however, appeared during the Thirty Years' War, pioneered by the Swedish commander Gustavus Adolphus. Adolphus placed a new emphasis on light, more maneuverable gun types. His 3pdr "leather guns," for example, were light enough (around 120lb/55kg) to be pulled around the battlefield by just two horses – the heaviest field guns could require no less than 14 horses. He also used 4pdr cannon, whose crews worked with ammunition that had both the

OPPOSITE: French horse-drawn light artillery goes into action during the Napoleonic period. The ease and speed with which guns could be used was a battlefield revolution. (akg-images)

ABOVE: The battle of Malplaquet on September 11, 1709, was one of the major engagements of the War of the Spanish Succession. The extensive use of artillery by the Allied army under the command of the Duke of Marlborough helped drive the French from the battlefield, although the Allies lost so many troops that the rivers reportedly ran red with blood for three days. (The Bridgeman Art Library)

powder (contained in flannel bags) and shot pre-packed in wooden cases to speed up loading times. These light artillery pieces could, in the hands of a well-trained crew, be fired faster than a flintlock musket.

Following Adolphus' lead, more professional armies bought into the use of light artillery, particularly the French, British, and Russians. Furthermore, investments in new carriage and barrel design reduced the weight of some larger-caliber weapons substantially – in Russia, for example, the weight of a 12pdr cannon was, during the early 18th century, reduced from around 4,036lb (1,835kg) to 1,081lb (491kg). The 18th century therefore saw artillery become increasingly mobile, the beneficiary of weight reductions and new designs in limbers. Light 3pdr and 4pdr pieces would sit amongst the ranks of infantry, and with skilled handling could move across the battlefield as fast as the men could, giving present direct-fire support at every stage of a battle.

ARTILLERY BATTLES

Certain names stand out in this evolution, particularly Jean-Baptiste de Gribeauval. In 1776 he became France's Inspector of Artillery, and pushed through a new method of barrel manufacture, casting guns as a single block then drilling out the bore. The result was an improved fit between bore and ball – making the guns more powerful – and thinner, therefore lighter, barrels of equal strength to the heavier barrels of the past. He also created a new system of standardized calibers, with an emphasis on lighter battlefield pieces ranging from a 1pdr through to a 12pdr.

The steady improvements in field artillery meant that gunnery became more central to the outcome of battles. Armies began to field artillery pieces numbering in the thousands (Russia, for example, had 13,000 artillery pieces by 1713), and these became more methodically organized into batteries and regiments. Frederick the Great pioneered horse artillery (in which all the artillerymen were mounted), forming the first battery in 1759.

BATTLEFIELD EFFECTS

The two primary ammunition types of field artillery were round shot and canister. Round shot was simply a solid metal ball. This was typically fired to make first graze in front of enemy infantry ranks – the ball would subsequently bounce through the tight-packed ranks, raking down whole lines of men. Canister consisted of a metal container filled with lead or iron balls (packed in sawdust for spacing), or other forms of shrapnel. When the canister was fired from a gun, the container disintegrated on leaving the bore and the shrapnel created a terrible short-range "shotgun" effect on enemy ranks. At close range, men and horses would literally be torn apart by canister shot. At the battle of Torgau on November 3, 1760, for example, some ten Prussian battalions were destroyed by canister as they led an attack. Artillery was a science for those designing the guns, but a horror for those facing them.

The upshot of all these developments was that field artillery began to emerge as *the* battle-winning arm. Mobility combined with firepower was now central. At the battle of Blenheim on August 13, 1704, for example, the Duke of Marlborough had two 3pdr guns attached to every English or Dutch battalion. Although the French had more, but heavier, guns, Marlborough managed to maneuver his lighter pieces to smash advancing French ranks, destroying around nine battalions of troops. Other battles in which field artillery was decisive included Malplaquet (1709), Liegnitz (1760), and Rossbach (1757). Field artillery had irrevocably changed the tactical reality of ground warfare, as much as air power would in the 20th century.

OPPOSITE: Gustavus Adolphus of Sweden, one of the true pioneers in the use of light artillery, who won several victories during the Thirty Years' War. (akg-images)

HOWITZER

THE HOWITZER OCCUPIES A DISTINCTIVE PLACE IN THE history and ranks of artillery pieces. In the modern world, in which direct-fire gun artillery has largely disappeared, the howitzer is the most influential artillery piece available, but its evolution to this status has been slow.

Howitzers sit between mortars and cannon in their capabilities being, in Early Modern history at least, as (or more) maneuverable as the former but of larger caliber than the latter. They are indirect-fire weapons, designed to lob shells at high trajectories at targets hidden from line-of-sight view.

FIRE SUPPORT

The origins of the howitzer, at least in etymology, date back to the Hussite Wars (1419–34), when the Hussite army deployed *houfnice* – mid-caliber defensive cannon mounted on carts – as

OPPOSITE: The howitzer of the 18th and 19th century was designed primarily to attack fortifications. This is the so-called "Howitzer of Belgrade" – the Hapsburg army of Prince Eugene of Savoy used this 6.7in (17cm) howitzer in the attacks on the Ottoman garrison of the city in 1717. (Getty Images)

part of their large artillery train. These guns were capable of delivering a punishing bombardment upon massed enemy ranks, and they were primarily used to defend gaps in the *Wagenburg* laagers. The word *houfnice* was in turn translated into German as *haubitze*, which went on to give us the English term "howitzer."

Although the Hussites laid the foundations, the howitzer proper was essentially an invention of the 17th century, with Sweden at the forefront. Howitzers were primarily designed for siege work, being able to lob shells over fortification walls. Yet they soon proved useful in other contexts. Being of relatively low weight and with a short limber trail, they could be wheeled around the active battlefield to provide heavy support fire at key points. For example, the howitzers under Marlborough's command in the early 18th century had a powerful caliber of some 8–10in (20–25cm), but only required eight horses to pull one gun; the British 6pdr field gun, by contrast, required 13 horses. Unlike many direct-fire guns, howitzers largely utilized "bursting shells," hollow round-shot filled with gunpowder and a fuse. Although the effect of such ammunition could be haphazard, howitzers ushered in the age of explosive artillery fire.

DIVERSE EMPLOYMENT

Throughout the 18th century, howitzers firmly established themselves amongst the ranks of artillery, and ranged from diminutive 7pdr guns through to hefty 24pdrs. Fielding a variety of howitzer calibers provided defensive and offensive flexibility, as illustrated by the British Army at the second siege of Badajoz, Spain, in 1812, when three different calibers of howitzer were used, each tackling specific defensive elements, from manned ditches to bastions.

Howitzer evolution post 1800 is too complex to relate here in full. Suffice to say that howitzers increasingly diversified,

BELOW: Boer troops photographed with a howitzer they used during the Siege of Ladysmith, Second Anglo-Boer War. (The Art Archive)

HOWITZER BY LADYSMITH

from light mountain howitzers small enough to be broken down into several components and strapped to a donkey, to the awesome German railway guns of World War I, such as the 17in (43.2cm) "Big Bertha," which had a crew of 200 men and a range of 9 miles (14.5km). From the second half of the 19th century, rifled barrels and developments such as improved propellants, recoil-absorption, and breech-loading produced the "gun-howitzer," an artillery piece capable of taking over the roles of both field and siege artillery. During the 20th century, the gun-howitzer steadily progressed to become the dominant artillery type, and self-propelled variants have given howitzers mechanized mobility.

In the battles of the 20th century, artillery emerged as the true killer of men, accounting for around 70 percent of the death toll inflicted on the enemy. The howitzer's pounding effects were central to this shift, and they remain much-respected weapons to this day.

ABOVE: A 12pdr howitzer of the American Civil War. (Getty Images)

BELOW: The howitzer of the Early Modern period was the direct forerunner of weapons such as "Big Bertha," a gun designed by the German industrialist Gustav Krupp capable of a range of 9 miles (14.5km). (Hulton Archive/Getty Images)

SHIP OF THE LINE

THE PERIOD BETWEEN 1500 AND 1800 ENCOMPASSED huge changes in many aspects of warfare, but nowhere were these greater than in the field of naval warfare. In what is known popularly as the "Age of Sail," warships were transformed from relatively lightly armed galleys and carracks carrying around a half-dozen cannon, to mighty ships of the line, the largest specimens bristling with more than 100 cannon set in powerful broadside arrangements. Allied to other changes in naval technology, these warships became oceanic in capability, and navies became the vehicles through which empires were built.

OPPOSITE: A naval cannon crew prepare to fire through the gunport of their warship. Ships of the line essentially operated as floating gun platforms, their primary function being to batter the enemy vessels into submission. (Philip Haythorntwaite)

MOUNTING GUNS

Cannon were first mounted upon warships in the 14th century, but the new weapons posed an immediate problem. Wrought-iron or cast bronze cannon, plus their carriages, were enormously heavy. Several of them set up on a main deck could cause serious instability problems by making the ship top heavy. Indeed, the sinking of the great *Mary Rose* in 1545 was probably in part due to the weight of ordnance aboard. For galleys, furthermore, increased weight from cannon put a heavier burden on those manning the oars, resulting in a significant decrease in maximum speed, and therefore ramming power.

From the 16th century, however, a number of maritime revolutions created warships that were far more stable gun platforms. In summary, the changes were broadly as follows. Galleys were replaced by three-masted carracks, "great ships," galleons, and "full-rigged" vessels. The numbers of decks, crew, and tonnage of supplies carried increased impressively, the changes represented by ships such as the British *Sovereign of*

the Seas, launched in 1669 with three decks, weighing 1,675 short tons (1,520 tonnes) and having a crew of 600 men. Navigational instruments improved, with both the quadrant and the sextant introduced in the 18th century. Later in the same century, the problem of determining longitude was solved by the marine chronometer of John Harrison.

OCEANIC WARRIORS

The increased capabilities of Early Modern sailing ships meant that the oceans of the world now became imperial playgrounds and battlegrounds. War galleys had classically sited the few guns they carried (around seven) on the bow pointing forward, with other small cannon at strategic points on the deck. The switch to large sailing vessels, however, meant that the biggest warships could carry up to and even exceeding 100 guns, arranged in broadside ranks and firing through lidded gun ports in the side of the hull. The muzzle-loading cannon were set on wheeled mounts, with the recoil controlled by thick breeching ropes to stop the gun flying uncontrollably backwards into the ship's interior. A system of ropes and pulleys returned the gun to firing position.

ENGAGING THE ENEMY WITH SHIP'S GUNS

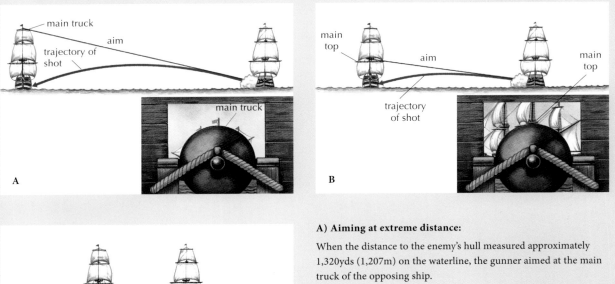

A) Aiming at extreme distance:

When the distance to the enemy's hull measured approximately 1,320yds (1,207m) on the waterline, the gunner aimed at the main truck of the opposing ship.

B) Aiming at moderate distance:

When the distance to the enemy's hull measured approximately 880yds (805m) on the waterline, the gunner aimed at the main top of the opposing ship.

C) Aiming at short distance:

When the distance to the enemy's hull measured 400yds (366m) or less, the gunner aimed directly at the hull of the opposite ship, since point blank range required no elevation of the gun. Broadsides delivered at less than 300yds (274m) were particularly effective.

ABOVE: Nelson's brilliant deployment of his fleet, as well as the superior British gunnery skills, led to a victory at Trafalgar that secured British dominance of the sea for the next 100 years. Eighteen out of 33 of the Combined Fleet ships were lost or destroyed, while the British lost none. Here the French ship *Redoutable* is shown sandwiched between *Victory* and *Téméraire*. (The Art Archive)

The huge, booming broadsides of these sailing ships were enormously destructive, but demanded new tactics. In the mid 1600s, the English and Dutch pioneered the "line of battle" tactic, in which fighting ships went into action in a coordinated line, hence could turn their broadsides on the enemy without friendly ships being in their line of fire. The ships who were powerful enough to take their position in the line of battle were known, appropriately enough, as "ships of the line." They came in numerous different sizes and varieties, but many navies established standardized systems of ranking the boats. The British Navy, for example, used a system of "rates" (see feature box), the "first rate" being the most potent.

Tactically, the ideal outcome for a squadron commander was to turn his line of battle so that it passed to the front or rear of the enemy ships, meaning that he could unleash his broadsides while the opponents were unable to bring their guns to bear.

BRITISH SHIP RATINGS

The following are ratings for British ships of the line of the 18th century, based on the number of guns carried by the warship:

First rate – three decks, 100 guns
Second rate – three decks, 90–98 guns
Third rate – two decks, 74 guns (the most numerous Royal Navy ship of the line during the second half of the 18th and early 19th centuries)
Fourth rate – two decks, 50–60 guns
Fifth rate – frigates, with two decks, 32–36 guns
Sixth rate – frigates, one or two decks, 28 guns
Unrated – any vessels ranked below sixth rate, such as sloops and fire-ships.

Yet such precision was relatively rare, and broadside engagements were typically brutal affairs, each side pounding the other with hails of round, bar, grape, and chain shot. The battles were destructive but frequently indecisive – victory could come as much through weather and navigation as gunnery.

Ultimately, it was the advent of the steam ship in the 19th century that ended the era of the ship of the line. Not bound by the winds, steam warships could express themselves in more diverse maneuver tactics, although as emblems of sheer naval power, the great sail ships have few rivals.

HMS *VICTORY*

Specifications:

Launched: May 7, 1765
Displacement: 3,500 UK tons (3,556 tonnes)
Length overall: 186ft (56.6m)
Keel length: 151ft 4in (46.1m)
Beam: 52ft (15.8m)
Draught: 21ft 6in (6.5m)
Armament: 30 x 32pdrs, 28 x 24pdrs, 30 x 12pdrs, 12 x 6pdrs

Key

1 Poop deck
2 Quarter deck
3 Upper deck
4 12pdr gun
5 68pdr Carronade
6 24pdr guns
7 Middle deck
8 Gun deck
9 Gun ports to 32pdr guns on deck
10 Spot where Nelson was mortally wounded at the battle of Trafalgar, 1805

IMPERIAL WARS
1800–1914

BAKER RIFLE

THE GERMAN STATES WERE PARTICULARLY FORMATIVE in both the technology and tactics of rifled firearms. Small units of Prussian *Jägers* – the name means "hunte'" – were in action by the 1740s, used as skirmishers, reconnaissance troops, and snipers. The classic *Jäger* rifle, as the weapon itself became known, had a caliber of around 0.75in, a barrel length of 30–32in (762–814mm), and a straight stock to help absorb recoil directly into the shoulder. It also came with an iron, rather than a wooden, ramrod to cope with the pressures of ramming the ball down a rifled bore.

OPPOSITE: A private of the 95th Rifles armed with a Baker Rifle, the first British unit to receive the new rifle designed by Ezekiel Baker. (The Bridgeman Art Library/Peter Newark images)

MARKSMEN AND SNIPERS

Via German and Swiss emigrants, *Jäger* rifles became extremely influential on the development of US rifles and marksmen. The "Kentucky" or "Pennsylvania" rifle utilized many of the same design features, but scaled down the caliber to between 0.40 and 0.54in. In the hands of American sharpshooters, who used

"unconventional" tactics of cover and concealment, these rifles inflicted worrying losses on British forces during the American War of Independence (1775–83), particularly amongst officers. The rifles were capable of hitting and dropping a man at 300–400yds (275–365m), and the effect on command-and-control could be profound. At the battle of Freeman's Farm on September 19, 1777, for example, an American sniper shot and killed General Simon Fraser, effectively producing a British retreat in what was a pivotal battle of the Revolutionary War.

LESSONS LEARNT

While many British officers still deplored the irreverence of a common soldier killing gentlemen officers, the lesson was not lost on army officials. The capabilities of rifle-armed skirmishers were reinforced when French versions were encountered in the early battles of the French Revolutionary Wars. A handful of British soldiers were equipped with breech-

loading Ferguson rifles in the late 1770s, but it would take until the beginning of the next century to make rifle-armed troops a more significant component of the British Army.

In 1798, the Board of Ordnance began to look for alternatives to the extremely expensive Ferguson. The *Jäger* rifle was a natural choice, and around 5,000 were issued to various light infantry units. Yet the following year gunmaker Ezekiel Baker received a commission to develop a new service rifle, based

BELOW: During the retreat from Corunna in the winter of 1808–09, the British riflemen were used as rearguards to slow down the pursuing cavalry. If the French cavalry, under the command of General Auguste-Marie-Francois Colbert, could break the rearguard, the British Army would be at their mercy. But on January 3, 1809, Rifleman Thomas Plunkett took aim from a back-position (more suitable for long-distance firing) and shot the general dead, throwing the French forces into disarray and allowing the escape of the British troops. (Artwork by Peter Dennis © Osprey Publishing Ltd.)

on the *Jäger* pattern but adapted to British use. The result was the now legendary Baker rifle, adopted for service in 1800, principally by the 95th (Rifle) Regiment. Initially produced in 0.7in caliber, the major production batch was in the smaller 0.62in, firing from a 30in (762mm) seven-groove rifled barrel. Overall length was 45.5in (1,156mm), considerably shorter than the Brown Bess musket, and therefore much more suited to nimble skirmishing work from behind cover.

The Baker rifle was in many ways little different from previous rifled firearms. Its significance, however, was that it helped begin the British Army's slow tactical shift away from uniform volleys to fire and maneuver. The 95th Rifles were known for their intelligent use of ground, and their ability to take shots at ranges in excess of 200yds (182m) – they were particularly fond of targeting enemy officers, NCOs, drummers, and artillerymen, taking out people of value and authority. The lessons of the 95th would take some time to filter out into the wider army, but with the introduction of unitary cartridges, cheaper methods of producing rifled weapons, and effective breech-loading later in the century, every soldier became capable of long-range attrition. In the rifled age, those who were exposed were dead.

SHARPSHOOTER

A British 95th (Rifle) Regiment soldier, Rifleman Harris, here recounts a battle with a French marksman during the Napoleonic Wars:

> **"** I was startled by the sharp report of a firelock, and at the same moment, a bullet whistled close to my head. Instantly starting up I turned and looked in the direction whence the shot had come ... but nothing could I see. I looked to the priming of my rifle ... when another shot took place, and a second ball whistled past me. This time I was ready, and turning quickly I saw my man; he was just about to squat down behind a small mound, about twenty paces from me. I took a haphazard shot at him, and instantly knocked him over. **"**

BELOW: A pair of *Jäger* military-pattern flintlock rifles *c.* 1750 – the direct forerunner of the Baker. (Martin Pegler collection)

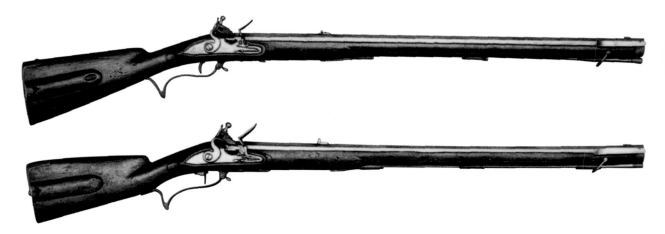

DREYSE NEEDLE-GUN

MUZZLE-LOADING FIREARMS COULD BE FRUSTRATING weapons to use on a battlefield. The downtime in reloading, for example, was considerable, and firepower ebbed and flowed in volleys, rather than maintained a constant attrition. Muzzle-loading was also generally ill-suited to rifled weapons, despite some innovations in ammunition types. Breech-loading firearms, however, changed the game entirely.

CARTRIDGE GUNS

The first modern breech-loading firearm was created by Swiss gunmaker Johannes Pauly in 1812. Pauly created a hinged-barrel sporting gun that took a self-contained paper cartridge, fitted with a brass head that contained a primer pellet. The cartridge was inserted into the opened barrel, the gun closed, and when the trigger was pulled a firing pin in the fixed breech hit the primer and fired the cartridge. The brass cartridge head expanded to provide obturation (a gas-tight seal). Remember that up to this point a skilled infantryman could probably fire three rounds per minute from a smoothbore musket. In one demonstration, Pauly fired 22 shots in the same time with his new weapon.

The idea was advanced by Frenchman Casimir Lefaucheaux, who in 1835 patented a new breech-loading cartridge known as the pinfire with the pinfire cartridge featured an entirely brass case holding the powder, primer, and bullet. A pin projected from the side of the case above the primer. Lefaucheaux's gun had a slotted chamber through which the pin protruded, and when the gun was fired a hammer struck the pin, driving it down onto the primer to fire the cartridge.

Pinfire cartridges worked well (although best in revolvers), and they went on to have huge commercial success for several decades. More importantly, they began the evolution to rimfire then centerfire cartridges, which became dominant in the second half of the century and remain so to this day.

BOLT-ACTION

Prussian gunmaker Johann Nikolaus von Dreyse utilized the "unitary" cartridge for a seminal leap in rifle design. In 1836, Dreyse was awarded a patent for the world's first bolt-action rifle – the Dreyse "Needle-Gun." The gun was loaded via a system that

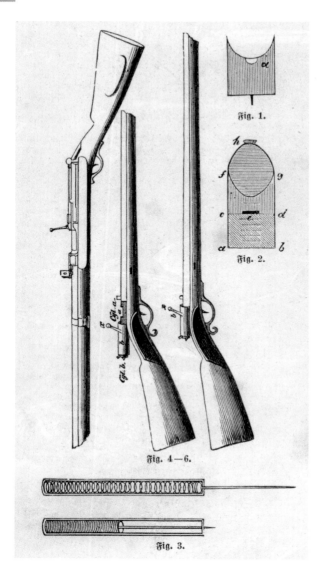

ABOVE: An original engraving shows the revolutionary new design of the Needle-Gun. (akg-images)

BELOW: A Needle-Gun carbine M1870, a Prussian design which used the Dreyse system but was a breech-loader produced two decades after the original. (Mary Evans Picture Library/Interfoto)

looked very much like a common door bolt, although the bolt had a spring-loaded firing pin running through its center. When the bolt handle was lifted and the bolt drawn back, it exposed the gun's chamber, which was loaded with a unitary cardboard cartridge. (Drawing the bolt back also cocked the firing pin.) The cartridge in itself was a bit of an oddity, with the percussion cap located at the rear of the bullet, rather than at the rear of the case. By pushing the bolt forward and locking the handle down into a recess in the frame, the gun was ready to fire. Pulling the trigger released the long, needle-like firing pin, which pushed through the bottom of the cartridge, drove through the powder charge, and struck the percussion cap to fire the gun.

Dreyse's breech-loading firearm was truly revolutionary. The Prussian Army adopted it in 1848 in 0.607in (15.42mm) caliber, and used it to inflict withering casualties upon Danish and Austrian troops during the wars of the 1860s. Its rate of fire was about one round every five seconds, and it had an effective range of more than 220yds (200m).

Bolt-action rifles took a while to catch on, but with the later introduction of centerfire cartridges the momentum became inexorable. By the end of the century, virtually every soldier in the world would go into battle with a bolt-action rifle, albeit one firing metallic centerfire cartridges. Bolt-action rifles are suited to rugged use yet also deliver exceptional range and accuracy, hence they are still in use today as hunting, target, and sniping weapons. The Needle-Gun itself had marginal impact, and was quickly superseded by better models. Yet Dreyse started a lineage of one of the most successful weapon types in history.

ABOVE: The battle of Königgrätz during the Austro-Prussian War of 1866, when Prussian troops used their Dreyse Needle-Guns to devastating effect. (Mary Evans Picture Library/Interfoto /Daniel)

DREYSE NEEDLE GUN – SPECIFICATIONS (1849 PRUSSIAN ARMY MODEL)

Caliber: 0.607in (15.42mm)

Operation: Bolt-action

Feed: Manual single-shot

Length: 56in (1,422mm)

Barrel length: 38in (964mm)

Rifling: 4 grooves, r/hand

Weight: 9lb (4.1kg)

Muzzle velocity: c. 950ft/sec (290m/sec)

US COLT NAVY 1851

Flintlock handguns had been around for three centuries by the turn of the 19th century. Their one-shot firepower, however, made them of limited use in a scrappy, close-quarters skirmish; once the shot in the chamber was fired, the best use for the pistol was to flip it around and use the butt as a club. Multi-shot "ducksfoot" and "pepperbox" handguns provided better defensive qualities, both using multiple barrels – the former set in a splayed horizontal arrangement, the latter in a cylindrical arrangement around a central axis. Both were awkward to handle and fire, and the pepperbox also ran the hand-destroying risk of "flashover," where the ignition of one chamber ignites adjacent chambers.

PERCUSSION REVOLVER

Once firearms entered the percussion age, however (see next entry), the revolver changed everything. Credit for the revolver does not actually belong to the great Samuel Colt, but arguably to Artemus Wheeler of Massachusetts. (Although there are extant diagrams of revolver-like matchlock, wheellock, and flintlock mechanisms from as far back as the 16th century.)

OPPOSITE: Samuel Colt (1814–62), founder of Colt's Patent Fire-Arms Maufacturing Company. (akg-images)

THE COLT BREECH-LOADING REVOLVER.

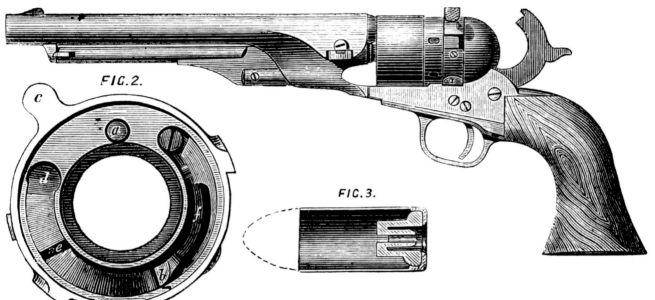

FIG.1.

FIG.2.

FIG.3.

ABOVE: The Colt breech-loading revolver. This illustration shows the revolver (Fig. 1), the breech-disk (Fig. 2), and the cartridge (Fig. 3). Illustration from *The Mechanics Magazine*, London, 1869. (akg-images/IAM/World History Archive)

In 1818, Wheeler acquired a patent for a single-barreled flintlock rifle fed from a multi-chamber cylinder. (Each cylinder contained an individual shot.) His design was not a commercial success, but one Elisha Collier used the cylinder principle with flintlock, then percussion cap technology to create a new type of firearm. The ingenious part of Collier's design was that the cylinder was rotated between shots by the action of cocking the hammer. Ingenuity did not translate into reliability, however, and the gun suffered from poor sales. Here entered Samuel Colt.

Colt revolutionized hand-held firearms. The first of his guns was the 1836 Colt Paterson, a 0.34in five-shot gun in which each chamber of the cylinder was loaded separately with powder, cap, and ball. It was "single-action" – the action of cocking the hammer rotated the cylinder between shots, and was a slightly awkward first attempt from Colt, but subsequent revolvers changed the game entirely, becoming bywords for power, reliability, and short-range accuracy. They included the massive "Whitneyville Walker" Colt of 1847 – 0.44in caliber, 15.5in (394mm) long, and weighing 4.5lb (2.04kg) – and what would be the definitive percussion cap revolver, the Navy 1851.

The Navy 1851 woke the world to the potential of the revolver. It was a manageable, well-balanced six-shot gun, in 0.36in caliber with a 7.5in (190mm) barrel. Importantly, it could be easily carried in a belt holster. In combat, it was

ABOVE: An 1851 US Navy Colt, which was used by an unknown member of the North Carolina Infantry Regiment during the American Civil War. (The Bridgeman Art Library © Civil War Archive)

smooth and accurate to fire, hence it sold in huge quantities to both domestic and military customers – total production, when it ended in 1873, was in the region of 250,000. Indeed, the British alone bought more than 41,000. It was the side-arm for which history had been waiting, providing meaningful back-up or short-range firepower to everyone from Texas Rangers (a major customer) to cavalry troopers.

Of course, weapons such as the Navy Colt were just the beginning of the revolver story. Eventually Colt patents lapsed and numerous competitors flooded in, including the likes of Remington and Smith & Wesson. Percussion cap revolvers eventually gave way to cartridge revolvers, radically improving the speed with which a handgun could be reloaded. The Colt company itself went on to produce cartridge revolvers such as the magnificent Colt Single-Action Army, which became known as the "Peacemaker" and was

produced in one form or another for 130 years. It is a tribute to the Colt design that its basic principles still underpin most revolvers that roll off production lines even today.

COLT NAVY 1851 SPECIFICATIONS

Caliber: 0.36in
Operation: Single-action revolver
Feed: Six-round cylinder
Length: 12.9in (328mm)
Barrel length: 7.5in (190mm)
Rifling: 7 grooves, r/hand
Weight: 2.4lb (1.1kg)
Muzzle velocity: c. 700ft/sec (213m/sec)

ENFIELD PATTERN 1853

THE ENFIELD PATTERN 1853 RIFLE IS IMPORTANT because of the invention that it represents. It was an invention that began the most profound change in firearms design since the introduction of the flintlock, and which eventually brought the flintlock's 300-year reign to an end.

PERCUSSION

The invention was the percussion system. Its origins lay with Scottish clergyman Reverend Alexander John Forsyth, who in the late 18th century looked for ways to improve sporting firearms. The problem with flintlocks, he found, was that the slight time lag between the ignition of priming powder and the main charge was large enough for alert prey to escape before the shot reached them. The solution was a chemical, fulminate of mercury, which would detonate under impact alone and produce a very fast, hot flame. Forsyth created a new "scent bottle" lock – so called because of its evocative shape – which placed measured amounts of the substance under a pin and hammer arrangement. There was no flint, and the lock time was, for practical purposes, almost instant.

Forsyth had ushered in the percussion age. Others soon tried to improve on it, creating locks that used fulminate contained in patches of paper or in pellets. Yet the great leap forward came in the 1820s, with the percussion cap. Several names are associated with its invention, including Joseph Manton (Britain),

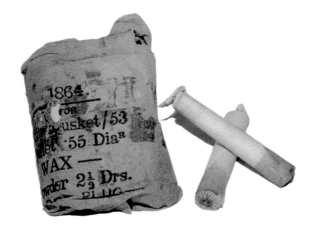

OPPOSITE: This photograph shows the cartridges of the Pattern 1853 rifle, and the packet that they came in. It is possible to make out some details on the packet. (Martin Pegler collection)

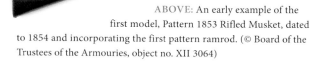

ABOVE: An early example of the
first model, Pattern 1853 Rifled Musket, dated
to 1854 and incorporating the first pattern ramrod. (© Board of the
Trustees of the Armouries, object no. XII 3064)

Joshua Shaw (United States), and François Prélat (France), but whatever the provenance it worked as follows. The fulminate mixture was contained in crushable copper cap. The cap was placed on a metal nipple, beneath which ran a hole through to the gun's chamber. When the trigger was pulled, a hammer fell onto the cap, crushing it, detonating the fulminate, and thereby igniting the main charge. The system required no flints, was more reliable than the flintlock (being more weather resistant), was quicker to load, and its faster ignition times meant the gun was more accurate.

THE MINIÉ BALL

The Minié ball was the invention (albeit building upon earlier precedents) of Frenchman Claude-Etienne Minié in 1847. Minié was looking for ways to improve the reloading times of muzzle-loading rifles. He developed a conical-cylindrical soft lead bullet that had a width slightly less than that of the bore of the gun, the dimensions making it easy to ram down the barrel. However, the bullet had a conoidal hollow in its base, and on firing, the gases pushed into the hollow, squeezing out the base of the bullet to provide a virtually gas-tight fit into the rifling grooves. The Minié gave the best of all worlds, being quick to load and accurate out to hundreds of yards, with formidable penetration. Along with the percussion system, it dramatically increased the lethality of rifled firearms.

DEFINING PATTERN

Flintlocks toiled on for much of the 19th century, but the percussion cap system instantly began to eat away at their use. One of the great firearms created for the percussion lock was the British Enfield Pattern 1853 Rifled Musket P53, which essentially became the British Army's first standard-issue rifle. Firing a heavy-caliber 0.577in bullet, the P53 was shorter and, at 8.6lb (3.9kg), lighter than most previous British Army weapons. Indicative of its range capabilities, it had a ladder backsight that could be set from 100yds to 1,000yds. The P53 was also an industrial success story, new developments in mass production resulting in 1.5 million of the firearm being produced between 1853 and 1867.

The P53 left a bloody trail across Britain's Empire, and was the second most widely used firearm during the American Civil War (1861–65). Firing Minié-type ball ammunition (see feature box), it was just as quick to reload as a smoothbore, while being far more accurate, and brought all the advantages of the percussion cap system. It also became the basis for the later Snider-Enfield breech-loading conversion, introduced in 1866. Guns such as the P53 steadily demolished the centuries-old authority of the flintlock.

BELOW: A group of unknown Confederate troops during the American Civil War. Over 500,000 P53 Enfields made their way to the United States for use by both the North and South. (Public domain)

> *Such a distracting row of thousands of rifles being fired without intermission I never heard, and such a sight of slaughter I never saw…*
>
> Arthur Moffat Lang, Indian Mutiny, 1857

BELOW: One of the most famous battle paintings of all time, *The Thin Red Line* by Robert Gibb, depicts the 93rd Highlanders standing firm in the face of a Russian cavalry charge. They are armed with P53 Enfields with bayonets fixed. Their commander reportedly said, "There is no retreat from here men. You must die where you stand." (Courtesy of the Council of the National Army Museum)

ABOVE: The same 93rd Highlands charge during the Indian Mutiny. The mutiny was in part a direct result of the distribution of Enfield rifles. To load the rifle, sepoys in the employment of the East India Company had to bite open cartridges that were reportedly lined with animal fat, which violated their religious principles. (Courtesy of the Council of the National Army Museum)

GATLING GUN

In 1718, Englishmen James Puckle presented an odd-looking firearm to the world. The Puckle Repeating Gun was innovative in that its single barrel was fed by a rotary, hand-operated, breech-loading, nine-cylinder magazine. By manually turning the magazine via a handle, the operator could load and fire one cylinder at a time without reloading. Although the system worked – in a test in 1722 one soldier fired an unheard of 63 shots in 7 minutes – it was neither a practical nor commercial success. It was, however, a first step on the road to the machine-gun.

BATTERIES AND VOLLEYS

The 19th century ushered in three technological revolutions that finally rendered "automatic" firearms possible: the percussion cap, unitary cartridges, and effective breech-loading. Progressively, these inventions made it possible to load and fire a gun with rapidity and consistency. In 1857, for example, Sir James Lillie introduced a 12-barrel firearm, each barrel having a hand-cranked multi-chamber revolving magazine behind it. During the American Civil War, other specimens emerged, including the 25-barrel Billinghurst-Requa Battery Gun and the Ager "Coffee Mill," the latter being a single-barrel gun fed with pre-loaded ammunition from a gravity-powered hopper. More significant was the Montigny Mitrailleuse, a Belgian invention introduced into French service in 1870. The Mitrailleuse had no less than 37 barrels, which were loaded by a steel plate holding 37 cartridges and fired by a separate breech-block with 37 firing pins. Cranking the gun's

OPPOSITE: An early British machine-gun firing on Boers in the midst of an ambush near Krantz Kloof during the Anglo-Boer War (1899–1902). (The Bridgeman Art Library)

BELOW: An 1870 front view and an 1872 rear view of a Gatling Gun. (Mary Evans Picture Library)

ABOVE: At the battle of San Juan Hill during the Spanish–American War (1898), the three Gatling guns commanded by Lieutenant John H. Parker supported the advance of the 1st Volunteers (the "Rough Riders") and the 10th Cavalry as they stormed up Kettle Hill. (The Bridgeman Art Library/Peter Newark Military Pictures)

handle fired each cartridge in turn, giving a practical rate of fire of 150rpm. The system worked quite well, but the French tactically mishandled the gun, using it like an artillery piece in the Franco-Prussian War and therefore losing the gun battle with actual field artillery.

> **"** We were exposed to the Spanish fire, but there was very little because just before we started, why, the Gatling guns opened up at the bottom of the hill, and everybody yelled, "The Gatlings! The Gatlings!" and away we went. The Gatlings just enfiladed the top of those trenches. We'd never have been able to take Kettle Hill if it hadn't been for Parker's Gatling guns. **"**
>
> Trooper Jesse D. Langdon, 1st Volunteer Infantry, 1898

NEW LETHALITY

The title of first genuinely effective manually powered machine-gun, therefore goes to Richard Jordan Gatling's infamous Gatling gun, which he began developing in 1861 and which finally reached maturity in 1864. The Gatling gun utilized multiple barrels (around ten), each with its own chamber, arranged in a rotary relationship around a central axis. When the operator turned the crank handle at the side, the barrel unit rotated. At the top of the turn, each barrel was loaded with a centerfire cartridge from a 240-round cylindrical magazine, and the round was fired when the barrel reached the 6 o'clock position. During the next 180 degrees of travel, the spent cartridge was ejected and the chamber made ready for a fresh cartridge. All the operator had to do to keep the gun firing, was to turn the handle.

The Gatling gun was adopted into the US Army in 1866 in 0.5in and 1in calibers, and subsequently sold across the world in a variety of other calibers and formats. It was groundbreaking on many levels. It could maintain a cyclical rate of fire of c. 400rpm, and its multi-barrel arrangement managed the problems of overheating that had plagued previous mechanical machine-guns. It was reliable, jamming infrequently. More importantly, it proved itself in combat in numerous different theaters and conflicts, from British colonial wars in Africa to Russian conflicts in Central Asia. During the battle of San Juan Hill in the Spanish-American War (1898), three Gatlings fired 18,000 rounds in 3.5 minutes at Spanish positions. Against those not similarly equipped, the effect was devastating.

Ultimately, the Gatling was rendered obsolete from the late 1800s by Maxim's first true (i.e. self-cycling) machine-gun, although the principle of rotary-barrel cannon is still very much alive today in electrically powered weapons such as the US Minigun and the Soviet-era AK-630. What Gatling essentially proved was the principle and the effects of automatic firearms, and by so doing increase the lethality of the battlefield.

Richard Gatling wrote to Elizabeth Jarvis, June 15, 1877, to explain his reasons for developing the gun:

" My Dear Friend,

It may be interesting to you to know how I came to invent the gun which bears my name; I will tell you: In 1861, during the opening events of the war, (residing at that time in Indianapolis, md.,) I witnessed almost daily the departure of troops to the front and the return of the wounded, sick, and dead. The most of the latter lost their lives, not in battle, but by sickness and exposure incident to the service. It occurred to me if I could invent a machine – a gun – which could by its rapidity of fire, enable one man to do as much battle duty as a hundred, that it would, to a great extent, supersede the necessity of large armies, and consequently, exposure to battle and disease be greatly diminished. I thought over the subject and finally this idea took practical form in the invention of the Gatling Gun.

Yours truly,
R.J. Gatling   **"**

CSS *HUNLEY*

The story of the CSS *Hunley* is one of sheer ingenuity in the midst of war. The year was 1863, and the United States was gripped in its terrible civil war. For the Confederate South, one of the greatest threats to its strategy and survival was the Union naval blockade around its coastline. By cutting off vital supplies, the Northern command not only restricted the flow of essential goods to the South, but it also led to a 95 percent decline in Southern cotton exports, thereby limiting the South's ability to trade cotton for armaments and goods.

MAN-POWERED SUBMARINE

Experiments with submersibles dated back to the 17th century, although history's first military submarine – a one-man, bubble-like craft called the *Turtle* – was designed in 1775 by American David Bushnell. Thereafter various experimental submarines appeared in the Americas and Europe, although none ever managed to sink an enemy vessel, and most ended up sinking or being abandoned on grounds of cost. The *Hunley*, however, would go to war.

The Union blockade gave a group of wealthy New Orleans citizens the impetus to revisit submarine designs. In 1862 and 1863, two prototypes were inauspiciously built – the first had to be scuttled, the second sank of its own accord. Yet the *Hunley* made it to testing in July 1863, and in August was moved to the embattled city of Charleston, which was being starved and shelled by Union warships.

The *Hunley* itself was a 40ft (12.2m) submersible, with an appearance not dissimilar to that of modern submarines. It had a crew of eight: one man steered the vessel, while the other seven hand-cranked the propeller. The fore and aft ballast tanks were also hand-pumped, making the *Hunley* an exhausting craft to operate. Two short conning towers with small portholes provided

OPPOSITE: CSS *Hunley*, the first submarine ever to sink a ship during war. (Naval Historical Center)

limited visibility. In terms of weaponry, the *Hunley* was armed with a "spar torpedo," which consisted of a 17ft (5.2m)-long barbed iron spar attached to a large copper canister containing a 90–130lb (41–59kg) black powder charge. The idea was to float the torpedo into the target ship, the spar embedding in its side, after which the *Hunley* would pull away and detonate the charge by lanyard.

The *Hunley*'s first year at Charleston was unpromising. On August 29, it sank when under tow, and had to be refloated in a lengthy operation. It sank again on October 15 during a demonstration dive, and was raised for a second time. On February 17, 1864, however, it sailed out on its first actual operation. Its target was the USS *Housatonic*, anchored off Sullivan's Island to intercept blockade runners.

GROUND-BREAKING ATTACK

Under the cover of darkness, at about 8.45pm, the *Hunley* approached the enemy vessel, tracking through the water just below the surface. It was spotted as it moved in, and mariners aboard the *Housatonic* opened up with rifle fire, to no avail. (The position of the *Hunley* in the water meant that the Union ship could not depress its cannon enough to engage it with heavier firepower.) Just short of her target, *Hunley* released its torpedo, which was mounted on the keel at the bow, and the iron spike embedded itself into the *Housatonic*. The *Hunley*'s crew then turned their craft about, and made off while spooling out the detonating lanyard.

When the *Hunley* was about 50yds (46m) from the *Housatonic*, the lanyard went taut and detonated the torpedo.

CSS *HUNLEY*

Key

1   Spar torpedo boom coupling
2   Forward ballast tank
3   Commander's station
4   "Snorkel" air tube
5   Vision port
6   After hatch
7   Propeller shaft flywheel
8   After ballast tank
9   Rudder
10 Propeller
11 Crew seating

Specifications

Crew: 8 (1 officer, 7 enlisted)
Displacement: 7.5 short tons (6.8 tonnes)
Length: 40ft (12.2m)
Beam: 3ft 10in (1.17m)
Propulsion: Hand-cranked propeller
Speed: 4 knots (7.4km/h) on the surface
Armament: 1 × spar torpedo

The subsequent blast of the warhead was powerfully augmented by the sympathetic explosion of the *Housatonic*'s magazine, ripping the ship apart and sinking it in less than five minutes.

The CSS *Hunley* goes down in history for being the first submarine to sink a ship under wartime conditions. Yet neither the submarine nor the crew returned from its mission. The reason for its sinking are uncertain. Possibilities include the sub being holed by small-arms fire, or its hull being fractured by the combined detonation of the torpedo and *Housatonic*'s magazine. Either way, the *Hunley* represents the crude beginnings of a weapon system that would one day become the biggest threat to shipping on the world's oceans.

In one final point of note, the wreck of the CSS *Hunley* was discovered in 1995 and raised on August 8, 2000. The remains of the submarine's crew were still inside, and they were buried in 2004 with full military honors in Charleston's Magnolia Cemetery.

ABOVE: An artistic impression of a Civil War-era submarine from *Harper's Weekly*. Newspapers frequently carried depictions of these "infernal machines" which were far from accurate. (Stratford Archive)

BELOW: An artistic representation of the CSS *Hunley* attacking USS *Housatonic*, Charleston Harbor, February 1864. The *Hunley* approached the *Housatonic* unseen until it was within 50ft (15.2m) of its target. Marksmen on the *Housatonic* fired on the strange "log-shaped" vessel, but were unable to prevent it placing its torpedo. (Artwork by Tony Bryan © Osprey Publishing Ltd.)

NAVAL MINES

Although submarines, surface warships, and aircraft tend to capture the press in naval history, the sea mine has been and remains one of the greatest practical threats to shipping. Sea mines are cheap to deploy, can remain operational for months, even years, and they allow a navy to exert control over certain waters without actually being present.

EARLY DEVICES

Naval mines have a surprisingly old lineage. Floating explosive devices were employed back in the 14th century by the Chinese, and in the 16th century the Dutch created a form of mine by packing unmanned vessels with explosives, floating these "bomb ships" into enemy harbors and sea lanes. Yet the first true mines were invented during the American War of Independence by American military engineer David Bushnell (also the inventor of the *Turtle* submarine mentioned previously). Actually called a "torpedo," Bushnell's mine consisted of watertight gunpowder kegs fitted with impact-sensitive flintlock mechanisms. The mines were deployed in action on the Delaware River in 1777, but without operational success.

Next up to the plate was Robert Fulton, also American, who in the late 1790s created drifting mines that were detonated by timer. These were impractical, so he then designed double mines connected by a cable, the idea being that a ship snagged the cable and drew the mines onto itself. After some experimentation, he also submerged the mines, which would ensure that they detonated well beneath the waterline. In 1805 and 1807, Fulton successfully tested these weapons on large warships, proving the mine concept.

OPPOSITE: A stockpile of German underwater mines, *c.* 1944. (akg-images/RIA Nowosti)

IMPACT DETONATED

It would be in the 19th century, however, that mine warfare truly came of age. Throughout the first half of the century, individuals such as Pavel Schilling (Russia) and Samuel Colt (United States) experimented with submerged mine detonation using electrical current. During the Crimean War (1854–56), Moritz Jacobi, a Prussian living in Russia, successfully created contact mines, triggered when a ship hit the mine's chemical fuse (a glass tube of sulfuric acid). One such mine damaged the British paddle steamer HMS *Merlin*.

ABOVE: A view of Port Arthur. Sea mines can be used both offensively and defensively and during the Russo-Japanese War the Japanese protected the entrance to Port Arthur by using a large number of mines. (akg-images)

LEFT: The Russian battleship *Petropavlosk* was sunk by sea mines laid by the Japanese. The Russo-Japanese War was the first time sea mines were used in large numbers. This was a portent of things to come in the two world wars. (akg-images)

By the 1860s, sea mines had entered the modern naval arsenal in significant numbers. They tended to come in contact or electrical-command detonated forms. The former could be employed out to sea, either free floating or anchored, while the latter were kept close to shore to protect harbors, anchorages etc – an electrical cable ran from the mine to a shore post. In terms of combat usage, mines were moderately influential in the American Civil War – a total of 50 ships (the vast majority being Union vessels) were sunk by this means. During the Russo-Japanese War (1904–05), mines were laid in even greater volumes, and did serious damage. The Japanese Navy, for example, lost three battleships and four cruisers to mines, while the Russian battleship *Petropavlosk* was sunk by Japanese mines laid across the entrance to Port Arthur – 638 sailors died. This conflict, more than any other, demonstrated the military value and strategic flexibility of naval mines. In World War I, therefore, nearly 310,000 mines were deployed in contested waters. The following world war brought the widespread introduction of influence mines, devices detonated by magnetic, pressure, or acoustic triggers rather than contact, increasing their effectiveness. More than 600,000 sea mines were laid in the Atlantic and European waters alone between 1939 and 1945, and across the world they accounted for millions of tons of shipping.

To this day, sea mines remain an international security problem, being sophisticated, durable, cheap, and easy to deploy by either ship or aircraft. Since the end of World War II, mines have damaged or destroyed numerous vessels both inside and outside hostilities, and they remain a problem that will dog all navies well into the future.

BELOW: Throughout the world wars Britain and Germany made extensive use of mines both to protect their own territorial waters and in an attempt to destroy enemy vessels. Mines frequently broke free of their moorings and washed ashore, where they would have to be tackled carefully by a mine disposal party. (IWM A 6355)

EXPLOSIVE SHELLS

Any firearm or artillery piece is, of course, only a delivery system for ammunition. Transformations in munitions technology, therefore, are just as important as changes in the weapons themselves. Nowhere is this more apparent than in the field of artillery shell development in the 19th century. Powerful high-explosive fills, and more effective propellants, changed artillery shells from being inert or low-power projectiles, through to being weapons of extreme destructive power, capable of blowing apart buildings, fortifications, and ships at beyond-visual distances.

OPPOSITE: Alfred Nobel not only invented dynamite but also ballistite, known to the British as cordite, a smokeless powder also used as the explosive in artillery shells, tank guns, and naval guns. (akg-images)

SHELL SHAPES

Right up until the mid 1800s, artillery ammunition was typically solid shot – and its variants such as canister and chain shot – or simple explosive spheres filled with gunpowder, detonated by a slow-burning fuse. The spherical shape of these projectiles reflected the smoothbore configuration of artillery, but from the 1850s and 1860s the introduction of rifled, breech-loading artillery pieces demanded very different projectiles indeed. Artillery shells became cylindro-conoidal in shape, with stabilized flight patterns. This reshaping had two immediate implications. First, as shells now landed nose-first, they could be fitted with

ABOVE: Filling a shell with its explosive content *c.* 1900
(akg-images)

percussion fuses, to detonate explosives on impact. Second, the elongated shells could, by increasing the density of metal at the front (or in the case of many early naval shells, making them totally solid), have significant armor-piercing capability.

What was needed now, however, was a more powerful explosive to go inside the shells. The history of 19th-century explosive developments is a complex one, and cannot be expanded on fully here. Specifically in terms of military explosives, however, there are salient points. In terms of propellants, a major step forward came in 1884 when a French chemist named Paul Vielle invented a nitrocellulose-based

ABOVE: A German high-explosive shell bursting near a British ammunition dump hidden in a wood, *c*. 1916. (Mary Evans Picture Library)

smokeless powder that was three times more powerful than gunpowder, and produced little obscuring smoke. At first the smokeless powder was only suited to small arms (and transformed their performance), but in 1887 the inventor of dynamite, Alfred Nobel, succeeded again by creating ballistite, which the British (ignoring Nobel's patent) called cordite. Ballistite/cordite gave artillery shells the powerful propellant they needed for long-range work, with improved versions in the early 20th century tweaking the power output even more.

EXPLOSIVE FORCE

Alongside developments in propellants, came advances in explosives themselves. The first major military high-explosive for shell fillings was picric acid, and related compounds such as Britain's lyddite. It entered service in the 1870s and saw use through to World War I. More stable and powerful high-explosives arrived in the early 20th century in the form of Trinitrotoluene (TNT), which had been discovered in the 1860s but wasn't applied as a shell explosive until 1902. Thereafter, it wasn't until World War II that explosive compounds moved forward again significantly, with the creation of substances such as RDX, PETN, and EDNA. (Note that all these explosives, however, were in part TNT.)

The final act in the evolution of explosive artillery shells was fuses. Three basic types of fuse had evolved by the beginning of World War I. The percussion fuse sat in the nose of the shell and detonated the explosive on impact (some more sophisticated versions could impose a slight delay), producing a useful shell for general anti-materiel and anti-personnel effects. Time fuses triggered the shell at a particular point in time, usually when it was over the heads of the enemy – combined with a heavy shrapnel content, such shells could have a devastating effect on unprotected troops. Armor-piercing shells, by contrast, tended to have delayed-impact base fuzes, to allow for some penetration before detonation. Fusing options would become highly sophisticated in the 20th century, and included proximity fuses, designed to detonate the shell when it sensed it was near the target.

Artillery development was scientifically fascinating, but physically appalling for those on the receiving end of the new shells. High-explosive shells became the great killers of the battlefield, against which there was little sure defense.

AMMUNITION CONFIGURATIONS

Historically, artillery ammunition comes in three different configurations. Fixed ammunition is rather like a rifle cartridge, the propellant, primer, and shell being in one unit. Such ammunition is most common for field guns, light naval guns, and small howitzers. In larger guns, however, fixed ammunition can become impractically heavy. The two options for these weapons are semi-fixed ammunition, in which the shell is separate from a powder and primer unit, and separate loading, in which shell, charge, and primer are all loaded individually (in that order). Semi-fixed munitions tend to be found in large-caliber howitzers, while separate loadings are most typical in major naval and coastal guns.

FRENCH 75mm M1897

THE WIDESPREAD INTRODUCTION OF BREECH-LOADING and rifled barrels during the 19th century had a profound effect on the nature of artillery. Neither phenomenon were new, but during the 1800s they were perfected in tandem, extending the range and accuracy of artillery considerably, and making possible the eventual application of indirect fire.

BREECH-LOADERS

Pioneers of the breech-loading, rifled field gun were William Armstrong in Britain and Alfred Krupp in Germany, who both introduced successful types in the 1850s. For naval guns, the French invention of the interrupted screw breech brought maritime forces fully into the breech-loading age.

Breech-loaders gradually brought more power, and with more powerful guns came the need for improved systems of recoil control, particularly if a gun crew was to avoid resighting after every shot. The 19th century saw triumphs in this field also. Larger guns in static emplacements were mounted on gun carriages that sat on upward-sloping platforms (the slope climbing to the rear). Gravity, plus a braking effect from compressor plates fitted on the side of the carriage, arrested the rearward travel of the gun, after which it could be run back to the firing position. The most important recoil control systems for field guns, however, were hydraulic buffers, these broadly consisting of fluid-filled cylinder and piston arrangements that absorbed the shock of the gun recoil, allowing a spring to return the gun to battery. From the 1890s, compressed gas was also used alongside oil in "hydropneumatic" systems.

OPPOSITE: During World War I the French 75mm gun was sometimes modified for an anti-aircraft role. (Private collection)

> *[The French fire] was monstrous... Everything was covered in columns of black smoke, so high and broad that I could hardly see anything; in between were white shrapnel bursts. Limbers and riderless horses emerged from time to time fleeing Montceaux.*
>
> **German artilleryman, first battle of the Marne, 1914.**

The final big change to artillery was in terms of sighting. In the late 19th and early 20th centuries various sighting devices – particularly the "goniometric" sight and the clinometer – were developed that enabled a gun crew to calculate the necessary angles to deliver accurate indirect fire. Now, for the enemy, death could come without warning, apart from the ranging shots of the first shells. Yet the psychological fondness for direct fire, plus the problems of correcting shots at range, meant that indirect fire would not reach its fullest expression until World War I.

LONG-SERVING GUN

The French 75mm M1897 is a perfect example of how all these elements came together in one weapon. An advanced hydropneumatic recoil system maintained the gun's precise position after each shot – the gun's trail and wheels didn't

BELOW: The crew of the French 75s bombarding the village of Montceaux-lés-Provins during the first battle of the Marne in 1914. First introduced in 1897, the guns would be ubiquitous in the early years of the war. (Artwork by Graham Turner © Osprey Publishing Ltd.)

> **" Artillery conquers: infantry occupies "**
>
> Marshal Pétain

ABOVE: The gun line of the 20e Régiment d'Artillerie (RA). The "Seventy-Five" was an accurate field gun but its trajectory was quite flat, which would prove problematic in the latter years of World War I. (Courtesy of Ian Sumner)

even move during firing. (Powerful smoothbore guns with no recoil system, by contrast, could roll back 3ft/2m on firing.) Combined with a rapid-action rotating screw breech-loading system, it could put 15 shells on target every minute, in the hands of a well-trained crew; the recoil cycle only took about two seconds. (The ammunition was also of the fixed type, which aided fast reloading.) High-explosive, anti-tank, or shrapnel shells could be delivered out to ranges of 7,500yds (6,900m), although with later boat-tailed ammunition the range of some shell types extended to 12,000yds (11,000m).

The M1897 was one of the best field guns available for the next 20 years, and was also used extensively by Polish, British, and American forces. It served with distinction during World War I, blowing apart German attacks at the battle of the Marne in 1914, and firing a total of 16 million shells during the battle of Verdun in 1916. Its destructive power against emplacements and barbed wire defenses was limited by its light shells, but

75MM M1897 – SPECIFICATIONS

Caliber: 75mm
Crew: 6
Barrel length: 106in (2,692mm)
Carriage: Horse/tractor drawn
Elevation: -11° to +18°
Traverse: 6°
Weight: 3,400lb (1,544kg)
Shell type: 75 × 350 mm; 13.13–15.95lb
    (5.97–7.25kg); high-explosive, shrapnel, anti-tank
Muzzle velocity: c. 1,600ft/sec (487m/sec)
Range: 7,440–9,350yds (6,800–8,550m)

its rapidity of fire made it devastating against infantry assaults. It also, intelligently, featured a shield for its crew, to protect them from small-arms fire. M1897s even soldiered on into the next world war, and the gun didn't entirely disappear from the world's battlefields until 1945. The gun was a triumph of engineering, including innovations of its own while incorporating the best of the 19th century's developments in artillery.

MAUSER GEWEHR 98 RIFLE

WHILE THE DREYSE NEEDLE-GUN DISCUSSED PREVIOUSLY was the beginning of the bolt-action system, it was a later Mauser rifle, however, that perfected it.

TUBULAR MAGAZINES

In 1884 weapons designer and industrialist Peter Paul Mauser, already known for the quality of his bolt-action designs, introduced an eight-round rifle with a tubular underbarrel magazine. It worked decently – the French Modèle 1886 followed a similar system, and would see service in the French Army until 1940.

Tubular magazine weapons were fine, but they always had to negotiate the safety issue of a bullet head resting against the primer of the cartridge in front of it. When fully loaded, they

OPPOSITE: Louis Botha (1862–1919), the commander-in-chief of the Boer forces from 1900 during the Second Anglo-Boer War (1899–1902). He is shown with his decorated Mauser rifle. (akg-images/IAM/World History Archive)

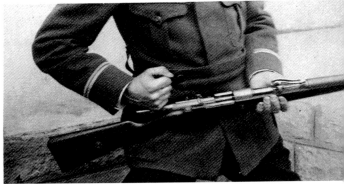

ABOVE: Loading a Mauser with its clip of five cartridges.
(© *Illustrated London News*/Mary Evans Picture Library)

were also front heavy, which didn't help for a steady aim. In 1885 another option arrived on the market, courtesy of Austrian gunmaker Ferdinand Mannlicher. In the Mannlicher system, the rifle featured an integral magazine beneath the bolt. Opening the bolt allowed the user to insert a clip of five rounds, and thereafter feed them one at a time by cycling the bolt. It was a major improvement over tubular magazines, and in a modified format was adopted as the German Army's standard rifle in 1888.

BELOW: A Mauser 98 from *c.* 1916 produced by the Prussian State Arsenal at Spandau. The rifle was the standard German infantry weapon of World War I. This particular rifle was captured by Colonel Webb of the Canadian Expeditionary Force from a German officer. (IWM FIR 7100)

MAUSER'S SOLUTION

There was a problem, however. Clip loading meant that once the gun was loaded, all cartridges had to be fired and/or ejected before reloading – you couldn't top up a part-emptied magazine with additional rounds. The man who solved this problem was Mauser. Mauser replaced clip loading with charger loading, in which the cartridges were pushed out of a thin clip into the magazine – the clip itself was not loaded into the gun. This meant that individual rounds could be added to the magazine in the heat of battle simply by opening the bolt and pushing fresh ammunition down on top of the stack.

The Mauser action became the model not only for a series of successful Mauser rifles, but for many bolt-action rifles to this day. In 1893 Mauser also refined the design of the bolt mechanism itself. These changes included a superior three-lug locking system and improved extractor.

In 1898, the German Army adopted the Mauser rifle in 7.92mm caliber as the Mauser Gewehr 98. This rifle, along with its shortened variant – the Kar 98K – were the standard-issue German rifles from the late 1890s until the end of World War II, such was the Mauser's qualities. From the deserts of North Africa to the winter steppes of Russia, the robust Mauser action kept working. Fitted with a telescopic sight, a Mauser rifle could achieve hits at more than 656yds (600m).

As combat weapons, the Gew 98/Kar 98K were not perfect. They were heavy and long (the Gew 98 measured 49.3in/1,250mm, and weighed 9lb/4.1kg), which made them awkward close-quarters weapons. Furthermore, while they had good command over long ranges, at practical combat distances – typically less than 220yds (200m) – submachine-guns and other automatic weapons had the rate of fire advantage over any bolt-action rifle. For such reasons, after World War II the assault rifle rendered the Mauser redundant, as it did all bolt-action rifles as standard issue weapons. Yet the fact remains that the bulk of the most professional infantry force in history, the German *Heer* of World War II, was principally armed with the bolt-action Mauser, which speaks volumes about its qualities.

BELOW: German Stormtroopers engaged in assault training, their Mausers at the ready. (IWM Q 55483)

LEVER-ACTION GUNS

Lever-action guns took a different route to the bolt-action. The US Sharps Carbine, invented in 1848, had a vertical sliding breech mechanism operated by a lever that was integral with the trigger guard, while the later British Martini-Henry rifle, used a hinged breech block, again lever operated, to expose and close the breech for loading/firing. Lever actions also provided the foundation for repeating rifles. The Spencer Carbine led the way in 1860. Here was a rifle that had a seven-round tubular magazine in the butt, each .56-caliber rimfire cartridge fed and (after firing) ejected by cycling a lever beneath the grip. Yet the greatest of the lever-action rifles were undoubtedly the Henry/Winchester repeaters, guns that virtually became synonymous with the Wild West. With the first model introduced in 1866, these rifles used a tubular magazine beneath the barrel rather than in the stock, giving an ammunition capacity of 15 rounds. In competent hands, these bullets could be loaded and fired in as many seconds.

COLT M1911

THE COLT M1911 WAS NOT THE WORLD'S FIRST automatic pistol, far from it. That accolade goes to a delayed-blowback weapon patented in 1892 by German Joseph Laumann, which was produced in 8mm caliber as the Schonberger-Laumann from 1894. It offered little advantage over the revolver, with its five-round capacity internal magazine, so sold in unconvincing numbers. A more significant design, therefore, was the 1894 7.63mm Borchardt pistol. In a crucial distinction from the Schonberger-Laumann, the recoil-operated Borchardt actually had a separate eight-round magazine that was inserted into the grip.

OPPOSITE: A US Marine recruiting poster illustrates the Marines Corps' trust in their M1911 pistols. (Library of Congress)

ENTER BROWNING

Yet the Borchardt was undeniably a monster, weighing 3lb (1.4kg) and of dimensions that made one-handed firing virtually impossible (in fact it came with a detachable butt-stock). Germany was now on a roll, however, and it eventually

BE A U.S. MARINE!

307 Evening Star Building, Washington, D. C.

established the automatic handgun as a type with models such as the Bergmann 1896, Mauser C/96, and the great Luger P08 of 1908, which fired the 9mm Parabellum cartridge that became one of the world's standard ammunitions for automatic handguns and submachine-guns. Other international companies also became semi-auto handgun producers, including Savage, Browning, Dreyse, Steyr, and Beretta, flooding the markets with this new form of firepower. Then came the Colt M1911.

The M1911 design actually belonged to the great gun designer John Moses Browning. In the early years of the 20th century, Browning had been working for the Belgian firearms company Fabrique Nationale (FN), for whom he had created legendary semi-auto firearms such as the Model 1900 and Model 1903. The latter used the same basic layout

ABOVE: Soldiers on the US Punitive Expedition into Mexico carry their M1911 pistols slung on their hips. (NARA)

BELOW: In a scene reminiscent of an earlier period, US cavalrymen charge with their M1911s drawn during maneuvers in 1941. Shooting from the saddle is one-handed, so the Colt was perfect for this role. (NARA)

REVOLVERS vs SEMI-AUTO HANDGUNS

It is worth reminding ourselves of why people use automatics in the first place, especially as revolvers have much to recommend them. Revolvers offer ultimate reliability – they rarely go wrong, and if a cartridge misfires you can always just pull the trigger again, or cock the hammer, to move on to the next round. Semi-auto handguns don't give such reliability – they can and do jam. Yet what they provide is enhanced firepower and fast reloading. Auto handgun magazines typically contain at least two more rounds than a six-shot revolver, and modern versions can carry more than 15 cartridges. Furthermore, once you empty a magazine it can be ejected and swapped for a fresh one in a matter of seconds, without the frequently fiddly reloading that accompanies a revolver. For these reasons alone, and other factors such as more controlled recoil, the semi-auto handgun today significantly outsells the revolver.

BELOW: A Colt M1911 shown with a World War II-era holster, pistol belt, and magazine pouch. (Courtesy of Leroy Thompson)

as the later M1911 – Browning gave FN rights to produce his pistol while he went back to the United States to create new designs for Colt.

.45 FIREPOWER

The M1911 was his masterpiece, ranking alongside his famous machine-guns. It fired a particularly powerful 0.45in ACP cartridge from a seven-round box magazine. The cartridge choice was based upon US combat experience during the Philippine Insurrection (1899–1902), during which US troops found .38in revolvers had limited man-stopping capabilities against a committed enemy.

The workings of the M1911 are simple and rugged. Its barrel features two locking ribs on top, just in front of the chamber, and these lock into corresponding grooves in the gun's slide. When the gun was fired, the barrel and slide recoiled back together for a short distance while the firing pressure dropped to safe levels, then a swinging link pulled the rear of barrel downwards, disengaging it from the slide grooves and leaving the slide to continue backwards against the return spring. During this process, the spent case was ejected, before the slide returned to battery, stripping off and chambering a new round as it did so.

The M1911's two virtues were its power and its simplicity. With few modifications, it was the US Army's standard handgun until the 1990s, serving with utter dependability in every conceivable theater, terrain, and environment. It is still produced today for the domestic market, and literally hundreds of other auto handguns are indebted to its basic design.

ABOVE: Despite being separated by several decades, US troops of two far-removed generations perform target practise with their trusty Colt M1911s (NARA and USMC)

IRONCLAD

THE 19TH CENTURY'S TRANSFORMATION OF NAVAL power could scarcely be more dramatic. Steam power, allied to the screw propeller, eventually freed navies from the vagaries of wind, and therefore gave them greater tactical maneuverability in action. (In balance, they become strategically dependent upon passage between coaling stations.) Furthermore, the developments in breech-loading artillery already outlined in this chapter profoundly altered the long-range accuracy of naval firepower, and in time gave birth to the turreted gun as the standard format for large naval artillery pieces.

VULNERABILITIES

All these changes took time, however, and sail warships and muzzle-loading guns persisted well into the second half of the century. Yet in the 1850s, another profound change began in the construction of naval vessels. On November 30, 1853, a Turkish squadron of wood-built ships – seven frigates, two corvettes, two steamers, and two transports – were set ablaze and destroyed within minutes by six Russian warships. The action greatly alarmed the world's navies, because it revealed the vulnerabilities of wooden warships to shellfire. By this time, iron merchant ships were already in production, so warship designers now reflected on the possibility of giving their vessels armored protection.

One way to achieve this protection was to create the "ironclad," essentially a wooden warship with the hull wrapped in iron plates for protection. The procedure was at first patchily applied, with sections of iron plate as much as 4in (10cm) thick emplaced around the ship's waterline. In 1859, however, the French launched the first true ironclad, the single-deck frigate *La Gloire* designed by Stanislas Charles Henri Dupuy de Lome. With a displacement of 6,206 short tons (5,630 tonnes), her oak hull was encased in iron armor 4.7in (119mm) thick and she was

OPPOSITE: This drawing shows the deck plan and side elevation of the USS *Monitor*, as produced by the Swedish designer John Ericsson in 1862. (NARA)

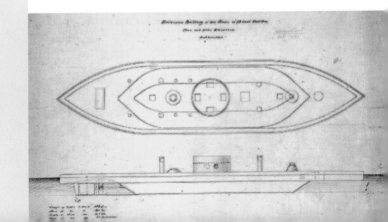

ABOVE: The close-range fighting between the rival ironclads, *Monitor* and *Virginia*, on March 9, 1862, is captured perfectly in this engraving. The damage to the smokestack, deck rails, and boat davits of the *Virginia*, much of which was caused during the action the previous day, is clearly visible. (Courtesy of Ron Field)

powered by a combination of steam and sail. The ship carried 36 breech-loading, rifled guns, and she frankly terrified the British. In response, therefore, they built the large iron-hulled *Warrior*. Launched in 1860, this vessel displaced 10,315 short tons (9,358 tonnes) and carried 40 guns, and was briefly the world's most powerful warship.

IRONCLAD BATTLE

Ironclads or iron-hulled warships steadily became the order of the day, and the world's great navies began to field increasing numbers. The world also soon saw history's first ironclad versus ironclad engagement. This occurred on March 9, 1862, at what is known as the battle of Hampton Roads during the American Civil War. The Confederate ironclad *Virginia*,

> ❝ On our gun-deck all was bustle, smoke, grimy figures, and stern commands, while down in the engine and boiler rooms the sixteen furnaces were belching out fire and smoke, and the firemen standing in front of them, like so many gladiators, tugged away with devil's-claw and slice-bar, inducing by their exertions more and more intense heat and combustion. The noise of the crackling, roaring fires, escaping steam, and the loud and labored pulsations of the engines, together with the roar of the battle above ... produced a scene and sound to be compared only with the poet's picture of the lower regions. ❞
>
> – Acting Chief Engineer Ramsay, CSS *Virginia*

1

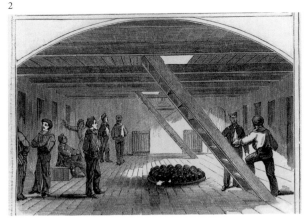

WHEEL HOUSE

2

3

4

6

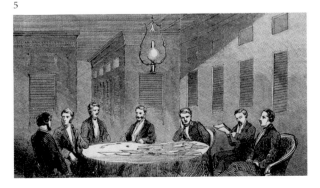

5

ABOVE: These engravings showing the interior of the *Monitor* were published in *Harper's Weekly* on April 12, 1862. Although partly inaccurate they offer a valuable insight into life aboard the ship. [1] An over-sized view of the interior of the pilothouse with the quartermaster standing at the ship's wheel. Note the viewing slits and speaking tubes. [2] View of the cabin berth, with ladders giving access to the turret and shot stored in the center of the deck. [3] The ship's galley, seen here with oval iron hathways and turret shaft mechanism overhead. [4] The captain's cabin luxuriously furnished. [5] The wardroom provided a communal area for the officers. [6] The engineer officer and assistants tending one of the two Martin boilers. (Courtesy of Ron Field)

ABOVE: The *Virginia* steams towards the *Monitor* and battle. The stricken frigate USS *Minnesota*, a symbol of an earlier era, is seen in the left middle distance. (*Ironclads* by Eaymond Bayless, US Navy Art Collection, Donation of Raymond Bayless, 1975)

(actually the rebuilt Union frigate *Merrimack*), met the innovative Union ironclad *Monitor* in action near Chesapeake Bay, Virginia. Although both ships shared a wood-and-iron construction, their layouts were dramatically different. The *Virginia* had a longitudinally triangular superstructure made from sloping iron sheets, with guns sticking out of circular ports. The *Monitor*, by contrast, had a iron deck almost flat to the waterline with a single iron turret in the center, this

BELOW: The passage of Vicksburg, April 1863. On April 16, 1863 Admiral Porter's ironclads were ordered to pass the city of Vicksburg and join the ocean-going fleet further downstream. Seven ironclads and three army transports made their way down river, while the Confederates lit tar barrels along the shore and fired flares to illuminate the Union ships, making them an easier target for their gunners. All of the ironclads survived the passage. (Artwork by Tony Bryan © Osprey Publishing Ltd.)

BATTLE OF TSUSHIMA

Despite the rise of new naval technologies, they remained no substitute for tactical authority, as was proven by engagements such as the battle of Tsushima, fought between Japan and Russia on May 27–28, 1905. The context was the Russo-Japanese War, and the battle occurred when a large Russian squadron of eight battleships, eight cruiser, nine destroyers, and three monitors attempted to sail through the Tsushima Strait between Korea and Japan. The Russian force, commanded by Admiral Zinovi Rozhdestvenski, was demoralized and disorganized after a long voyage, whereas the Japanese forces that suddenly attacked them were well-trained and highly motivated, and led by an intelligent and enthusiastic commander, Admiral Heihachiro Togo. The Japanese fleet had only four battleships but more cruisers and destroyers, plus better range-finding technology for their guns. Using advantages in speed, maneuverability, and night-fighting, and building upon Russian panic, the Japanese sank 17 Russian vessels and captured five, for a cost of only three torpedo boats sunk. As the Russians found out, in the age of steam, steel, and rifled guns, there were few places to hide from tactical mistakes.

mounting two 11in Dahlgren guns. The battle itself was rather inconclusive, a four-hour slogging match in which the armored hulls resisted the penetration of the opponent's shells. Both ships ended up withdrawing, but the value of armor had been proven.

In 1873, the Royal Navy commissioned HMS *Devastation*. This ship, if anything, truly represented the general pattern in naval warship design that would dominate the modern world. It was an ocean-going ship powered purely by steam – no auxiliary sails were fitted. Its armament, initially, consisted of two above-hull turrets, each turret mounting two 12in muzzle-loading guns. (In 1891 these were replaced by 10in breech-loaders.) Within 20 years of *Devastation*'s launch, almost all capital ships followed this pattern, made with iron then steel armored hulls. The great battleship arms race had begun.

WORLD WAR I
1914–18

HAND GRENADE

In one form or another, hand grenades have been with us as long as there has been gunpowder. From the 1st millennium AD, the Chinese were using rudimentary grenades made from clay or paper, and in the medieval period spherical cast-iron grenades had limited explosive force, but delivered potentially lethal fragmentation at close ranges. Grenades adopted a variety of forms between the 16th and 19th centuries, even including fin-stabilized percussion-fused types used during the American Civil War. Yet from the 18th century, grenades became tactically peripheral, especially with the decline in fortress siege warfare. World War I, however, made the grenade a fundamental part of almost every soldier's kit.

CRUDE DEVICES

Grenades are essentially an infantryman's own personal, hand-thrown artillery. While limited by the thrower's own muscle power – maximum range for a light grenade is about 50yds (46m) – they are ideally suited to clearing enemy troops from confined spaces, such as dugouts or rooms. Once the Western Front had bogged down into static warfare in late 1914, such confined spaces were in abundance. Grenades were ideal tools for attacking bunkers and trenches, a lesson that had already emerged from the Russo-Japanese War of 1904–05. Yet the types and availability of grenades in the first year of the war varied significantly amongst the combatants.

The Germans were best prepared, having stockpiled some 70,000 hand grenades and 106,000 rifle grenades. French and Russian forces also had decent numbers of grenades, but the British had limited amounts of the distrusted Mk I impact-detonated grenade, which once armed could go off in the user's hand if it received a knock. Improvised grenades were also produced by all

OPPOSITE: A female worker inspects Mills hand grenades in a British factory during World War I. As the war progressed, women increasingly filled more traditional male roles, including working in armaments factories. (IWM Q 54615)

ABOVE: German soldiers throwing grenades from their trenches, *c.* 1915. The soldier to the foreground throws a ball grenade while the soldier to the rear uses a stick grenade. World War I saw the hand grenade become an essential piece of kit for the ordinary soldier, a development that continued in World War II. (akg-images)

combatants to satisfy the insatiable demands of trench warfare. These varied in both quality and ingenuity. A common British grenade, for example, consisted of nothing more than a tin can packed with gun cotton and pieces of shrapnel and fitted with a friction igniter fuse. German and French equivalents often attached packets of explosive to long wooden handles, providing extra range in the throw through principles of leverage.

Such devices were ad hoc and unpredictable, but as grenades demonstrated their value in combat, that situation would change.

STANDARD EQUIPMENT

In 1915, new official models of hand grenade entered service, ones that established basic patterns of design and use for the next century. Most influential was the British No. 5 "Mills"

bomb, designed by William Mills from Sunderland. The grenade had a basic pineapple outline, made from cast iron but with the surface serrated to produce effective (although somewhat erratic) fragmentation upon detonating. To use, the operator withdrew a safety pin securing a spring-loaded striker lever. The soldier typically kept a grip on the lever until he threw the grenade, at which point the lever flew off and ignited a four-second delay fuse.

Weighing only 1.25lb (0.57kg), the Mills bomb fitted conveniently in the hand and could be thrown to about 15yds (14m). Its popularity, therefore, was assured, and more than 70 million were produced by the war's end, and many more thereafter (the 36M variant was the standard British Army grenade in the next world war). Germany also produced its own landmark hand grenade in 1915, the Model 24 *Stielhandgranate*, which had its explosive head fixed to the end of a long wooden handle. The pullcord of a friction-ignited fuse ran through the handle, but the handle also meant that the Model 24 could be thrown to distances double that of the Mills bomb.

Collection "Patrie"

B. ANDRÉ

40 c.
Le récit complet illustré.

LA PRISE
de COMBLES

BATTLE AT POZIÈRES RIDGE

The battle for Pozières Ridge in 1916 illustrates just how integral grenades became to infantry warfare in the first two years of the war. On July 23, the battle of the Somme having raged for three weeks, I ANZAC Corps and various British formations began an assault on the strategically important Pozières Ridge. (It offered one of the highest geographical points on the Somme front, making it ideal for artillery observation.) The attack secured its initial objectives, but subsequent German counterattacks resulted in numerous close-quarter engagements with small-arms and grenades. On the night of July 26–27, Australian and British forces exchanged grenades with the Germans for more than 12 hours, with the Allied contingent alone expending 73,000 grenades.

The following is an extract from the war diary of the Australian 5th Infantry Brigade, referring to the fighting at Pozières Ridge on July 26:

" There was no preliminary bombardment. The enemy detected the advance as soon as it began and very heavy casualties resulted, as the hostile artillery and machine gun fire grew very intense. When the raiders approach the wire it was found almost intact and only one party (the right) managed to reach the enemy trench. Immediately after affecting an entry this party commenced to bomb [attack with grenades] both ways but owing to heavy casualties among the carrying platoon the supply of bombs soon ran out and after holding the trench for about 1 hour the party was compelled to withdraw. "

These, and many other types of delay-fuse grenades became central to infantry tactics in World War I and beyond. The British, for example, assaulted trenches with nine-man "bombing parties," two of the men hurling grenades into the trenches and bunkers at regular intervals, two other men serving as grenade carriers, and the rest providing support or mop-up with their small arms. In World War II, grenades were essential for urban fighting, being one of the best methods of instant room clearance.

The same tactics are seen today in troops operating in Afghanistan and other war zones, demonstrating that some elements of warfare remain resolutely low-tech.

OPPOSITE: A French contemporary impression of a *poilu* doing his part in the attempt to retake the village of Combles during the battle of the Somme, 1916. (akg-images)

BELOW: A quarter of a century later, a different generation of German soldiers throw their own stick grenades during World War II. (akg-images/Ullstein Bild)

TORPEDO

On September 5, 1914, only a few weeks into World War I, the British scout cruiser HMS *Pathfinder* was returning from a patrol off the east coast of Scotland. At 3.45pm, the afternoon sunny and unthreatening, lookouts aboard the ship reported a torpedo wake off the starboard bow. The officer of the watch gave the command for urgent evasive action, but it was too late. A single German torpedo, fired from the submarine *U-21*, slammed into the ship beneath the bridge and exploded. The detonation in turn caused the ship's magazine to erupt, blowing *Pathfinder* apart and causing it to sink in just four minutes with the loss of more than 200 lives. HMS *Pathfinder* was the first ship – the first of hundreds – to be sunk by a submarine-launched torpedo.

OPPOSITE: A Royal Navy 320 Seaplane here drops an 18in torpedo. The aircraft was developed specifically to tackle U-boats, and was the first aircraft to sink such a vessel. Its overall success was marginal, however, although torpedoes themselves became one of the most influential weapons of the war. (IWM Q 27453)

UNDERWATER KILLER

Torpedoes were the product of the ever-fertile 19th century. "Spar torpedoes" were the earliest versions, consisting of nothing more than an explosive charge sticking out from the bows of a ship or early submarine on the end of a long wooden spar. The first true self-propelled torpedo, however, was developed by English marine engineer Robert Whitehead in 1867. Driven by compressed air, it had a maximum speed of 6 knots (11km/h), a range of a few hundred yards, and an 18lb (8kg) dynamite warhead. The Austrian government that had commissioned the project actually declined to take on Whitehead's torpedo, but the British Admiralty was far more impressed, and bought the rights to develop and manufacture the weapon.

Over the next 40 years, all maritime powers embraced torpedoes, and worked on improving launch systems for both surface vessels and submarines. By the time war broke out in 1914, torpedoes had improved tremendously, now featuring

gyroscopic direction control, hydrostatic depth gauges, and more powerful propulsion. A typical torpedo at the start of the war could travel at speeds of up to 44 knots (81km/h) to ranges of nearly 10,000yds (9,144m). Now they were to be tested in war.

UNDERWATER HUNTERS

The grim effectiveness of modern torpedoes was fully demonstrated by the destruction of *Pathfinder* and in the subsequent sinking of millions of tons of shipping. The Germans were at the forefront of submarine warfare, sporadically launching campaigns of unrestricted warfare against both merchant vessels and warships. These assault overturned the principles of naval warfare. In the space of one hour on September 22, 1914, for example, *U-9* sank the British cruisers *Hogue*, *Aboukir*, and *Cressy*. In 1917 alone, U-boats sent 6 million long tons (6,096,000 tonnes) of Allied shipping to the bottom, and only the adoption of the convoy system saved the Allies from disaster.

Torpedoes were not only launched from submarines. Torpedo boats and destroyers could fire them from deck-mounted tubes, and on August 12, 1915, a Short 184 seaplane became the first aircraft to sink an enemy ship with an air-dropped torpedo.

PREVIOUS PAGE: A US Navy recruitment poster. (akg-images)

BELOW: A torpedo being fired from the British light cruiser HMS *Cordelia* during World War I. (IWM SP 1613)

RMS *LUSITANIA*

One of the most famous sinkings was that of the passenger liner RMS *Lusitania* on May 7, 1915. The German submarine *U-20* put one gyroscopic, contact-detonated torpedo into the liner's side, at a range of 766yds (700m) with the torpedo running at 10ft (3m) depth. *U-20*'s commander, Kapitänleutnant Walther Schwieger, later reported in his log: "Torpedo hits starboard side right behind the bridge. An unusually heavy explosion takes place with a very strong explosive cloud. The explosion of the torpedo must have been followed by a second one [possibly the boiler]... The ship stops immediately and heels over to starboard very quickly, immersing simultaneously at the bow ... the name *Lusitania* becomes visible in golden letters." A total of 1,198 people died, and the incident was a horrifying demonstration of how a single torpedo could sink a ship with a displacement of 44,000 long tons (44,706 tonnes).

Torpedoes and submarines had, by the end of the war, altered the very nature of naval warfare, suddenly making huge battleships look like little more than tempting and costly targets. That perspective would be reinforced during the next world war.

DREADNOUGHT

THE INTRODUCTION OF DREADNOUGHT BATTLESHIPS had a similar effect on the global strategic security situation as the appearance of atomic weaponry in the mid 1940s. With the launch of HMS *Dreadnought* in 1906, almost all other battleship types were rendered obsolete overnight.

ALL-BIG-GUN SHIPS

By the late 19th century, battleship design had largely settled on mixed-armament configurations, each ship displaying a variety of calibers ranging from a few heavy long-range guns down to numerous short-range quick-firing weapons. The theory was that by being thus armed a ship could engage threats across the full range spectrum, from long-distance shots at enemy capital ships down to close-in engagements with enemy torpedo boats. As combat revealed, however, the idea didn't work. Battles during the Russo-Japanese War in particular revealed that having multiple calibers simply complicated effective fire-control. Furthermore, the most profitable gunnery was that of the largest-caliber guns (around 12in), which could engage targets at nearly 20,000yds (18,300m), well before other weapons could come into play.

A new idea took hold – that of a battleship armed purely (apart from minor defensive armament) with big guns of uniform

OPPOSITE: HMS *Royal Oak*, a so-called "super dreadnought" due to improvements in armament and design, was launched in 1914 and completed in 1916. She saw action during the battle of Jutland in 1916 and was sunk on October 14, 1939, in a surprise attack by the German submarine *U-47* while under anchor at Scapa Flow. (Stratford Archive)

caliber. The Japanese actually began laying down such a battleship in 1905, but it was the British who would reveal the first completed example. HMS *Dreadnought* had a displacement of 18,120 long tons (18,410 tonnes), armor plate up to 12in (30.5cm) thick, a fast top speed of 21 knots (39km/h) and, most importantly, ten 12in guns arranged in two-gun turrets. Here was a warship the likes of which the world had never seen.

POWER AND VULNERABILITY

Dreadnought was launched on February 10, 1906. At a stroke, the design made all other vessels obsolete, including the Royal Navy's. The result, fuelled by various imperial tensions, was a huge and costly arms race – by 1918 Britain alone had built 48 dreadnought-type battleships, and Germany constructed 26. "Dreadnought" became a British blanket term for all big warships, which over the next three decades grew ever faster, larger, more heavily armored, and with bigger guns. There were

variants on the theme, such as the "battlecruiser," still armed with heavy guns but with a reduced armor component to increase speed. One of the most famous battlecruisers was HMS *Hood*, which displaced 46,680 long tons (47,430 tonnes), carried eight 15in guns, and ran at a maximum speed of 31 knots (57km/h). Her lack of deck armor, however, would prove her undoing – she was blown apart on May 24, 1941, when a shell from the German pocket battleship *Bismarck* detonated the ship's magazine, killing all but three members of its crew.

The fate of the *Hood* illustrates one of the great, sad ironies of the age of the battleship. For these majestic, highly visible emblems of imperial power became little more than vulnerable burdens to the state. Engagements between major capital ships in World War I were relatively few, the greatest example being Jutland in May 1916 (see feature box). Battleships were so costly that all sides were wary of committing them to risky battles. Over time submarines and aircraft also proved

BATTLE OF JUTLAND

The battle of Jutland was the greatest clash of capital ships in modern history. The full might of the German and British battlefleets met for the first, and only, time in battle in the North Sea off the Danish coast, on May 31, 1916. The German *Hochseeflotte* (High Sea Fleet) commander, Vizeadmiral Reinhard Scheer, wanted to avoid engaging the Royal Navy's entire Grand Fleet, which was covering a battlecruiser force led by Vice Admiral Sir David Beatty. A major battle developed between Beatty's warships and a German battlecruiser force, the clash eventually drawing in the main fleets in a thunderous big-gun engagement. Both sides struggled to gain the advantage, and Scheer eventually managed to escape from the clutches of the Grand Fleet. The costs to both sides were high – the British lost three battlecruisers, three cruisers, and eight destroyers, while German losses were one battleship, one battlecruiser, three cruisers, and five destroyers. Although the battle itself was rather inconclusive, the losses had a greater strategic effect on the Germans.

LEFT: The ship that gave its name to a generation of battleships: HMS *Dreadnought*, seen in 1914 when she was flagship of the 4th Battle Squadron. Powered by turbines, capable of higher sustained speeds than reciprocating machinery, and armed with 12 x 12in (305mm) guns, this revolutionary warship rendered all contemporary battleships obsolete. (IWM Q 22184)

BELOW: The impressive sight of dreadnoughts in line astern. The view is from the British flagship *Iron Duke* at 1830hrs during the battle of Jutland. The dreadnought *Royal Oak* fires on the German battlecruisers. (Artwork by Howard Gerrard © Osprey Publishing Ltd)

ABOVE: A rare photo of the battle of Jutland underway. HMS *Invicible* is shown exploding after being hit by German battlecruisers. Jutland was the last major sea action of the war. (IWM SP 2468)

themselves to be confident battleship killers, particularly during World War II. As a result, following the loss of the *Bismarck* on May 27, 1941 (destroyed by the Royal Navy in retaliation for the *Hood*), the German Navy basically retained its major warships in safe home waters for the rest of the war, most to be bombed into destruction by the RAF. The largest battleships ever built – the Japanese monsters *Yamato* and *Musashi*, displacing 72,000 long tons (73,000 tonnes) and armed with nine 18.1 in guns – were both obliterated by US air attacks in the Pacific. By the end of World War II, battleships were most useful as floating anti-aircraft batteries to protect aircraft carriers, or for providing shore bombardment. Big guns, it appeared, were no longer decisive in a world of torpedoes and bombs.

SHORT MAGAZINE LEE-ENFIELD

THE SMLE HAS AN ARGUABLE CLAIM TO BEING THE best bolt-action service rifle in history. It was the primary weapon of most British infantrymen in two world wars, and Lee-Enfield variants would soldier on in the British Army until 1954, when they were replaced by the L1A1 semi-auto rifle. Such longevity alone should command our respect.

NEW DIMENSIONS

The Lee-Enfield evolution began back in 1888, when the British Army adopted the Lee-Metford bolt-action rifle as its standard service weapon. The name came from the designers of the gun's major components – James Paris Lee developed the bolt-action and the magazine, while the barrel and the rifling were the responsibility of one William Metford. The Lee-Metford was a decent enough rifle, chambered in the rimmed 0.303in cartridge that would serve the British Army for decades. Yet once cordite replaced gunpowder as a small-arms propellant in the 1890s, the Lee-Metford's barrel and rifling had to be reconfigured. This was done by the Royal Small Arms Factory (RSAF) at Enfield Lock, near London, hence the new rifle was called the Lee-Enfield.

The Lee-Enfield Mk I was introduced in November 1895, but in 1903 a new version was brought out, named the ".303in Rifle, Short, Magazine, Lee-Enfield Mk I." The "Short" part of the title was justified, taking the length of the rifle down to 44.57in (1,132mm) from the Lee-Metford's 49.5in (1,257mm). The reason given for the reduction was that the new dimensions

OPPOSITE: Snap-shooting instruction at the School of Musketry in Kent, England, *c.* 1915. The Lee-Enfield was not the most convenient weapon for close-range combat, but it gave the British infantryman reliable and accurate medium-range firepower. (IWM Q 53552)

suited both the infantryman and the cavalryman, but many experts were incensed by what they saw as nothing more than a cost-cutting exercise. Their negative evaluations would soon be proved wrong.

BATTLE TESTED

The SMLE's strengths were its fast bolt-action, a robust design in which wooden furniture ran to the very end of the muzzle, a ten-shot charger-loaded box magazine, and a powerful round. It could hit and kill someone at ranges in excess of a mile, although over open sights it was at its best up to about 400yds (365m). In short, the SMLE was durable, dependable, and hard hitting, and it was those qualities that made it a superb combat rifle on the battlefields of World War I.

BELOW: The three US divisions who served with the British during World War I were all issued British weapons, including the SMLE. Here men of Company K, 111th Infantry, 28th Division, have recently received their own No.1 Mark III Lee-Enfields. (NARA)

Early proof of the Lee-Enfield's power came at the battle of Mons in August 1914, the first clash between British and German troops on the Western Front. The highly trained riflemen of the British Expeditionary Force (BEF) delivered such withering fire from their Lee-Enfields that the German commander, General von Kluck, assumed that the British were using machine-guns. In fact, the troops were simply

LEE-ENFIELD SMLE MK I – SPECIFICATIONS

Caliber: 0.303in
Operation: Bolt-action
Feed: 10-round detachable box magazine
Length: 44.57in (1,132mm)
Barrel length: 25.19in (640mm)
Rifling: 5 grooves, l/hand
Weight: 8.18lb (3.71kg)
Muzzle velocity: 2,025ft/sec (617m/sec)

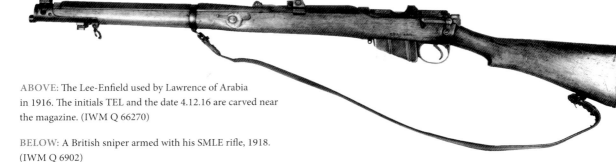

ABOVE: The Lee-Enfield used by Lawrence of Arabia in 1916. The initials TEL and the date 4.12.16 are carved near the magazine. (IWM Q 66270)

BELOW: A British sniper armed with his SMLE rifle, 1918. (IWM Q 6902)

sending out around 15 aimed shots per minute from their rifles. Later British conscript soldiers would be hard-pushed to achieve such rates, but 12rpm was perfectly viable.

The SMLE was in many ways well suited to the conditions of trench warfare. It was particularly robust in dirty conditions, and was dependably accurate across the typical distances of no man's land. Although it was fitted by some with telescopic sights, and served as a sniper weapon, it was not ideally suited to shots of more than 1,000yds (914m), as the all-encasing woodwork could distort the barrel depending on environmental conditions. Yet as a battlefield rifle, it had few equals.

FLAMETHROWER

As we have seen, armies have been using fire in combat since antiquity. Its introduction onto the battlefields of World War I in 1915, however, marked a new era in flame weaponry.

GERMAN FLAMETHROWERS

Germany has the dubious credit of introducing manportable, battlefield-mobile flamethrowers into modern warfare. In 1901, engineer Richard Fiedler pitched the idea for a flamethrower to the German Army, promoting it as an irresistible tool for clearing enemy positions, destroying strongpoints, and defending against infantry attacks. His audience bought into the idea, and between 1908 and 1914 Fiedler (aided by engineer and soldier Bernhard Reddemann) developed two principal models of *Flammenwerfer* (flamethrower). The first was the portable *Kleinflammenwerfer* (small flamethrower). This consisted of a large tank of oil, worn on the back, to which was attached a smaller tank of high-pressure gas (air, nitrogen, or carbon dioxide). When a valve was depressed, the gas was released and forced a stream of the fuel through a hand-held lance. The fuel was ignited at the muzzle of a lance to project a fearsome jet of oily, smoky flame to a range of up to 20yds (18m). Burn time was just a few seconds, however. His other model, the *Grossflammenwerfer* (large flamethrower), by contrast, was a far larger device suited only to static defense emplacement, and operated by a small crew. It could burn for up to 40 seconds, and throw its flame out to 40yds (36m).

OPPOSITE: The first encounter with a flamethrower must have been truly terrifying for the opposing troops. Here a German flamethrower is shown in action with some Stormtroopers *c.* 1918. (Mary Evans Picture Library/Robert Hunt Collection)

ABOVE: Here flamethrowers are shown in an anti-tank role on the Western Front. Early models of flamethrowers had to be lit manually, which was highly dangerous. As a result, later versions included an automatic ignition system. (Mary Evans Picture Library)

BELOW: Although the Germans were pioneers of flamethrowing, the Allies soon followed their lead. Here German troops are shown with a captured French portable flamethrower.

First combat testing came in minor engagements in 1914, but in 1915 the German high command created Flammenwerfer-Abteilung Reddemann (Flamethrower Unit Reddeman), a specialist assault formation. It first went into action against the French at Malancourt in February 1915, the opposing lines being scorched by huge tongues of flame prior to the attack, rendering the French soldiers largely incapable of reacting when the infantry assault came. Impressed by the flamethrower unit's performance, the army leadership formed a full flamethrower battalion in March, which eventually grew to become a 3,000-man regiment.

SCORCHED EARTH

Flamethrowers became an established element of German assault tactics for the remainder of the war. Two-man flamethrower crews would attempt to burn out defenders from forward trenches, suppressing or killing them to provide an opening for attacking infantry. There were some notable successes. On July 30, 1915, for example, an attack of 20 German flamethrowers on the British lines at Hooge forced the defenders from their

ABOVE: Portable flamethrowers would continue to be used in World War II. Here a German Pioneer soldier is shown destroying a house somewhere on the Eastern Front. (IWM COL 176)

trenches, although the lost ground was later retaken in a counterattack. Flamethrowers worked at their best alongside other assault troops, men armed with grenades and machine-guns – they were not intended to be applied unilaterally.

Soon the Allies also had their own flamethrowers and dedicated teams. The British developed the Hall Projector, which had a 33yd (30m) range, while the French had the *Schilt* flamethrower, which worked off gasoline and naptha. Both models were introduced in mid 1916, and were used with similar tactics and units to those of the Germans.

Flamethrowers could be horribly effective. Even if the defenders were not directly burnt to death, they could be suffocated in bunkers by oxygen depletion. Yet in balance, flamethrower operators were highly vulnerable. To use a flamethrower, they had to close to very short range with large tanks of flammable liquids attached to their backs – all it took was a single bullet to strike the tank, and the operator could be incinerated. Actual casualties caused by flamethrowers were relatively low, much of their effect coming from defenders being displaced from their trenches to be cut down by small-arms fire as they fled. For such reasons, the US forces never formally adopted flamethrowers during World War I, although willingly embraced them in World War II, where they proved ideally suited to attacking well-defended bunkers and other inaccessible installations. Flamethrowers largely fell out of use after 1945, partly because air-dropped napalm took away their rationale. Yet they are not banned by any convention, so they could well appear again in the future.

MK I/IV TANK

In February 1915, the British Admiralty established an unusually titled organization known as the "Landship Committee." Its purpose was to oversee the design and production of armored vehicles – known as "landships" – that might be capable of breaking the grinding trench deadlock on the Western Front. The idea was spurred by British experience of using armored cars in various imperial policing and combat roles. The new vehicles, however, had to be heavily armed, resistant to enemy small-arms fire, and have a genuine cross-country capability.

FROM "LITTLE WILLIE" TO THE MK I

The Landship Committee's first vehicle was the whimsically named "Little Willie." It had a boxy iron superstructure pushed along by two continuous tracks, and directed mainly by two wheels on a steerable axle projecting from the back. Powered by a 105hp (78kW) Daimler six-cylinder engine, it could achieve a magnificent road speed of 2mph (3.2km/h), and less than half that cross-country. Armament consisted of various machine-guns and, in the original configuration that had a fixed, dummy turret, a 2pdr automatic cannon.

"Little Willie" never rolled into combat, but it was undoubtedly a pioneer in tank design, and laid the groundwork for what was to follow. For on January 16, 1916, the Landships Committee ran another design, known variously as "Mother" or "Big Willie." This vehicle was designed by Lieutenant W.G. Wilson, and it was designed to meet a War Office demand for an armored vehicle capable of crossing a trench 8ft (2.44m) wide and a parapet 4ft 6in (1.37m) high. "Mother" fulfilled those conditions, and became the Mk I tank, the first British Army tank to go into action.

OPPOSITE: Close-up frontal view of a Female Mark I, probably of A Company during the November 1916 actions. So called "female" tanks were armed with five machine-guns. In contrast, the more common "male" tanks were armed with two 6pdr guns and four machine-guns. (Tank Museum, Bovington)

ABOVE: King George V and senior officers watch two new Mark IV tanks (one male, one female) tackle a steeplechase course in July 1917, the same month the Tank Corps came into being. (Tank Museum, Bovington)

EARLY ACTIONS

The Mk I had a distinctly different appearance from "Little Willie." From the side it was rhomboidal in shape, the caterpillar tracks running around the entire outer edge of the tank (it retained the two rear steering wheels, however). The tank was built in two versions. The "Male" tank was armed with two 6pdr quick-firing (QF) guns and four Hotchkiss machine-guns, while the "Female" version – designed specifically to repel swarming infantry attacks – was equipped with five machine-guns. Speed was still sluggish – maximum pace was 3.7mph (6km/h) – but these dinosaur-like creatures were sent into action at Flers-Courcelette on September 15, 1916, during the Somme offensive. The first experience of battle sent mixed messages.

Of the 49 tanks committed, most did not reach their objectives because of mechanical breakdown. Those that did get through, however, routed the defenders in their sectors. The tank had proven itself in action.

The Mk I went through several stages of modification before it became the definitive British tank of World War I – the Mk IV. The Mk IV entered service in June 1917, and was the beneficiary of numerous improvements to powerplant, ventilation, armor, steering (the external rear wheels were gone), and operability, but the eight-man crew inside still endured a horrible experience. These early tanks were baking hot – temperatures easily exceeded 32°C (90°F) – filled with poisonous engine and gun fumes, violently loud (hand signals were often the only way of communicating), and hard-edged (impact injuries were commonplace). The impact of bullets on the outside of the tank peppered those inside with "splashes" of razor sharp metal fragments. Visibility was extremely poor.

BELOW: *Little Willie* during trials. (Artwork by Tony Bryan © Osprey Publishing Ltd.)

Despite such internal ghastliness, however, the tanks nevertheless made an impact on the battlefield. At Cambrai in November 1917, some 476 tanks accompanied a major offensive thrust across a 6-mile (10km) front. Aided by the tanks' guns and ability to grind through barbed wire defenses, the attack cut through the Hindenburg Line for the first time and made gains of 3.7 miles (6km). The gains of the battle were subsequently lost to German counterattacks, but the ability of tanks to change the outcome of a battle was no longer doubted.

By the end of the war, all of the combatant armies were fielding tanks on the battlefield in various numbers. During the inter-war years, the armored component of land forces became utterly central to army maneuver warfare, as would be proved by the German Blitzkrieg in 1939.

LEFT: The first tanks stunned the world and postwar they were shipped to a number of countries for publicity purposes. The tank Britannia was part of a procession down Fifth Avenue and the of "Heroland" spectacle. (Artwork by Tony Bryan © Osprey Publishing Ltd.)

OVERLEAF: A British Mark IV tank as it would have appeared to occupants of German trenches during the battle of Cambrai – the first occasion on which tanks were launched en masse in a surprise attack. (IWM Q 6284)

THE ROLE OF TANKS

The following is an excerpt from the introduction to a British booklet entitled *Instructions for the Training of the Tank Corps in France*, issued December 1, 1917:

" The guiding principle to be remembered when considering the role of fighting tanks is that they, like all other arms, must be mainly employed to assist the infantry both in attack and defence. The infantry is the only arm which can seize and hold a position and upon its skill and endurance depends the security of the defence.

The employment of tanks, therefore, does not entail any essential modifications in the recognized offensive and defensive tactics of the infantry. It is their duty, just as it is the duty of the artillery, machine guns and trench mortars, to assist the infantry to gain superiority of fire. Owing to their imperviousness to rifle and machine gun fire, to their ability to develop rapidly a powerful volume of fire, to their mobility and moral effect, tanks can materially assist the infantry by destroying the enemy's strong points and machine gun emplacements, by overcoming his resistance and by protecting the flanks of the attack. In defence they can be employed in counter attack either independently or in co-operation with the infantry and can be used, if necessary, to cover a withdrawal. "

ZEPPELIN

THE ZEPPELIN AIRSHIPS ARE SOMETHING OF AN ODDITY in this book. While other weapons studied here often had a profound impact on the history of warfare, combat dirigibles were a passing, and not terribly effective, phase. Yet they remain amongst the first serious attempts at long-range strategic bombing, the later practice of which would have far more serious consequences for millions of people.

OPPOSITE: In response to the first Zeppelin bombing raids the *Daily News* offered a leaflet on what to do during an attack, as well as free "Zeppelin Bombardment Insurance." (Courtesy of Charles Stephenson)

NAVY AND ARMY

At the beginning of World War I, Germany's small force of dirigibles (seven operational craft) was divided between army and navy service. The two services had, and would maintain, very different attitudes to the use of airships in combat. The army looked upon them principally as low-level bombers,

POLICE WARNING.

WHAT TO DO WHEN THE ZEPPELINS COME.

Sir Edward Henry, the Commissioner of the Metropolitan Police, has issued a series of valuable instructions and suggestions as to the action that should be taken by the ordinary householder or resident in the event of an air raid over London.

New Scotland Yard, S.W.
June 26, 1915.

In all probability if an air raid is made it will take place at a time when most people are in bed. The only intimation the public are likely to get will be the reports of the anti-aircraft guns or the noise of falling bombs.

The public are advised not to go into the street, where they might be struck by falling missiles; moreover, the streets being required for the passage of fire engines, etc., should not be obstructed by pedestrians.

In many houses there are no facilities for procuring water on the upper floors. It is suggested, therefore, that a supply of water and sand might be kept there, so that any fire breaking out on a small scale can at once be dealt with. Everyone

should know the position of the fire alarm post nearest to his house.

All windows and doors on the lower floor should be closed to prevent the admission of noxious gases. An indication that poison gas is being used will be that a peculiar and irritating smell may be noticed following on the dropping of the bomb.

Gas should not be turned off at the meter at night, as this practice involves a risk of subsequent fire and of explosion from burners left on when the meter was shut off. This risk outweighs any advantage that might accrue from the gas being shut off at the time of a night raid by aircraft.

Persons purchasing portable chemical fire extinguishers should require a written guarantee that they comply with the specifications of the Board of Trade, Office of Works, Metropolitan Police, or some approved Fire Prevention Committee.

No bomb of any description should be handled unless it has shown itself to be of incendiary type. In this case it may be possible to remove it without undue risk. In all other cases a bomb should be left alone, and the police informed.

E. R. HENRY.

EXTRACT FROM
LATEST POLICE WARNING:
KEEP SAND AND WATER HANDY.

Press Bureau.

In view of the possibility of further attacks by hostile aircraft, the Commissioner of Police deems it advisable to call attention to the public warning published on June 26 recommending residents to

remain under cover, and advising them for dealing with incendiary fires to keep a supply of water and sand readily available.

(Signed) E. R. HENRY,
Commissioner of Police of the
Metropolis.

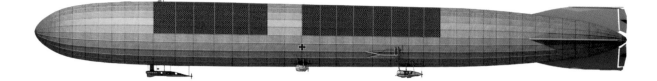

using them to attack cities such as Liege and Antwerp in the early months of war. Yet the army quickly lost enthusiasm for this application of these huge, vulnerable craft, in which they proved lumberingly vulnerable to anti-aircraft fire. Tactical bombing was therefore abandoned after the battle of Verdun in 1916.

The *Kaiserliche Marine* (Imperial Navy), by contrast, had a different overall approach, using them for long-range maritime reconnaissance and also for early attempts at strategic bombing against British towns and cities. Both the army and the navy would use airships in this latter role, capitalizing on the fact that for much of the war, dirigibles flew at greater altitudes than fighter aircraft could reach.

ZEPPELIN RAIDS

There were actually two principal manufacturers of dirigibles during the war: Zeppelin and the Schutte-Lanz Company – "Zeppelin" simply became the popular shorthand for all German airships. In charge of the airship campaign was Korvettenkapitan Peter Strasser, head of the *Luftschiffer*. The first Zeppelin raid was conducted on January 19, 1915, when two airships (L3 and L4) attacked Great Yarmouth, Sheringham, and King's Lynn. The damage was not extensive – two people were killed, 16 injured, and a few buildings hit – but the shock to the British psyche was instant.

After this first action, Zeppelin raids became relatively frequent to British shores (the first raid over London was on May 31, 1915), and had cumulatively appreciable results. In total, 181 people were killed and 455 injured by Zeppelin attacks in Britain in 1915, and they caused hundreds of thousands of pounds of damage.

ABOVE: Luftschiffbau Zeppelin (LZ) 62 – the first of the "Super Zeppelins" that took to the skies in May 1916. Sixteen of these vessels were created during the war and they would be the mainstay of the strategic bombing offensive against the Allies. (Artwork by Ian Palmer © Osprey Publishing Ltd.)

At first, the British air defenses were rather impotent against the Zeppelins. Fighters struggled to reach the airships' altitude, and were often unable to down one if they did – inert rifle and (later) machine-gun ammunition had surprisingly little effect on the huge airframes. Anti-aircraft gunners had trouble detecting and spotting the giant but silent craft during night-time raids. Yet steadily, the tide started to turn against the Zeppelin. Fighter

RIGHT: Count Ferdinand von Zeppelin, a German general who enjoyed his greatest success as an aircraft manufacturer and founder of the Zeppelin Airship company. (akg-images)

ABOVE: Bomb damage caused by a single 660lb bomb dropped by a Zeppelin on part of London. Two men were killed. (IWM LC 30)

ABOVE: The Zeppelins were ultimately halted by improved air defenses over London. A contemporary postcard shows SL11 caught by searchlights and under attack by anti-aircraft guns. (Courtesy of Ian Castle)

performance improved, and equipping machine-gun aircraft with explosive and incendiary ammunition made it much easier to start the fires that were so disastrous to airships. If they couldn't attack over British airspace, the Royal Flying Corps (RFC) pilots would wait until the airships were descending to their bases over France before attacking. The German Army abandoned raids over Britain in 1916, but the navy persisted

until 1918, utilizing new airships that could achieve even higher altitudes, although at the expense of near hypothermic or frostbitten crews.

Yet for the little damage they caused – just £90,000 worth in 1917 (several single raids in 1915 exceeded that figure) – the losses were too high. Some 115 Zeppelins were deployed during the war, and more than a third were either destroyed or damaged beyond repair. Strasser himself died on August 5, 1918, when L70, conducting one of the last raids over Britain, was shot down over the Norfolk coast. Strasser's Zeppelins had not shaped the outcome of the war they fought, but they did shape the wars that were to come.

ZEPPELIN WARSHIPS

The Zeppelins were huge creatures – the 1914 versions measured up to 525ft (160m) in length, and later versions exceeded these dimensions significantly. Zeppelin L59, for example, was 743ft (226.5m) long, had a 78ft (23.9m) diameter, and a gas volume of 2,420,000ft³ (68,500m³). (The hydrogen or, less commonly, helium gas was contained in individual air bags inside the outer covering and metal skeleton frame.) Power came from engines attached to nacelles or gondolas bolted to the frame, and the airships could have impressive lift capabilities for ordnance or other supplies – L59 had a maximum useful lift of 51,900lb (23,500kg). Airships also had excellent endurance capabilities, but navigation was heavily influenced by weather conditions. Their maximum speeds were also around 50mph (80km/h), making them slow-moving targets for enemy fighters and gunners.

VICKERS MAXIM

In August 1916, during the battle of the Somme, soldiers of the British 100th Machine Gun Company opened fire with ten Vickers machine-guns. They maintained the fire, directed onto an area of land they wished to deny to the Germans, for an ear-breaking 12 hours. During this half-day marathon of fire, the ten Vickers fired just shy of one million rounds, saturating the ground 2,000yds (1,800m) away and using up 100 barrels in the process. None of the guns broke down, the only stoppages coming from faulty ammunition.

MAXIM'S REVOLUTION

This epic display of firepower at the Somme was part of a revolution in firearms technology that began in the late 19th century, courtesy of US-born, British citizen Hiram Maxim, an inventor and engineer.

In 1884, Maxim demonstrated an entirely new type of weapon – the machine-gun. Whereas previous "automatic" weapons, such as the Gatling, were powered by hand, Maxim's weapon actually used the force of recoil to cycle the gun, removing the need for human muscle. Also gone were the awkward gravity-fed magazines; his gun was fed by a fabric belt of cartridges, drawn into the gun mechanically by the recoil-powered action. The barrel was necessarily cooled by a large water jacket.

The Maxim gun could fire at a cyclical rate of around 550rpm, astounding those who witnessed early demonstrations. In 1885 Maxim refined the design further, introducing a simpler "toggle lock" system of locking and opening the breech block,

OPPOSITE: Six men usually acted as a full Vickers gun detachment: two manned the weapon while others brought up ammunition and spare parts or acted as reserve personnel. Here a team from the Machine Gun Corps are shown near Orvilles during the battle of the Somme, 1916. (IWM Q 3995)

ABOVE: Two new members of a Vickers machine-gun section from the 1st Battalion Cameronians (Scottish Rifles) receive training on the Western Front, 1915. (IWM Q 51584)

BELOW: The Vickers saw widespread use until the end of the war. Here it is shown in May 1918 during the final major German offensive before the conclusion of hostilities. There was clearly no time to dig in and the Vickers is simply sited in a local barn. (IWM Q 6571)

and thereby making the gun more reliable and better suited to battlefield repairs and maintenance. Around this time Maxim also entered into partnership with British Vickers company, which would go on to produce the perfect variant of Maxim's invention.

INDUSTRIAL WARFARE

By the beginning of World War I, the world's great armies had all accepted the technology and logic of machine-guns. Although not all machine-guns at this time used Maxim's principles, the Germans were equipped with virtually a direct copy of the Maxim, named the MG08. The British also used Maxim's design, but revised the internal layout to make a gun that was lighter and more manageable. This was the Vickers machine-gun, adopted by the British Army in 1912.

The Vickers demonstrated the full-power of the new machine-gun technology. It fired 0.303in rounds at a cyclical rate of 500rpm, the barrel still cooled by the bulky water jacket (the barrel would need replacing after every 10,000 rounds or so, less if the rate of fire was high). For infantry use it was mounted on a heavy tripod, and sight fittings were configured for either direct or indirect fire. The former could be delivered at ranges of up to 2,000yds (1,828m), but for the latter the gun's range could go as far as 3,800yds (3,475m). (Such extreme ranges, however, were rarely entertained.) The 0.303in rounds could eat through brick, concrete, and sandbag defenses. Against exposed infantry attempting to cross no-man's land, the effect could be like a scythe, cutting down ranks of men. The Germans, of course, visited similar horrors on the British with their machine-guns.

The Vickers' design was so robust and workmanlike that the gun would stay in British service in one form or another until 1968. It was mounted on tanks, ships, and aircraft, respected as a light anti-aircraft gun as well as an infantry weapon. Guns such as the Vickers demonstrated that industrial-scale firepower would be the decider of many battles.

VICKERS MAXIM – SPECIFICATIONS

Caliber: 0.303in
Operation: Short recoil
Feed: 250-round fabric belt
Cyclical rate: 450–500rpm
Length: 45.5in (1,155mm)
Barrel length: 28.5in (723mm)
Rifling: 4 grooves, r/hand
Weight (gun): 33lb (15kg)
Weight (tripod): 50lb (22.7kg)
Muzzle velocity: 2,240ft/sec (682m/sec)

BELOW: Vickers were also used by American "doughboys" – here shown receiving instruction from a British sergeant of the Machine Gun Corps in May 1918. (Stephen Bull)

LEWIS GUN

ALTHOUGH WORLD WAR I IS PRIMARILY REMEMBERED for its static trench works, there was regular movement either in the form of periodic massive offensives or in numerous localized attacks and fighting patrols. Heavy machine-guns like the Vickers and the Maxim were excellent in a relatively fixed supporting role, but much too heavy to move with the infantry in the assault. If footsoldiers wanted to take automatic firepower with them, then they would need a machine-gun suited to the purpose.

MACHINE-GUN TYPES

Machine-gun design by 1914 had broadened considerably since Maxim's early offerings. New automatic operating mechanisms emerged in the 1880s and 1890s, including one that would create an entirely new stratum of machine-guns. Gas-operated firearms utilized the gas pressure produced when a gun was fired to cycle the weapon. It was first pioneered by John Moses Browning in 1889, but the great breakthrough was made by Captain Baron A. Odkolek von Augeza of Austria. In the machine-gun he designed, propellant gas was tapped off from the barrel via a port, and directed into a cylinder, in which there was a piston. The piston was connected to the bolt by an operating rod, and as the rod was forced back by the gas pressure the bolt was unlocked and pushed to the rear against the force of a return spring, ejecting the spent cartridge case as it went. Once the bolt had reached the rear of its travel, the return spring drove it back to battery, loading a new round as it went. In effect, the design worked on similar principles to an internal combustion engine. Moreover, the gun was cooled by air, not water, removing the need for the weighty water jacket.

OPPOSITE: A gunner from the New Zealand Rifle Brigade fires a Lewis gun on the Western Zealand Front, using the front bipod in the classic light machine-gun mode. (IWM Q 10506)

ABOVE: The ubiquitous Lewis gun. Here a German machine-gun crew is shown with captured British Lewis guns during the second battle of the Somme, 1918. (IWM Q 55482)

Gas-operation would become the dominant operating mechanism for many of the world's machine-guns. Such weapons not only had manageable recoil – the gas system absorbed much of the rearward force – but they could also be made lighter than recoil-operated guns, opening the possibility for true assault machine-guns.

LEWIS FIREPOWER

What we now know as "light" machine-guns (LMGs) emerged in the early years of the 20th century, one of the first being the Danish Madsen of 1902, which weighed 22lb (10kg) and was fed by a 30-round box magazine. The Lewis gun arrived on the scene exactly ten years later. It was also gas-operated, designed by American Colonel Isaac Lewis (building on an earlier design by Samuel McLean), and featuring some distinct

innovations. The barrel was surrounded by a large shroud, into which cooling air was drawn by the expansion of the muzzle blast. A clock-like return spring could be adjusted for tension, making it possible to adjust rates of fire slightly.

LEWIS GUN (UK) – SPECIFICATIONS

Caliber: 0.303in
Operation: Gas
Feed: 47-round pan magazine (97-round magazine in aircraft fittings)
Cyclical rate: 500rpm
Length: 49.2in (1,250mm)
Barrel length: 26in (661mm)
Rifling: 4 grooves, r/hand
Weight (gun): 26lb (11.8kg)
Muzzle velocity: 2,440ft/sec (744m/sec)

It was fed from a 47-round top-mounted pan magazine. For the infantryman, one of its best features was its weight – just 26lb (11.8kg).

Finding no initial buyers for the weapon in the United States, Lewis took the gun to a war-ready Europe, where he sold thousands to the Belgians (from 1914) and the British (from 1915).

By 1917, every British Army infantry section had a Lewis gun, dramatically increasing the infantry's fire-and-maneuver capabilities. Mounted on a simple front bipod, the Lewis could be set up wherever required and spray out 0.303in rounds to an effective range of about 650yds (594m). The value of such convenient firepower meant that Lewis guns found new roles in aircraft, tanks, armored cars, and even on motorcycles. In addition, six Lewis guns could be produced in the time it took to make a single Vickers, hence more than 50,000 had been made by the end of the war. These included 0.30in versions, belatedly taken into US service.

Surplus stocks of Lewis guns would serve in World War II, despite the British adopting the superb Bren gun as its replacement. (The US forces replaced the Lewis with the Browning Automatic Rifle – BAR.) World War I ended with the LMG firmly established as part of infantry tactics, in large part due to the Lewis proving the concept.

OPPOSITE, ABOVE: Australian soldiers learn to fire the Lewis gun. (IWM E(AUS) 683)

OPPOSITE, BELOW: A Lewis gunner firing through a wooden box on the banks of the Lys canal, near Marquois, during the German Spring Offensive of 1918. (IWM Q 6528)

POISON GAS

THE USE OF POISON GAS DURING WORLD WAR I WAS one of the most unpalatable aspects of an already terrible conflict. Despite the fact that the Hague Declaration of 1899 and the Hague Convention of 1902 forbade the use of poisonous weaponry, the battlefields were soon choked with gas, killing or wounding thousands of soldiers. Yet despite its prevalence between 1914 and 1918, it was subsequently abandoned as a conventional weapon of war, the conflict revealing its limitations as much as its possibilities.

BREAKING THE STALEMATE

By the end of 1914, the war on the Western Front had largely devolved into static trench warfare. Both sides looked for tactical and technical solutions to break the deadlock, and on April 22, 1915, at the second battle of Ypres, the German forces turned to gas in an attempt to do so. Strictly speaking, this was not the first time that gas had been used by the combatants. In 1914, both the French and Germans had experimented with tear-gas and another irritant chemicals, contained in both hand grenades and artillery shells. Combat tests were not particularly successful, but at Ypres the Germans switched to using lethal chlorine gas, pumping it out towards British, Canadian, and French lines as preparation for the infantry attack. Up to 1,400 Allied troops were killed by the gas, and another 4,000 injured. (Chlorine gas works by irritating the lungs, causing them to fill with fluids and effectively drowning the victim.) Despite the Allied condemnation of the attack, the British responded in kind at the battle of Loos on September 24, 1915, releasing the

OPPOSITE: A German Jäger and an infantry officer charge with grenades wearing the *Linienmaske*, designed to protect against Allied gas attacks. The infantryman on the right has a Mauser C96 pistol at his hip in its wooden holster-stock, and appears to be brandishing the bayonet that by 1915 had usually replaced the officer's sword. (Courtesy of Simon Jones)

LEFT: Although the Germans first introduced the use of gas, it was rapidly adopted by all combatant armies. Here the chlorine gas from a French attack during the battle of the Somme is drifting over the German lines, but the risk of the wind direction changing was high. (Courtesy of Simon Jones)

BELOW: A French trench at Poelcapelle captured in the first gas attack on April 22, 1915. Chlorine gas victims were described as lying on their backs with their fists clenched with a blue cast to the eyes and lips. (Courtesy of Simon Jones)

contents of 5,900 chlorine gas canisters. The fact that gas deployment was wind dependent became painfully apparent as much of the gas blew back into British lines, causing more than 1,000 British casualties.

DEADLY MIX

Although gas did not bring the hoped-for strategic breakthroughs, from 1915 it was nonetheless part of the regular arsenal of weaponry. Two more types of gas were "weaponized" – phosgene and mustard gas. Both were appalling chemicals. Phosgene gas caused devastating respiratory damage, and it could be inhaled for some time without detection, the casualty succumbing to the poison up to 48 hours after breathing it. Mustard gas was first used by the Germans on the Eastern Front in September 1917, and although odorless it was a grim blistering agent, causing blindness, mutilation, lung damage, and death. During the first German mustard gas bombardment of British lines on July 12/13, 1915, 15,000 British soldiers were injured, and up to 450 later died from their injuries. Often different types of gases would be deployed simultaneously, along with smoke to increase confusion in the enemy lines.

Initially, gas was deployed directly from pressurized canisters, but by the end of 1915 artillery shells were the primary delivery method. Shells had the advantage not only of accuracy, but also of dumping the gas well away from friendly lines, although the wind was still capable of carrying it backwards. Protection against the gas was of almost medieval crudity in the early years of the war, consisting of little more than thick cotton or gauze pads wrapped over the face, these being soaked in a variety of mixtures from urine to bicarbonate of soda. By 1917, however, more sophisticated gas masks, respirators, and hoods were available. Partly for this reason, and partly because the element of surprise was gone, casualties from gas attacks plunged significantly after 1915.

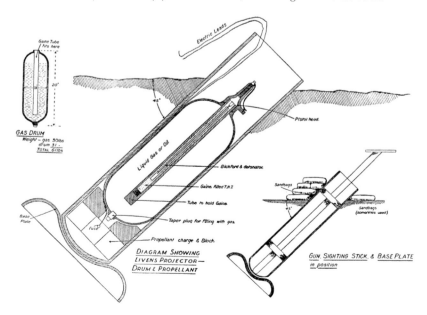

ABOVE: *Gassed* (1919) – the haunting depiction by John Singer Sargent of the survivors of a gas attack who were suffering from temporary blindness. (IWM ART 1460)

LEFT: The Livens projector consisted of a tube dug into the ground at an angle of 45 degrees. It acted similarly to mortars in that it could fire drums of gas towards enemy lines. It was the standard British Army means of delivering gas attacks. (From Foulkes, *Gas!*)

RIGHT: German 15cm T-shell, the first gas shell used in action. Approximately 0.5 gallons (2.3 liters) of liquid tear-gas were held in a lead container with a bursting shell in the head. (From Prentiss, *Chemicals in War*, 1937)

Once the war had ended, the world resumed being outraged by gas warfare, and it was banned in the 1925 Geneva protocol on chemical warfare. Yet the threat of chemical weapons has never subsided, and training to combat such attacks remains an integral part of modern military training.

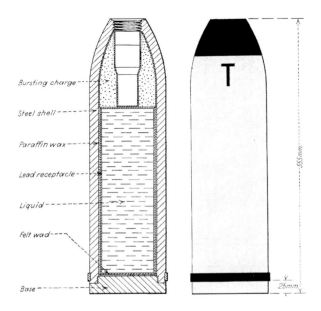

Bursting charge

Steel shell

Paraffin wax

Lead receptacle

Liquid

Felt wad

Base

" DULCE ET DECORUM EST

Bent double, like old beggars under sacks,
Knock-kneed, coughing like hags, we cursed
    through sludge,
Till on the haunting flares we turned our backs
And towards our distant rest began to trudge.
Men marched asleep. Many had lost their boots
But limped on, blood-shod. All went lame;
    all blind;
Drunk with fatigue; deaf even to the hoots
Of disappointed shells that dropped behind.

GAS! Gas! Quick, boys! – An ecstasy of fumbling,
Fitting the clumsy helmets just in time;
But someone still was yelling out and stumbling
And floundering like a man in fire or lime...
Dim, through the misty panes and thick green light
As under a green sea, I saw him drowning.
In all my dreams, before my helpless sight,
He plunges at me, guttering, choking, drowning.

If in some smothering dreams you too could pace
Behind the wagon that we flung him in,
And watch the white eyes writhing in his face,
His hanging face, like a devil's sick of sin;
If you could hear, at every jolt, the blood
Come gargling from the froth-corrupted lungs,
Obscene as cancer, bitter as the cud
Of vile, incurable sores on innocent tongues,
My friend, you would not tell with such high zest
To children ardent for some desperate glory,
The old Lie: Dulce et decorum est
Pro patria mori. "

Wilfred Owen

MORTAR

THE ORIGINS OF THE MAN-PORTABLE MORTAR (AS opposed to the venerable siege mortar) lie in the Russo-Japanese War of 1904–05. Russian artillery officer Lieutenant-General Leonid Nikolaevich Gobyato designed a mortar device that could throw naval shells at a high-angle from a closed position. The capabilities of Russian mortars so impressed German observers that the German Army began developing its own versions, with 160 produced just prior to the onset of war in 1914.

THE MORTAR ADVANTAGE

World War I, being a war in which trench-bound stalemate was a norm, was a conflict totally suited to the development and application of mortars. Mortars are traditionally short-range and rather inaccurate weapons, but it is worth reminding ourselves of the many advantages they confer. By delivering indirect fire at a high-trajectory, a mortar can be operated from a totally protected position – the gunners can remain out of sight. Most (not all) mortars are muzzle-loading, meaning that they are convenient to use in confined positions and can also deliver a high rate of fire simply by dropping bombs rhythmically down the tube. As low-velocity projectiles, mortar bombs can also contain a higher proportion of explosive content than high-velocity artillery shells (the shell wall doesn't need to be as thick). They are also more portable than conventional artillery, having no recoil mechanism (they typically transfer recoil forces directly into the ground), large carriage, and hefty breech or shells. Taken together, mortars provided the trench-bound infantry of World War I with an immediate means of bringing heavy fire down on the enemy, while remaining in the protective confines of the trench.

OPPOSITE: A German *Minenwerfer* in action in the dunes of the Flanders coast during the summer of 1917. (IWM Q 50665)

TRENCH WARFARE

German wartime mortars were collectively known as *Minenwerfers* ("bomb throwers"). Three versions were produced: a light 76mm, a medium 170mm, and a massive 250mm. The medium and heavy mortars were not the last word in mobility, but they could deliver substantial firepower – the 170mm mortar, for example, could fire 35 shells weighing 110lb (50kg) every hour, to a maximum range of 325yds (300m). The German enthusiasm for mortars is evidence that by 1918 they had nearly 16,000 mortars of all types in use.

It was the British, however, who changed the nature and capabilities of mortars. In January 1915, one Wilfred Stokes designed the 3in Stokes Mortar, which weighed just 104lb (47.17kg) in total, making it light enough for two men to carry and operate. (The German mortars required between six and 21 men to operate.) The base of the mortar tube was fixed to a baseplate that sat on the ground, while the upper part of the tube was stabilized and adjusted on a bipod. Each 10lb

ABOVE: Another German mortar crew pose with the 76mm German light *Minenwerfer*. Fired from a traversing plate, it was capable of reaching distances of 800yds (731m) and could launch both high-explosive and gas shells. (Courtesy of Stephen Bull)

BELOW: Men of the King's Own Yorkshire Light Infantry fuse shells for the Stokes trench mortars during 1917. (IWM Q 6025)

ABOVE: Australian soldiers shown loading the British 9.45in trench mortar, known to the troops as the "flying pig," during 1916. (IWM Q 4092)

(4.5kg) bomb had an impact cartridge at its base. To fire the mortar, the gunner simply dropped the armed bomb down the tube; when the bomb hit the bottom of the tube, the impact cartridge detonated and threw the bomb out to a maximum range of 800yds (731m). Moreover, the gunner could send out these shells at a rate of 25 rounds every minute.

The Stokes Mortar was a game-changer. It provided even small infantry units with a truly portable indirect-fire capability, and by the end of the war every division contained 24 Stokes Mortars. The British also fielded 2in medium and 9.45in heavy mortars, to provide more substantial firepower.

By the end of the war, mortars had become an integral part of infantry firepower for all sides, and remain so to this day. Throughout World War II and the postwar era their capabilities changed dramatically, increasing their range, accuracy, and

explosive force. Some of the latest varieties of GPS-guided mortar round, for example, have a circular error probable (CEP) of just 11yds (10m) at ranges of several miles. Many mortars are now rivaling heavier tube artillery in terms of their power, and by being far cheaper to produce, their place on the future battlefield is assured.

STOKES MORTAR – SPECIFICATIONS

Caliber: 3in
Crew: 2
Length: 51in (1,295mm) tube
Weight: 104lb (47.17kg)
Elevation: 45°–75°
Bomb weight: 10.6lb (4.84kg) for high explosives (HE)
Effective range: 750yds (686m)
Maximum range: 800yds (731m)
Maximum rate of fire: 25rpm

SOPWITH CAMEL

THE PRINCIPAL APPLICATION OF AIR POWER IN THE early years of the war was reconnaissance. Aircraft, from their high vantage point, were ideally placed to report on enemy troop movements or positions and, with the addition of later two-way radio technology, to act as airborne artillery observers, correcting fire onto a target.

BIRTH OF THE FIGHTERS

Flying was initially a civilized business – opposing pilots might salute one another if they met in the skies, or if aggressive take pot-shots with a rifle or revolver – but over time military authorities soon realized that enemy reconnaissance aircraft posed a serious threat to military operations. For this reason, aircraft were developed to destroy other aircraft. Machine-gun armament was added. In the spring of 1915, French aviator Roland Garros adopted the "deflector gear," an mechanism developed by Raymond Saulnier in which metal deflector plates were fitted to the back of the propeller blades, allowing a machine-gun to fire directly through the propeller without fear of the occasional round shattering the blades. Thus equipped, the Morane-Saulnier Type L became one of history's first fighter aircraft, immediately racking up a string of victories.

Yet the advantage would not rest long with French. Within weeks the Germans, courtesy of Dutch aircraft designer Anthony Fokker, had designed an "interrupter gear," which synchronized the machine-gun with the position of the propeller blades, only firing when the blades were out of the bullet's path. It was

OPPOSITE: A view across the cockpit and engine cowling of the Sopwith Camel, clearly showing the two Vickers machine-guns mounted to fire directly through the propeller arc. (Courtesy of Philip Jarrett)

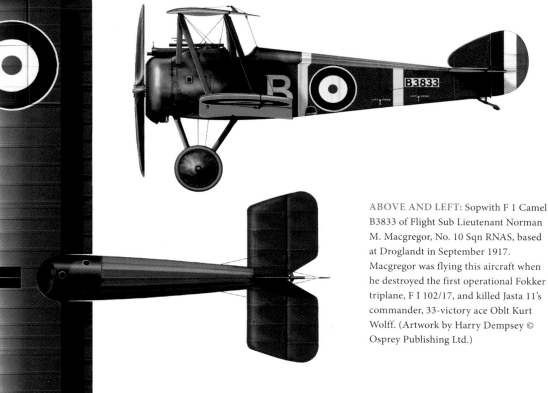

ABOVE AND LEFT: Sopwith F 1 Camel B3833 of Flight Sub Lieutenant Norman M. Macgregor, No. 10 Sqn RNAS, based at Droglandt in September 1917. Macgregor was flying this aircraft when he destroyed the first operational Fokker triplane, F I 102/17, and killed Jasta 11's commander, 33-victory ace Oblt Kurt Wolff. (Artwork by Harry Dempsey © Osprey Publishing Ltd.)

a revolutionary step forward. Now the pilot of a single-seater aircraft had direct line of sight down his machine-gun, meaning he could take straight aim with the target. Both sides quickly adopted the interrupter gear.

Fighter aircraft differed from other types by emphasizing speed, maneuverability, and a high power-to-weight ratio. New designs came out thick and fast, with the advantage passing quickly from one side to the other. In 1915, for example, the Fokker Eindecker temporarily ruled the skies, then dominated by the British FE2 series and French Nieuport and Spad VII aircraft. Then, in early 1917, the Germans introduced the

Albatros D-series biplanes, which completely outclassed anything then in the skies. In "Bloody April" of 1917, the Allies lost some 30 percent of aircrews and aircraft, with pilot life expectancy dropping to just 11 days. A corrective was needed.

SOPWITH SUPERIORITY

The Sopwith Camel is, for many aviation historians, one of the best all-round fighters of World War I. (It has a competitor – see next entry.) Introduced into action in June 1917, it had a top speed of 118mph (190km/h) – the Albatros D III's max speed was 109mph (175km/h) – and a service ceiling of 19,000ft (5,790m). It was exceptionally maneuverable, possibly excessively so – accidents amongst inexperienced pilots were high. Furthermore, it was armed with not one but two synchronized Vickers machine-guns, meaning that any aircraft in its sights was in serious trouble. It also had the option of fitting underwing racks for four 25lb (11.3kg) bombs, making it a nimble ground-attack aircraft also.

ABOVE: This Camel has been fitted with an underfuselage rack to allow it to carry 25lb Cooper bombs. The Camel was used in a trench-strafing role from September 1917 onwards, as its agility meant it was more able to dodge ground fire than other aircraft types. (Museum of Flight, Peter Bowers Collection)

NAVAL ACE

Flight Sub-Lieutenant Lawrence Coombes, DFC, of the Royal Naval Air Service (RNAS), claimed 15 "kills" as a fighter pilot, mainly from the cockpit of a Sopwith Camel. Here he recounts one action on May 11, 1918:

“ A patrol of 24 British and Australian Camels did a high offensive patrol on this date. We drops 92 bombs on Armentières and set fire to an ammunition dump. About eight enemy aircraft dived on us, and about 20 more attacked on our level. There was a general dogfight, one Australian Camel going down in flames while Alexander [Flight Lieutenant William Alexander] of 210 got an enemy aircraft also in flames. I shot down an Albatros out of control.

Turning for home, we discovered that a ground mist had suddenly come up, covering a huge area of France. Nine of our squadron crashed – including myself – trying to land in fields, one being killed and one severely injured. Quite a number of allied aircraft were taken by surprise and suffered similar fates.[6] ”

The Sopwith Camel had an immediate effect on the air superiority situation over the Western Front. In total Camels shot down 1,294 enemy aircraft, plus three Zeppelin airships. Nearly 5,500 Camels were produced. Indeed, alongside other great Allied fighters such as the SE5A, Bristol F.2B, and the Spad, the sheer numbers of Camels meant that even when better German Fokker fighters appeared in 1918, they were still tactically disdvantaged. The combination of firepower, speed, and maneuverability in the Camel, perfectly embodied the aerial combat ethos, and subsequent British aircraft would seek to build on those qualities.

ABOVE: A highly successful Camel ace, Captain John L. Trollope claimed 18 victories, including six in one day on March 24, 1918. However, only a fraction of these claims can be borne out by actual German losses. The same can be said for the 1,294 victories credited to Camel pilots overall. Trollope did not claim a single Dr I victory. (Courtesy of Jon Guttman)

BELOW: Sopwith Camel D1777 piloted by 2nd Lieutenant Cecil F. King engaged in a dogfight on March 28, 1918. He successfully claimed one Albatros DV before he was "jumped" by a Fokker Dr I and was forced to land. (Artwork by Mark Postlethwaite © Osprey Publishing Ltd.)

FOKKER D VII

In the second half of 1917, the *Deutsche Luftstreitkräfte* (German Air Strike Forces) were looking for ways to correct the Allied combat advantage provided by aircraft such as the Sopwith Camel. The subsequent designs of Reinhold Platz, Fokker's chief designer, would come too late in the day to change the outcome of the air war, but they were superb examples of contemporary fighters.

TRIPLANE WARRIORS

In early 1917, the RFC introduced the Sopwith Triplane into service, a three-winged aircraft armed with a single Vickers machine-gun. Although the Triplane was superseded later in the year by the Camel, the type certainly impressed the Germans with its extreme maneuverability and aerodynamics. In response, Reinhold Platz designed the Fokker Dr I triplane, which was delivered in modest quantities to frontline squadrons from the August. The Dr I subsequently became famous as the favored mount of German ace Manfred von Richthofen, who in his combat career would down 80 enemy aircraft before his death on April 21, 1918. There was much to recommend the Dr I. It could turn on a dime, and had an excellent rate of climb. Two 7.92mm Maxim LMG 08/15s provided aircraft-wrecking firepower. Yet in balance, the Dr I was a rather slow aircraft – its top speed was 103mph (165km/h) – meaning that it performed best only at low altitudes, and in the hands of a skilled aviator. Although it gained some impressive kill tallies, it did not give an air superiority advantage back to the Germans.

OPPOSITE: On its nose and partially stripped of fabric, a Fokker D VII displays its wooden cantilever wing structure. (Courtesy of Greg VanWyngarden)

CROWNING DESIGN

In late 1917, Platz once again put his mind to creating a new aircraft. This time the aircraft had a more dramatic effect on the power struggle above the Western Front. The D VII had a speed that matched that of the Camel when fitted with its original Mercedes D.IIIa engine, but a later BMW powerplant took its top speed up to 124mph (200km/h). Speed, indeed, was becoming the holy grail of fighter performance for many, giving an aircraft the ability to attack fast and disappear quickly. The aircraft also retained its performance across the altitude range (its service ceiling slightly exceeded that of the

FOKKER D VII – SPECIFICATIONS

Type: single-seat biplane fighter

Length: 22ft 10in (6.95m)

Wingspan: 29ft 2in (8.9m)

Height: 9ft (2.75m)

Weight (empty): 1,508lb (684kg)

Weight (max take-off): 2,006lb (910kg)

Powerplant: Mercedes D.IIIa generating 180hp
    (134kW), later BMW IIIa

Maximum speed: 116mph (187km/h) with D IIIaü

Armament: 2 x 7.92mm Maxim LMG 08/15
    machine-guns

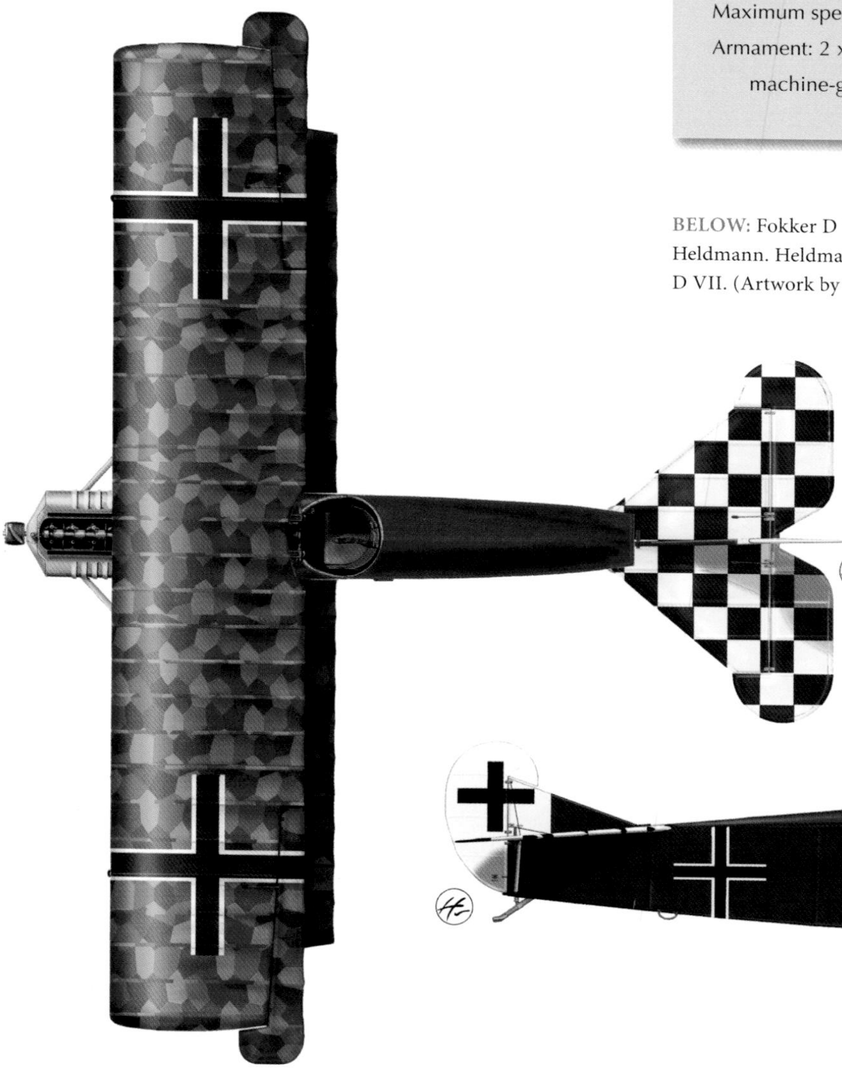

BELOW: Fokker D VII (F) 4264/18 of Lieutenant D.R. Aloys Heldmann. Heldmann scored ten of his 15 victories in the Fokker D VII. (Artwork by Harry Dempsey © Osprey Publishing Ltd.)

Camel), and it was maneuverable as well. It has been noted that such was the respect the Allies had for the D VII, that it was the only aircraft specifically named in the Armistice agreement of 1918 to be surrendered.

Had the D VII arrived earlier in the war, and in greater numbers, the outcome of the air battle might have been different. Individual pilots became aces in the aircraft, such as Carl Degelow, who shot down 22 aircraft in a D VII between July and November 1918. Yet wars and battles are decided on many other issues than talented pilots, and the D VII must simply rest on its laurels as one of the best fighter aircraft of the conflict.

BELOW: A postwar Fokker D VII under inspection by the United States Air Service. Its 180hp (134kW) BMW engine is on display. It was primarily the speed generated by this engine that made the Fokker D VII a remarkable aircraft and difficult to best in a dogfight. (R. Watts Album via Greg VanWyngarden)

ABOVE: The second-highest scoring German ace, Lieutenant Ernst Udet, poses in front of his Fokker D VII. He scored 62 victories in total during World War I before later becoming a senior figure in the Nazi party and the Luftwaffe. (Courtesy of Greg VanWyngarden)

WORLD WAR II
1939–45

LAND MINE

MINES SERVE A VARIETY OF PURPOSES. ATTRITION OF enemy personnel and vehicles is obviously one, but minefields also control, retard, or otherwise limit enemy tactical movement. They can, for instance, deny the enemy use of certain tracts of land or routes of travel, or direct him into a killing ground of choice. Furthermore, a minefield can defend a defined feature or area even without ground forces being present.

Mine warfare actually has a venerable history. Gunpowder-based mines date all the way back to 13th-century China (they were command detonated by fuse), for example, and the first mechanically triggered mines were developed in the American Civil War. During World War I, the Germans produced crude anti-tank mines – artillery shells fitted with pressure fuses or pressure-activated wooden box mines. It was World War II, however, that would truly establish the era of modern mine warfare, and transform huge tracts of land into lethal landscapes.

ANTI-PERSONNEL MINES

Anti-personnel (AP) mines, laid in their millions during World War II, became the soldier's nightmare. This was particularly so for the Allies, as the Germans were masters of AP mine design. "Jumping" mines such as the S-Mine 35 were especially feared. It could be activated by pressure, tripwire, or electrical

OPPOSITE: An American GI conducts a delicate operation to clear an anti-tank weapon that has been mined. During the dying days of World War II the retreating German Army made considerable use of booby traps. (Getty Images)

> *Risks must be taken, but losses will be lessened considerably if all personnel are alert, and are trained to search visually for mines at all times.*
>
> US Army Directive during World War II

PREVIOUS PAGE: A member of a British mine detector squad uncovers a landmine, *c.* 1944. (Getty Images)

ABOVE AND RIGHT: The Germans led the way in mine design. This Tellermine TMi 42 was first manufactured in 1929 and saw service until the end of World War II. It could be used both as an anti-tank and anti-personnel mine. (Courtesy of Stephen Bull)

command, after which there was a short delay before an inner casing, containing about 360 steel balls, was projected several feet into the air, where it detonated. The effect was a lethal cloud of shrapnel spraying out in all directions. Responding to the Allied introduction of electronic mine detectors in 1942, the Germans also developed the Schü-Mine and the Glas-Mine, with their bodies made from wood and glass respectively to make them virtually undetectable to electronic devices.

Combined with the dozens of other AP mines developed by the Germans, such weapons made large areas of land death traps for the unwary, or at least time-consuming obstacles to clear. Schü-Mines, for instance, were sometimes laid 12 rows deep and only 20in (51cm) distance apart. In return, however, the Germans also suffered in extensive Allied minefields, particularly on the Eastern Front and in North Africa. The Soviets alone laid two million mines by the end of the war, despite only accepting the value of the mine in 1941. US minefields, in accordance with their tactical theory, tended to be covered by machine-guns and mortars, so those attempting to cross them had to cope with much more than just underfoot explosives.

LEFT: A line of German TMi 35 anti-tank mines fitted with a pressure bar for simultaneous detonation. (Courtesy of Stephen Bull)

ANTI-TANK MINES

It was the advent of armored warfare, more than any other cause, that spurred the development of mine warfare. Apart from the German World War I experiments, the Italians were the first to use anti-tank (AT) mines in the form of the Type 9 – essentially a long wooden box containing 7lb (3kg) of explosive, detonated via pressure on the box lid. The Germans, continuing their talent for mine warfare, produced some of the best AT mines of the war, including four models of Tellermine, each capable of destroying an Allied tank, or at least shattering its tracks. Many of these models came with either integral anti-handling devices, or secondary fuse wells for fitting the same (such as secondary AP mines), to multiply the danger and problems of defusing them.

ABOVE: A British ordnance disposal engineer holds a German Teller AT mine. Although this image is clearly posed, AT mines were frequently attached to AP mines (in this instance the so-called "Bouncing Betty") to hinder clearance operations. (US Military)

MINE ADVICE

The following advice was given by a soldier in the British *Infantry Training Memorandum* of May 1944:

" I had been given to understand that if you stepped on an anti-personnel mine, the only thing to do was to hold the foot down, lean well back, accept that the foot might be blown off, but hope that the mine would not explode above ground level. Eighth Army engineers who had a good deal of experience with S-mines told me that though this idea had been current for some time it was quite erroneous. The anti-personnel mine has a delay of three or four seconds. When you step on it there is a muffled click in the ground. Between three and four seconds after this click – that is, after the cap has fired – the cylinder blows four feet or five feet into the air [to detonate]... It is probably best to move three or four yards away from the mine and lie down. "

The British were slow to produce decent quantities of AT mines, the first being the Mk IV, which was essentially a cake tin filled with 8.25lb (3.75kg) of TNT or Baratol and fitted with a pressure fuse. Being easily triggered by nearby explosives, however, it was replaced by the less sensitive Mk V. The US Army used AT mines such as the M1, M1A1, and M4.

This brief run through World War II mine technology does not do justice to the sheer numbers of casualties and problems mines caused. Many AP mines, for example, contained only enough explosive to remove a foot or leg, purposely designed to drain enemy manpower through casualty evacuation and lengthy rehabilitation. Mines were laid in mixed AP/AT fields, or were linked to booby traps of fiendish ingenuity. Up to 30 percent of all tanks destroyed or damaged during the war were accounted for by mines, and to this day thousands of people across the world die through both "legacy" mines and those laid in fresh conflicts.

DEPTH CHARGE

THE DEPTH CHARGE WAS A BRITISH INVENTION, introduced during World War I to combat the emerging threat of German submarines. By World War II, in fact, the fundamental structure of the depth charge had changed little, being essentially a large canister of high-explosive – the British Mk VIII model, for example, weighed 410lb (185kg) in total, of which 396lb (179kg) was explosive charge. The war against U-boats, however, would soon bring major changes.

DESTRUCTIVE PRESSURE

Depth charges were pre-set to explode at a certain depth by means of a hydrostatic pistol. These settings varied according to the tactical situation and the type of depth charge employed, but some models had formidable reach – the British Mk 10 had a maximum setting of 1,500ft (457m). The commander's aim was to estimate/detect the depth and heading of the enemy submarine and "bracket" that position with a pattern of depth charges. A direct contact was not usually necessary – a heavy depth charge could explode within 30ft (9m) of an enemy submarine and generate enough pressure to crush the hull.

The heaviest users of depth charges in World War II were the Allies, in the context of their intensive war against the German U-boats. If a U-boat was on the surface, it could be detected by centimetric radar, but once it dived the most useful locating device was ASDIC sonar detection. Returns from the sonar gave an escort commander a reasonable indication of the submarine's

OPPOSITE: US sailors with the most basic form of a depth charge – a steel drum filled with explosive. (NARA)

ABOVE: A depth charge party on board HMS *Viscount* prepare fresh charges. Depth charges were often simply rolled off the stern of an escort vessel into the sea. A direct hit was not required as even the pressure from a near miss was enough to cause considerable damage. (IWM A 13370)

position, and in response would lay down a pattern of about five depth charges. The depth charges were generally either rolled off the stern of the ship, or fired over the sides by spigot-type throwers.

MEANS OF DELIVERY

One problem with this system, however, was that ASDIC lost contact with a submarine within 197yds (180m) range. A solution was found in the British "Hedgehog" weapon, which entered service in 1942. This consisted of 24 small

depth charges fired ahead of a ship from a six-row launcher, falling into the water in a circular pattern about 130ft (40m) in diameter. The Hedgehog's mines were contact detonated, meaning that if an explosion was heard, it was likely that the submarine had been damaged or destroyed. A more powerful British launcher, the "Squid," entered service late in 1943. This fired three heavy depth charges, each with a 200lb (91kg) explosive charge, in a triangular pattern, with the bombs being pressure detonated. The key advantage of systems such as Hedgehog and Squid was that ASDIC contact with the enemy submarine could be maintained while deploying the weapon. As well as ship-delivery, depth charges were also dropped in significant numbers by aircraft during World War II, though these weapons tended to be lighter devices set to explode at shallow depths around 30ft (9.1m).

Depth charges could be basic weapons, but they were still responsible for sinking 43 percent of all U-boats destroyed in the war. In the postwar era they have taken on all manner of sophistications, from nuclear-warhead varieties to air-dropped weapons that actually home in on the enemy submarine. Today, as always, a submarine's best defense is not to be detected in the first place.

DEPTH CHARGE EXPERIENCE

Werner Ritter von Voiglände, a U-boat crewman, here remembers the experience of being targeted by Allied depth charges, and the attempts at evasion:

❝ We listed and heard "Bloop!" and ... the depth charges were on their way... We used to count the depth charges. They came in series of five ... one, two, down came the third and the fourth. Once the fifth had exploded – "Whoomph!" – then everything was switched off and we stood there in our socks going at 1.5mph. Often we thought: "We're not going to get away! We've had it!" One hour, not even that, three quarters of an hour at full speed would take us seven and a half miles, and then the battery was empty. We crept along and it was a real game of cat and mouse.[7] ❞

OPPOSITE: The sea erupts as a depth charge deployed by HMS *Starling* explodes. Over 30,000 British merchant seamen were lost bringing vital supplies across the Atlantic, 69 percent to submarines. Without the development of anti-submarine tactics and weapons, particularly depth charges, the figure would have been far higher and Britain's ability to remain in the war extremely unlikely. (IWM A 22031)

ABOVE, TOP: A depth charge is readied for deployment from the stern of HMS *Eskimo*. (IWM A 7414)

ABOVE: A US Navy official poster. (NARA)

THOMPSON SUBMACHINE-GUN

THE THOMPSON, MORE POPULARLY KNOWN AS THE "Tommy Gun," was not the world's first submachine-gun. That honor arguably goes to the twin-barrel Italian Villar-Perosa of 1914 or, more convincingly, the German Bergmann MP18 of 1918. Yet the Thompson was the gun that truly introduced both military and civilian worlds to the potential of mass-produced submachine-guns. Including all variants, some 1.7 million have been manufactured since 1921, making it one of history's most successful and credible firearms.

TRENCH GUN

The Thompson submachine gun was the brainchild of John T. Thompson (1860–1940), a US Army officer and firearms expert. Thompson had worked as Chief of Small Arms for the US Ordnance Department and as Chief Design Engineer for the Remington Arms Corporation before, in 1916, he founded his own venture, the Auto-Ordnance Corporation. Once the United States joined World War I in 1917, Thompson was drawn back into the Army in his old position. There he vented his frustration at the combat deficiencies of the standard US Army issue rifle, the Springfield M1903, but he also saw a solution: "Our boys in the infantry, now in the trenches, need a small machine gun, a gun that will fire 50 to 100 rounds, so light that he can drag it with him as he crawls on his belly from trench to trench, and wipe out a whole company single-handed. A one-man hand held machine gun."

OPPOSITE: A soldier from 3 Commando at Largs in Scotland during a training exercise. He is armed with an M1 Thompson. The squat design made it easy to carry close to the body. It became famed for its rugged dependability and knock-down fire-power, ensuring that it was deservedly popular amongst many Commandos. (IWM H 12271)

OPPOSITE PAGE: "Sold only to those on the side of law and order," Auto-Ordnance's 1927 price list for the Thompson.

Form P281

ABOVE: A British patrol in Italy 1944. The patrol leader carries a Tommy gun as does the second man in the line. (US Military)

BELOW: Okinawa 1945. A BAR gunner ducks to one side as the Tommy-man lets rip with his M1A1. (SSgt Walter F. Klein, NARA)

Thompson and a team of talented engineers set about creating this weapon. Early models emerged in 1919, but the first production version was the M1921. Here was a hand-held, friction-delayed blowback weapon firing the powerful .45 ACP pistol cartridge at cyclical rates of about 850rpm (later models tended to work at about 600rpm). Ammunition was fed from either straight box magazines or the visually distinctive 50- or even 100-round drums. The gun was a true man-stopper, but the war ended before it could be tested in combat. Consequently, the early Thompsons went primarily into the civilian and law enforcement markets.

GANGSTERS AND SOLDIERS

Hollywood has immortalized the Thompson as the roaring gangster weapon of the Prohibition era (1920–33). Yet the gun also, eventually, attracted the attention of the military. The most prevalent pre-World War II model, the M1928, was purchased in limited numbers by the US Navy and Marine Corps during the 1930s, and in 1938 the US Army itself became a major Thompson buyer, along with international customers such as Britain.

❝ *No-one hit by those bullets ever put up any further resistance* ❞
Anonymous Tommy Gun user, Second World War

ABOVE: The distinctive 50-round "L" drum designed by Oscar Payne, illustrating the positioning of the cartridges with the front plate and winder removed.

It was during World War II, of course, that the Thompson reached its fullest expression. In 1942 a simplified version entered service with US forces, the M1. Gone were the expensive drum magazines, front pistol grip and the friction-delayed blowback system, replaced by a rationalized and cheaper design suited to war production. Further simplification led to the M1A1, and more than a million of these weapons were distributed by 1944. Soldiers grew to love the Thompson as a close-quarters weapon, a convincing mix of portability, power, and reliability. Like all firearms, it was not perfect, but it was a weapon on which you could depend.

The end of World War II, and the spreading international adoption of assault rifles, did not kill off the Thompson. Many law enforcement units retained their stocks – the FBI did not get rid of theirs until 1976. Thompsons were also widely distributed across Asia, particularly China, Korea, and Vietnam, where they gave service during various Cold War conflicts. Civilian models of the Thompson are still produced today, while vintage weapons have become true collectors' items. The Thompson makes a good case for being history's greatest submachine-gun, a pioneer in the expression of portable firepower.

MAJOR THOMPSON VARIANTS – SPECIFICATIONS

Model 1921
Cartridge: .45 ACP
Muzzle velocity: 920 fps (280 mps)
Weight empty: 10lb 4oz (4.6kg)
Overall length: 25in (635mm) without butt, with butt
31.8in (807mm)
Barrel length: Finned type, 10.5in (268mm)
Barrel with Cutts compensator: 12.5in (317mm)
Sights: Lyman ladder rear, blade front
Cyclic rate: 800rpm
Magazines: 20 round box, 50 and 100 round drums

Model 1928A1
Cartridge: .45 ACP
Muzzle velocity: 920 fps (280 mps)
Weight empty: 10lb 12oz (4.8kg)
Overall length: 33.75in (857mm)
Barrel length: Finned type, 10.5in (268mm)
Barrel with Cutts compensator: 12.5in (305mm)
Sights: Lyman ladder rear, blade front
Cyclic rate: 600–725rpm

Model M1/A1
Cartridge: .45 ACP
Muzzle velocity: 920 fps (280 mps)
Weight empty: 10lb 7oz (4.7kg)
Overall length: 32in (813mm)

BELOW: A view of the Model 1921AC, showing its very distinctive silhouette. Many collectors and firearms historians believe this to be the most classic of all the Thompson models.

BROWNING M2HB

SOME FIREARMS ACHIEVE SUCH PERFECTION IN DESIGN that they endure in service well beyond the typical life cycles of most weapons. The Browning M2HB is a case in point. It is still the primary heavy machine-gun of many armies, including those of the United States and Britain, some 80 years after its original model was introduced. The fact that it has sustained this career largely without modification is remarkable.

OPPOSITE: John M. Browning himself test fires the very first .50-cal machine-gun. This early prototype was essentially an up-scaled version of the .30-cal M1917 Browning. (US Army)

OPPOSITE PAGE: The waist gunner of an American B-17 bomber firing his Browning M2. This is almost certainly a posed shot taken on the ground, for he wears no oxygen mask, goggles, or flying helmet. (Library of Congress)

HEAVY BARREL

John Moses Browning's first forays into machine-gun design, during the late 1800s, focused principally on gas operated systems. In 1900, however, he switched his attentions to recoil operation, and in 1910 unveiled a prototype 0.3in, tripod-mounted, water-cooled weapon. Firing at a rate of 500rpm from a robust mechanism, the gun should have captured immediate interest, but pre-war apathy meant it failed to attract orders. When the United States joined World War I in 1917, however, the focus changed, and Browning's gun went into production and service as the M1917. (A demonstration in which one gun fired 20,000 rounds without stoppage helped to convince the authorities.)

The M1917 was the beginning of an important series of Browning machine-guns, which included the air-cooled M1919 versions. They went on to become standard US Army firepower in numerous roles, from bipod-mounted infantry assault weapons through to armored vehicle guns. Yet towards the end of World War I, the head of the American Expeditionary Forces (AEF), General John Pershing, had requested a heavy machine-gun for long-range use against aircraft, tanks, and artillery crews.

AUDIE MURPHY

Audie Murphy was the most decorated US soldier of World War II, and he went on to become a famous Hollywood film star after the war. The following extract is from his Medal of Honor citation, won for an action in France in January 1945. Note the role of the 0.5in machine-gun in this action:

❝ Second Lt. Murphy commanded Company B, which was attacked by six tanks and waves of infantry. 2d Lt. Murphy ordered his men to withdraw to a prepared position in a woods, while he remained forward at his command post and continued to give fire directions to the artillery by telephone. Behind him, to his right, one of our tank destroyers received a direct hit and began to burn. Its crew withdrew to the woods. 2d Lt. Murphy continued to direct artillery fire, which killed large numbers of the advancing enemy infantry. With the enemy tanks abreast of his position, 2d Lt. Murphy climbed on the burning tank destroyer, which was in danger of blowing up at any moment, and employed its .50 caliber machine gun against the enemy. He was alone and exposed to German fire from three sides, but his deadly fire killed dozens of Germans and caused their infantry attack to waver. The enemy tanks, losing infantry support, began to fall back. For an hour the Germans tried every available weapon to eliminate 2d Lt. Murphy, but he continued to hold his position and wiped out a squad that was trying to creep up unnoticed on his right flank. ❞

Browning therefore scaled up his existing M1917 design for use with a 0.5in cartridge, leading to the M1921. The sheer power of the 0.5in round meant the M1921 more than fulfilled the brief, but heat build-up in the barrel was a problem, particularly in the air-cooled version, known as the M2. For this reason, a heavy-barreled model was introduced (the thicker, heavier barrel helped absorb and dissipate heat), known appropriately enough as the M2HB.

SUCCESS STORY

In terms of a heavy machine-gun, the M2HB approaches perfection. It has an effective range of about 2,200yds (2,011m), but a maximum range for indirect fire of at least double that distance. The destructive power of the round is fearsome, smashing through most building structures with relative ease – standard armor-piercing rounds can puncture 0.75in (19mm) of hardened steel armor plate at 547yds (500m).

During World War II, the capabilities of the M2 and its variants were embraced to the full. The guns found themselves everywhere, from B-17 Flying Fortress bombers (or the wings of

ABOVE: Men of the 102nd Infantry Division armed with their trusty .50cal, Germany, Spring 1945. (NARA via Tom Laemlein)

BELOW: Marines man the Okinawa coastline with a Browning M2HB. Note the .50-cal ammunition alongside them in the ammunition cans. (United States Marine Corps Historical Division via Tom Laemlein)

US fighters) through to the turrets of Sherman tanks. One or two M2s could inflict serious damage or delays on enemy formations (see feature box), particularly when ensconced in sandbagged positions. As well as severe anti-personnel effects, M2s were more than capable of smashing the engine block of a German half-track or Bf 109 fighter. Their most fearsome expression in US service was the quad mount – four M2HBs set together, often on an M16 half-track – which had devastating applications against aircraft or ground positions.

The M2HB has its limitations – it is weighty and awkward to handle off its mount, for example. What it delivers, however, is powerful, long-range, sustained fire, and it is for these reasons that it remains a standard weapon in many armies to this day.

AIRCRAFT CARRIER

EXPERIMENTS WITH FLYING AIRCRAFT FROM WARSHIPS began on November 14, 1910, when American aviation pioneer Eugene Ely took off and landed from an improvized flight deck fitted to the light cruiser USS *Birmingham*. The Royal Navy installed similar platforms on several vessels during World War I, although in most cases these were suited only to launching seaplanes – the returning aircraft landed on water and were retrieved by winch. Arguably the world's first aircraft carrier, however, was HMS *Argus*, commissioned in 1918. Holding up to 20 aircraft, *Argus* had a full-length flush deck from which aircraft could take off and land. In 1920 HMS *Eagle* was launched, which again had a flush deck but with the superstructure offset to one side, setting a pattern for future carrier design.

During the inter-war years, it was the British, Americans, and Japanese who pushed ahead with aircraft carriers in earnest, although within the limitations of the Washington Naval Treaty of 1922. Once the treaty's authority lapsed in the late 1930s, the three powers began to develop more formidable carrier fleets, although it would take war to confirm the carrier revolution.

OPPOSITE: The basics of carrier operations as depicted in a training manual. (Courtesy of Angus Konstam)

ABOVE: The aircraft carrier continues to play a crucial role in the United States' defense policy. Here USS *George Washington* is shown off the coast of South Korea in 2010. (Getty Images)

BELOW: Hurricanes inside the hangar of British carrier HMS *Argus*. Aircraft with folding wings would take up considerably less space in later aircraft carriers. (Courtesy of Angus Konstam)

LONG-RANGE WAR

On December 7, 1941, an Imperial Japanese Navy (IJN) carrier force attacked the US Pacific Fleet at Pearl Harbor, Hawaii. The attack by dive- and torpedo-bombers sunk or

damaged 19 major US vessels. The attack was a stunning illustration of naval air power, and practical proof of anti-ship bombing, as first demonstrated by the US general Billy Mitchell in the 1920s. From this point, carriers became the most important warships on the waves.

Carriers offered unique abilities over other surface craft. First and foremost was their remote strike capability, the carrier's aircraft being able to engage targets hundreds of miles from the ship. Yet other tactical abilities emerged – long-range reconnaissance; anti-submarine escort roles; preparatory attacks for amphibious landings; support for naval vessels in surface engagements. To satisfy these demands, three basic carrier types emerged: escort carriers, light fleet carriers, and large fleet carriers, each holding increasing numbers of aircraft. The British preferred smaller, more heavily armored carriers, while the US and Japanese carriers tended to have reduced armor, to maximize the aircraft holding capacity (combat experience meant protection improved later in the war). The largest US carriers could hold more than 100 aircraft, giving them enormous strike potential.

USS *ENTERPRISE*

Launched in 1936, the Yorktown-class USS *Enterprise* was one of the greatest carriers of the Pacific War. It had a full-load displacement of 25,500 short tons (23,133 tonnes), an overall length of 824ft 9in (251.38m), and a speed of 32.5 knots (60.2km/h). A full complement of more than 90 aircraft made it one of the most powerful carriers on the waves. *Enterprise* was involved in some of the greatest naval battles of World War II, including Midway (June 4–7, 1942), Eastern Solomons (August 24–25, 1942), Philippine Sea (June 19–20, 1944), and Leyte Gulf (October 23–26, 1944). The carrier suffered severe damage on several occasions, including hits by *kamikaze* aircraft, but nonetheless survived the war to be decommissioned in 1947. The carrier was given a Presidential Unit Citation for her service.

BELOW: USS *Independence*, July 1943. (US Navy Historical Center)

STRENGTH AND WEAKNESSES

In battle, carriers proved themselves to be both potent and vulnerable. The British, for example, lost the carriers *Courageous, Glorious, Ark Royal, Eagle,* and *Hermes* between 1939 and 1942. The United States lost four carriers in a year, and the Japanese suffered the catastrophic destruction of carriers *Akagi, Kaga, Hiryu,* and *Soryu* in a single battle, at Midway in June 1942.

Yet most carrier losses in World War II were inflicted by other carrier aircraft. Particularly in the Pacific, the naval surface war became a cat-and-mouse game between opposing carriers. The Japanese had the advantage of longer-range carrier aircraft, meaning they could attack the US carriers at greater distance, while the US had, eventually, better fighter aircraft in the Vought Corsair, well-trained pilots, radar-vectored fighter response, and radar-controlled anti-aircraft guns. For these reasons, amongst others, the United States progressively won the carrier battle in the Pacific. In the Atlantic, where there was less of an air threat, escort carriers became vital in providing trans-oceanic air cover for the Allied convoys, sinking or damaging dozens of U-boats in the process.

Since World War II, aircraft carriers have retained their dominance of the seas, US nuclear-powered vessels such as USS *Nimitz* and *Ronald Reagan* reaching vast proportions, with complements of more than 5,000 personnel and air wings of 90 modern jet aircraft. These have become the greatest national systems of power projection, although history and technology often have a habit of overturning such status.

FLAK 88

DEVELOPMENT OF THE FLAK 88 BEGAN UNDER THE strictures of the Versailles Treaty in the late 1920s. Responding to an army demand for a 75mm anti-aircraft gun, a German team from Krupp went to Sweden to design such a weapon, working alongside engineers at Bofors. By the early 1930s, however, the German engineers switched their focus to a more powerful 88mm shell.

CORE MODELS

The first gun they designed for the shell was the *Flugabwehrkanone 18* (Flak 18; Anti-aircraft Cannon 18), which went into service in the German armed forces in 1933.

The gun was visually arresting, standing high on a cruciform carriage and sporting a particularly long barrel. Its performance was excellent from the outset, having a muzzle velocity of 2,690ft/sec (820m/sec) and a maximum ceiling of 32,482ft (9,900m), and firing (in the anti-aircraft role) a time-fused shell containing 1.92lb (0.87kg) of high-explosive. These shells could be fired at a rate of 15rpm.

The Flak 18 received combat testing in the Spanish Civil War, where it also hinted at its practicality as an anti-tank weapon, made possible by a barrel elevation range of -3° to +85°. Subsequent pre-war versions – the Flak 36 and Flak 37 – improved on the Flak 18's carriage, barrel change method, and fire-control system, although basic performance characteristics stayed the same.

OPPOSITE: An 88mm fires on British tanks during the battle for El Alamein, October 23, 1942. (akg-images)

OPPOSITE PAGE: Flak 88 being towed by a SdKfz7 in Afrika, Spring 1941. (Bundesarchiv, Bild 101I-783-0109-19 / Dörner)

TANK KILLER

In 1939, Germany produced just 189 Flak 88 guns, but its rising popularity is clear from the production figures of subsequent years, which rose to 1,998 in 1941 and 6,482 in 1944. At first the "88" was applied mainly in its designed role as an anti-aircraft gun, but during the Libyan campaign of 1941–42 its competence as an anti-tank weapon emerged, easily dispatching most Allied tanks in service. With its high muzzle velocity, and equipped with appropriate anti-tank rounds, the Flak 88 could achieve penetration of around 4.3in (110mm) at 1,095yds (1,000m), and could engage and hit ground targets out to a maximum range of 16,202yds (14,815m).

It was this combination of availability and flexibility that made the Flak 88 famous. Amongst Allied armored troops, 88s became especially feared, although many kills attributed to 88s were in fact caused by some of the other excellent German anti-tank guns in service. Yet 88s undoubtedly accounted for thousands of British, American, and Soviet armored vehicles, and their crews. For Allied pilots, particularly those involved in the US and British strategic bombing campaign over Germany, Flak 88s also threw up blistering clouds of explosions over target areas.

Sergeant James Fraser of the Royal Tank Regiment later recalled coming under heavy fire from German anti-tank guns in the deserts of North Africa:

> " It was a place called the Knightsbridge Box, and we came under heavy fire. The tracks were blown off the tank. The tank commander gave the order to bale out. We baled out and we got underneath the tank – which normally one wouldn't do, because the tank is a main target – but we had no option. There was machine-gun fire and heavy shellfire, so we got underneath the tank.
>
> One would say it was a thousand-to-one chance, but a heavy explosive came underneath the tank, lifted it. I blacked out and when I came to, dazed, I looked round to find three of the tank crew had been killed. That left myself and another lad. In making our way away from the tank, we were fired on by a machine gun, and I was hit on the leg. I was picked up by one of our own squadron's tanks, taken back to the line, and then to the advanced field ambulance for treatment.[8] "

FLAK 18 – SPECIFICATIONS

Caliber: 88mm
Length (gun): 194.09in (4,930mm)
Weight: 10,992lb (4,985kg)
Breech mechanism: semi-auto sliding block
Rifling: 32 grooves, r/hand
Traverse: 720º
Elevation: -3º to +85º
Muzzle velocity: 2,690ft/sec (820m/sec)
Maximum ceiling: 32,482ft (9,900m)
Maximum ground range: 16,202yds (14,815m)

We must not overstate the 88's capabilities. In many ways, its performance was no better than guns such as the British 3.7in Mk 3 or the US 90mm M1. Its high mount, furthermore, made it easy to spot and kill if it wasn't camouflaged or positioned properly. During the war years, however, the basic 88 model became the foundation for other excellent weapons, including the Flak 41 anti-aircraft gun and the Pak 43 anti-tank gun. Yet regardless of the type, for those on the receiving end of 88s, the experience was unnerving at best, lethal at worst.

ABOVE: A gun crew of an 88 in the Western Desert, May 1942. The gun is lowered on to its base and the crew are in the process of unloading ammunition. (IWM)

BELOW: The Royal Artillery deploying 88mm guns against their former owners, December 1944. (IWM B 13292)

M1 GARAND

THE M1 GARAND WAS NOT THE WORLD'S FIRST SEMI-automatic rifle. In the early 1900s, for example, a Danish gun designer aptly called Soren H. Bang designed a muzzle-blast-actuated rifle, although the weapon never reached a standardized model nor went into production. In France, by contrast, the gas-operated 8mm R.S.C. Modèle 1917/1918 was manufactured in small numbers and issued to the French Army, while the Czechs and Soviets also established several innovative semi-auto designs during the 1920s. Yet the US M1 Garand takes a unique place in this history as the first semi-auto firearm to be issued as the standard weapon of an entire army.

NEW PERSPECTIVE

The designer of the rifle was John C. Garand, who started exploring semi-auto designs in 1920. His timing was fortuitous, as during the 1920s the US Ordnance Board began trials to find a replacement for the Springfield 1903 bolt-action rifle for the Army. While working for the Springfield Armory, Garand developed the rifle that would bear his name, which then underwent a series of trials. The 0.276in Pedersen, another semi-auto, was a frontrunner in the trials until the early 1930s, when slowly the Garand won through for a variety of technical and political reasons. It was adopted into US Army service in .30-06 caliber in 1936, and given the name US Rifle M1.

LEFT: A Marine fires his M1 rifle through the trees at Japanese snipers, Cape Gloucester, 1942. The .30-06 ammunition had the necessary power to punch through thick jungle foliage. (US Marine Corps Historical Division via Tom Laemlein)

ABOVE: A Marine armed with his trusty M1 Garand rifle.
(US Marine Corps Historical Division via Tom Laemlein)

The Garand could not be further from the Springfield it replaced. It was gas-operated, loaded by first drawing back the operating rod then pushing an eight-round clip down through the open breech into an internal box magazine in the receiver. The operating rod was then pushed forward and the gun was good to go. Every pull of the trigger discharged a shot, and when the last cartridge was fired the clip was ejected with a resolute "ping." The gun was robust, serviceable, and it could fire its eight rounds in about the time it took to fire two from a bolt-action gun.

M1 GARAND – SPECIFICATIONS

Caliber: .30-06
Operation: Gas, semi-auto
Feed: 8-round internal box magazine
Length: 43.4in (1,103mm)
Barrel: 24in (610mm), 4 grooves, r/hand
Weight (empty): 9.5lb (4.37kg)
Muzzle velocity: 2,800ft/sec (853m/sec)

INTO ACTION

By 1941, much of the US Army had been re-equipped with the Garand rifle. Once the United States entered into the war, the M1 was combat tested in the most extreme terrains: the humidity and heat of the tropical Pacific; the rain and mud of Italy; the freezing conditions of Northern Europe in the winter. In none of these environments was the Garand found wanting. In fact, the Garand gave the US infantryman a distinct advantage over the enemy in terms of firepower. In a typical US 12-man squad, up to 11 of those men would carry M1s (one man would be armed with a BAR or M1919A1). Theoretically, each of those 11 men could fire 30rpm from their M1s, making a total of 330 rounds every minute. If they were armed with bolt-action rifles, however, the total rounds fired would probably be less than 150. The firepower advantage was borne out on numerous occasions, and enemy and Allied soldiers often looked enviously at the US infantryman for his M1.

There were a few problems with the M1. Once loaded with the eight-round clip, it could not be topped up with additional rounds until the gun was empty, and the sound of the clip ejecting could be a useful auditory alert for an enemy that his opponent's gun was empty. It was also a heavy rifle, and the top-loading method meant it could not be fitted with a sniper scope. Yet compared with its benefits, the disadvantages were

trifling. All the nations of the world took note, and following World War II every country abandoned its bolt-action rifles for semi-auto designs.

ABOVE: An M1 Garand adapted for sniper use featuring the M84 sight and M2 flash-hider. (Getty Images)

BELOW: A recruit trains with the M1 Garand. (Tom Laemlein)

SPITFIRE

THE FAME OF THE SUPERMARINE SPITFIRE IS undoubtedly helped by its looks. Designed by R.J. Mitchell, the Spitfire's slender fuselage, long nose, and large, elliptical wing suggested the supreme aerodynamics that it indeed delivered. Yet aesthetics were matched by its capacity to fight, and it crucially placed Britain on an equal footing against the German, Italian, and Japanese air forces for the duration of the war.

MITCHELL'S CREATION

The Spitfire was a development of Mitchell's Supermarine S6B seaplane, which won the Schneider Trophy in 1931. When the British Air Ministry issued a specification for a new fighter aircraft in 1934, Mitchell adapted the seaplane to meet the purpose, fitting it with a new Rolls-Royce Merlin II engine and eight .303 machine-guns. The design was first flown on March 5, 1936, with excellent results. Tragically, given the Spitfire's subsequent history, Mitchell died the following year, but the Spitfire was developed further and it entered RAF service in 1938.

A year later, Britain was at war with Germany, and here the Spitfire began its journey to becoming an aviation legend. Many myths have accrued around the Spitfire's role in the early war years, particularly in relation to the Battle of Britain, fought in the summer of 1940. For example, the lion's share of Britain's fighter response was in fact borne by the more numerous but slower and less agile Hurricane. (At the beginning of the battle, there were 27 squadrons of Hurricanes and 19 squadrons of Spitfires.) The Hurricane also provided a more stable gunnery platform. Yet what the Spitfire gave the RAF was a combat aircraft that was

OPPOSITE: Spitfires of No. 610 Squadron flying in "vic" formation on July 24, 1940. In this outmoded tactic used in the early stage of the war fighters flew so close together that only the lead pilot had time to search for the enemy while the rest had to focus on formation flying. The harsh realities of warfare ensured that many pilots learnt the hard way to use their Spitfires to their best advantage. (IWM CH 740)

OPPOSITE PAGE: Three Spitfires of No. 19 Squadron grace the skies in 1939 shortly before the outbreak of war. (IWM CH 20)

able to take on the German Bf 109E fighters on equal terms. The Messerschmitt may have had a slightly faster top speed, particularly at high altitudes, and a better climb rate, but in practical combat conditions the Spitfire displayed a higher rate of turn and a smaller turning circle. This maneuverability advantage, once loosened from inappropriate tactics, meant the Spitfires were able to inflict severe losses on the Luftwaffe formations. Without the Spitfire, the outcome of the Battle of Britain could have been very different indeed.

Of course, Germany improved its aircraft – both the Bf 109F and the Focke-Wulf Fw 190 outperformed the Spitfire when they initially appeared on the scene. Hence the Spitfire itself went through numerous variants during the war. Armament configurations changed, many Spitfires receiving two 20mm cannon in place of four of the .303 machine-guns, and fighter-bomber versions such as the Mk VC could deploy 500lb (227kg) of bombs. Powerplants were frequently upgraded (Griffon engines eventually replaced the Merlins), which allied to minor airframe and wing profile adjustments brought improved altitudes and speeds. For example, a late-war variant, the Mk XVIII fighter-reconnaissance aircraft, had a top speed of 442mph (711km/h), more than 50mph

❝ *I've never flown anything sweeter* ❞
George Unwin, No. 19 Squadron

RIGHT AND BELOW: A Spitfire 1A flown by No. 234 Squadron ace Australian Flight Officer Paterson Hughes. He claimed two Bf 109Es off the Isle of Wight on the afternoon of August 18, 1940, while flying this aircraft. (Artwork by Jim Laurier © Osprey Publishing)

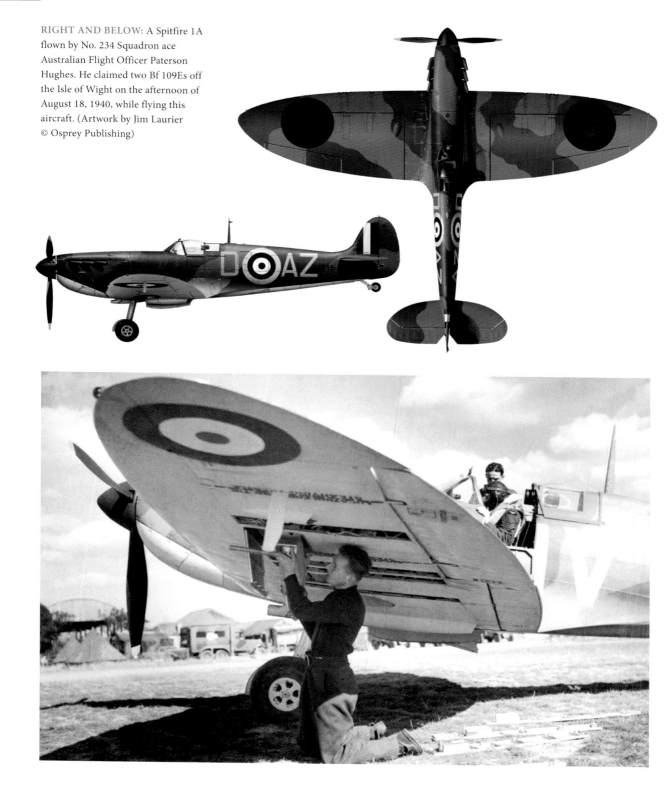

SUPERMARINE SPITFIRE MARK IA – SPECIFICATIONS

Powerplant: 1,030hp Merlin III
Span: 36ft 10in (11.2m)
Length: 29ft 11in (9.11m)
Height: 12ft 8in (3.8m)
Wing area: 242ft^2 (22.4m^2)
Weight (empty): 4,517lb (2,048kg)
Weight (max take-off): 5,844lb (2,650kg)
Maximum speed at 15,000ft: 346mph (556km/h)
Range: 415 miles (667km)
Climb: to 20,000ft (6,096m) in 7.42 min
Service ceiling: 30,500ft (9,296m)
Armament: 8 x 0.303in machine-guns

SUPERMARINE SPITFIRE MK VB – SPECIFICATIONS

Powerplant: 1 x 1,440hp Rolls-Royce Merlin 45/46/50 V-12 piston engine
Length: 29ft 11in (9.11m)
Height: 11ft 5in (3.48m)
Wingspan: 36ft 10in (11.23m)
Weight (empty) 5,100lb (2,313kg)
Weight (max take-off): 6,785lb (3,078kg)
Maximum speed: 374mph (602km/h)
Service ceiling: 37,000ft (11,280m)
Armament: 2 x 20mm cannon; 4 x 0.303in machine-guns

(80km/h) greater than that of the original Mk I. The Fleet Air Arm also had its own version, known as the Seafire.

In total during the war years, 20,351 Spitfires were produced. They were flown in action across all theaters of the conflict, and by pilots of many nations – Czechs, Poles, Australians, South Africans, Indians, and New Zealanders, amongst others. The aircraft was the making of numerous aces. For example, famous No. 74 Squadron pilot Adolph "Sailor" Malan's final tally in Spitfires was 27 individual kills, 7 shared kills, 2 unconfirmed, 3 probables, and 16 damaged. More than 1,000 Spitfires were also provided to the Soviet Union, where many Red Air Force pilots preferred them to indigenous fighter types.

The excellence of the Spitfire design meant that the aircraft soldiered on around the world for at least a decade after the end of World War II, seeing combat in conflicts such as the Korean War, the 1948 Arab–Israeli War, and the 1947 Indo-Pakistan War. Today, only a handful of flying examples remain in existence. Yet even in the age of hyper-sophisticated jet fighters, there is something instantly appreciable, elegant, and powerful about the Spitfire.

LEFT: An armorer re-arms a Spitfire at RAF Fowlmere. The distinctive shape of the elliptical wing is clearly visible. This was the ideal shape as it created the least amount of drag and had the required strength to hold the guns and the retractable undercarriage. (IWM CH 1458)

The Bf 109 could outdive a Spitfire, but the Spitfire had a smaller turning radius and this saved many RAF pilots' lives during the Battle of Britain. Flight Sergeant George Unwin later recalled getting tangled up with some Messerschmitts during a dogfight in the summer of 1940 when the Spitfire's turning ability was crucial.

> …in the distance I saw some ack-ack, and I went, I was at about 25,000 feet, and I went towards it and suddenly saw these waves of German bombers coming in. It was a fascinating sight and I was watching these things and I wondered whether anyone was going to attack them. There seemed to be hundreds of them pouring in and I forgot all about the fact that they may have an escort… Damn fool, I was lucky again! Anyway, I went into a tight turn and stayed in it and shot at several of them as they went through my sights and I actually shot two of them down… That was what probably saved me; you kept on turning and turning because the Messerschmitt couldn't turn like a Spitfire and I got away with it.[9]

TYPE VII U-BOAT

OF ALL THE THREATS FACED BY THE ALLIES DURING World War II, the British Prime Minister Winston Churchill said it was the U-boats in the Atlantic that he feared the most. The concern was well-justified, for during the course of the war the German U-boat arm sank around 14.5 million long tons (14.7 million tonnes) of Allied shipping. The workhorse of this terrible campaign was the Type VII submarine.

MARITIME HUNTER

The Type VII was not the best of the German U-boats, but it was nevertheless a proficient hunter available in large numbers – 709 in total. To put this figure into perspective, note that Britain and the United States together built only 370 submarines of all types between 1939 and 1945. (Germany's total was 1,141.)

OPPOSITE: No space on board a Type VII was left unused. Here one crewmate clamps a torpedo while another reclines on his bunk. Most German submariners did not complain about the lack of space in the Type VII compared to other classes as its small size and increased speed frequently ensured a successful escape when under attack. (Royal Navy Submarine Museum, Gosport)

The Type VII entered service in 1936, and was the Kriegsmarine's first serious long-range U-boat since the Nazis came to power in 1933. In its initial incarnation, the Type VIIA, it had a crush depth of 656ft (200m), a surface range of 4,300nm (7,964km) at 12 knots (22km/h), and a submerged range of 90nm (167km) at 4 knots (7.4km/h). Only ten of these boats were made, however, as designers quickly sought to make improvements. The Type VIIB, introduced in 1936, had its range extended dramatically to 6,500nm (12,038km), and the 21in torpedo capacity taken from 11 to 14. The most numerous of the Type VIIs, however, was the Type VIIC, of which 568 were commissioned between 1940 and 1945.

PREDATORS AND PREY

The Type VIIC U-boats really came into their own when France fell to the Germans in 1940. With French coastal bases under Kriegsmarine control, the U-boats could now range

RIGHT: Keeping watch. Watches lasted for an exhausting four hours in all weather conditions. Before the use of effective radar systems this was the only means of spotting enemy vessels. (Royal Navy Submarine Museum, Gosport)

BELOW: A Type VII moves at speed through the high seas. (Courtesy of Gordon Williamson)

deep into the Atlantic, hunting the Allied convoys in Wolf Pack missions that lasted weeks on end. Type VIICs benefited from numerous improvements over their predecessors, and the Type VIIC/41 sub-type had its crush depth increased by another 164ft (50m) to help it escape more efficient Allied depth charges. The submarine could dive in less than 30 seconds.

LEFT: The foredeck of a Type VII sub complete with 88mm deck gun. (Courtesy of Gordon Williamson)

BELOW: Thanks to increasingly superior Allied anti-submarine tactics the Type VII was not invincible. Here the crew of the frigate HMS *Conn* celebrate another successful "sub kill." It was obviously an eventful voyage as the crossed scapels indicate that a surgical operation was also performed at sea. (IWM A 28198)

ABOVE: A recruiting poster for the Germany Navy. The submarine service was considered the elite branch of the navy. (Courtesy of Gordon Williamson)

TYPE VIIC – SPECIFICATIONS

Length: 202ft (61.7m)
Beam: 20.3ft (6.2m)
Draught: 15.7ft (4.8m)
Displacement: 690 tonnes (761 tons)
Speed: surfaced: 17 knots (31.4km); submerged:
    7.6 knots (14.07km)
Range: 6,500nm (12,038km)
Crew: 44
Armament: 14 torpedoes, 2 x twin 2cm Flak guns,
    1 x quad 2cm Flak gun

THE SINKING OF *BARHAM*

On November 25, 1941, *U-331* – a Type VIIC captained by Hans-Diedrich von Tiesenhausen – torpedoed the British battleship HMS *Barham* off Bardia, Libya. One of the crew, Heinrich Schmidt, remembered the event:

❝ Our commander was at the periscope and saw the English fleet... Then the *Barham* turned away and all we saw was a white-grey wall. The commander ordered all four tubes to be made ready, which we did and then we fired a salvo of four.

We hit the *Barham* from a distance of 500 to 700 meters with a salvo of four torpedoes. The third "eel," as we called our torpedoes, penetrated the *Barham*'s ammunition chamber and the ship sank within a few minutes. It was sad. We heard later that 846 people on board had been drowned. After the *Barham* was hit, the *Valiant* approached, intending to ram us, but at that moment the *Barham* exploded and she had to turn away.[10] ❞

Individual Type VII U-boats became famed for their numbers of kills. *U-96*, for example, served between September 1940 and February 1945, and during that time it conducted 11 patrols and sank 27 major Allied vessels, plus damaged five others. Many other U-boat crews had similar success rates. Yet as Allied anti-submarine technologies and tactics improved during the war, the fate of most U-boat crews was an underwater grave. By the end of the war, nearly 80 percent of operable U-boats had been sunk, making losses of U-boat crew proportionately higher than losses amongst any other German arm of service. Other, more sophisticated U-boats were produced in an attempt to counteract the shift, but by the end of 1943 the battle for the Atlantic was effectively won.

B-17 FLYING FORTRESS

THE BOEING B-17 REPRESENTED WHAT CAME TO BE the specifically US approach to the strategic bombing campaign against Germany – daylight attacks by very heavily armed (and initially unescorted) bombers, as opposed to the RAF's night-time campaign. Whether this tactic was judicious is debatable, but the aircraft itself became a dominant player in the attempt to crush Nazi Germany from the air.

DAYLIGHT RAIDER

Throughout the 1930s a sense of absolute faith in the abilities of bomber aircraft to wage mass destruction and win wars was fostered by all the major powers. In the United States this belief was encouraged by a group of officers at the US Army Air Corps Tactical School. As a result, in 1934, the US Army Air Corps (USAAC) issued a requirement for multi-engine long-range bomber. With remarkable speed, Boeing developed such an aircraft in just a year, the Boeing Model 299 a four-engine bomber low-wing monoplane with a 4,800lb (2,200kg) bombload that made its maiden flight on July 28, 1935. Legend has it that a local newspaper reporter who witnessed this flight commented that it had the appearance of a "flying fortress" and the nickname stuck. US production orders were placed for what officially became known as the B-17, only for very small numbers at first, but increasing as the war in Europe escalated from 1939.

OPPOSITE: A silhouette of a Flying Fortress at sunset. (Library of Congress)

The first major production model was the B-17E. Introduced into service in September 1941, it featured numerous improvements over predecessors – a double-gun tail turret; power-operated ventral and dorsal turrets; and a hugely increased tail surface to provide better control at high altitudes. Defensive armament kept climbing until the most prolific model, the B-17G (8,680 produced), had a total of 13 0.5in Browning machine-guns. The "Flying Fortress" appellation was well deserved.

HARD WAR

In total, nearly 18,000 B-17s were produced by the end of the war. They served in both the European and Pacific theaters, but are particularly remembered for their role in the strategic bombing campaign against Germany between 1942 and 1945. Against the Reich's heavy air defenses – which included radar-vectored fighters and integrated anti-aircraft systems –

ABOVE: A staged photograph of a B-17 bomber crew receiving a briefing at sunrise before another raid over Germany in the final months of the war. (Library of Congress)

BELOW: A prewar flight of B-17s over New York City in February 1938. (Courtesy of Robert Forsyth)

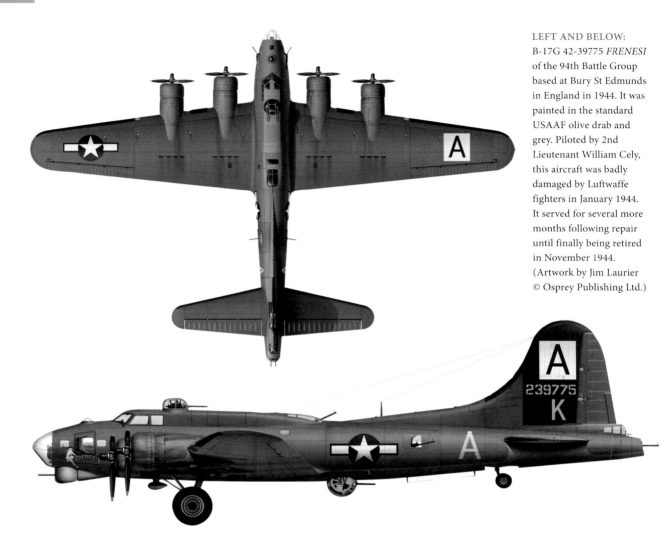

LEFT AND BELOW:
B-17G 42-39775 *FRENESI*
of the 94th Battle Group
based at Bury St Edmunds
in England in 1944. It was
painted in the standard
USAAF olive drab and
grey. Piloted by 2nd
Lieutenant William Cely,
this aircraft was badly
damaged by Luftwaffe
fighters in January 1944.
It served for several more
months following repair
until finally being retired
in November 1944.
(Artwork by Jim Laurier
© Osprey Publishing Ltd.)

GERMAN ATTACK

Adolf Galland was a German fighter ace and Luftwaffe commander, and a pioneer of fighter tactics throughout the war. Here he describes an attack on a straggling B-17:

" I was a hundred yards behind on his tail. The B-17 fired and took desperate avoiding action. The only thing that existed in the whole world was this American bomber, fighting for its life, and myself. As my cannons blazed away, pieces of metal flew off, smoke poured from the engines, and they jettison the entire bomb-load. One tank in the wings had caught fire. The crew was baling out. Trautloft's voice cried over the radio: "*Achtung, Adolf! Mustangs! I'm beating it! Guns jammed!*"

And then – with the first bursts from four Mustangs – I sobered up. There was no mistake about the B-17; she was finished, but I was not. I simply fled.[11] "

the US policy of high-altitude daylight raids was tested to its limits. The costs were extremely high. During the infamous raids against Schweinfurt and Regensburg in 1943, for example, each US mission was met by swarms of high-performance German fighters, often outnumbering the attackers. In the attack of August 17, 60 B-17s were shot down, and a repeated attack on Schweinfurt on October 14 resulted in 77 B-17s destroyed out of an attacking force of 291 aircraft. A further 121 bombers needed major repairs. These raids alone resulted in a temporary suspension of US operations over Germany.

Only the introduction of long-range fighter escorts in 1943–44 (see "Mustang" entry on pp.260–263) balanced the equation for the B-17s, although the daylight policy remained costly throughout the war. At the same time, losses amongst RAF bombers operating at night also grew severe, but the B-17s and the RAF's Lancasters undeniably did heavy damage to German industry. Furthermore, the heavy defensive firepower made the B-17 respected by the fighter pilots who attacked them. A typical 21-aircraft "combat box" of B-17Gs had a total of 273 machine-guns, which together could throw out more than 150,000 bullets every minute. (The total weight of these bullets was more than the weight of an entire Focke-Wulf Fw 190.) Indeed, more B-17s were lost due to engine failure as a result of the difficulties of flying such lengthy missions at extreme altitude and in extreme cold than were lost to enemy fighters during the course of the war.

The B-17 is historic not only because of its critical role in bombing the Axis, but also because it represents the end of an era in terms of aerial bombing. After World War II, the age of jet and missile rendered mass, daylight raids of hundreds of aircraft unthinkable.

RIGHT: A training photograph of a bombadier at Fort Benning, Georgia. American B-17 bomber crews were responsible for precision daylight bombing raids from high altitudes throughout the European Theater of Operations. For this they used their Norden Bombsight, first developed in 1932. But in reality precision bombing was almost impossible to achieve. (Library of Congress)

BOEING B-17G – SPECIFICATIONS

Crew: 10
Powerplant: 4 x 1,200hp (895kW) Wright Cyclone
   R-1820-97 radial piston engines
Length: 79ft 9in (22.78m)
Height: 19ft 1in (5.82m)
Wingspan: 103ft 9in (31.62m)
Maximum speed: 287mph (462km/h)
Service ceiling: 35,600ft (10,850m)
Range: 2,000 miles (3,220km) with 6,000lb (2,722kg)
   bombload
Armament: 13 0.5in Browning machine-guns arranged
   in twin-gun nose, tail, ventral, and dorsal positions
   and single machine-gun stations along the
   fuselage; maximum bombload of 17,600lb
   (7,983kg), although typical bombload was less
   than half that figure

T-34

On June 22, 1941, more than four million Axis troops and 600,000 vehicles surged across the Soviet border as the Germans launched Operation *Barbarossa*. That very day, German forces in Belorussia encountered a new Soviet tank that stunned them with its speed, armor, and gunnery. This was the T-34, and by the end of the war more than 80,000 would have been produced, making it the most prevalent – and influential – tank in history.

SOVIET DESIGN

The T-34 was designed and developed during the late 1930s. The Soviet Army was looking for an improvement for the BT-7 fast tank, which although speedy – partly by virtue of its suspension system, designed by the American J. Walter Christie – was poorly armored and had an inadequate gun. Through progressive design stages, the T-34 emerged, which retained the Christie suspension but revolutionized tank design in almost every other aspect.

The virtues of the T-34/76A, the first production model, were numerous. It had unusually wide tracks, which combined with the suspension system gave it a low ground pressure that made it possible to move over deep mud or snow. It was encased in thick armor with steeply sloping surfaces; the slopes both enhanced the presented depth of armor, and also increased the likelihood of shot deflection. It delivered its power through a V-2-34 V12 diesel engine that ran in all temperatures and conditions, delivering good range but with the low risk of catching fire if hit by an enemy shell. Top speed was 34mph

OPPOSITE: A T-34 under construction. The Russian tanks were often inferior to the best German tanks fielded, but their overall qualities and sheer weight of numbers gave them the ascendancy. It took just 3,000 man-hours to create a T-34 compared to the 55,000 hours it took to complete a Panther. (Tank Museum, Bovington)

ABOVE: The Soviet T-34/76 Model 1943. (Artwork by Jim Laurier © Osprey Publishing Ltd.)

BELOW: A tank crew clear the gun barrel in preparation for another battle. Throughout 1943 the Red Army lost 14,000 T-34/76 tanks. Only about 25–30 percent of tank crews survived the destruction of their vehicles. However, despite such high losses, the Red Army's ability to maneuver large tank formations ensured that they retained the initiative. (Tank Museum, Bovington)

(55km/h), about 10mph (6km/h) more than the maximum pace of a Panzer III or IV. The armament was like nothing ever seen on a tank before – a high-velocity 76mm long-barreled gun capable of killing any tank then in service.

WAR WINNING

The appearance of the T-34 stunned the Germans. At first, it completely out matched the German Panzers, and the T-34's armor made it resistant to most vehicular or towed anti-tank guns in the Wehrmacht's arsenal. Once winter set in,

T-34 BATTLE

Johann Huber, a gunner on a German Pz IV, here recounts an engagement with T-34s in East Prussia in 1944:

❝ We pull off the congested Rollbahn and make no further progress. Suddenly, at about 1500, all motors are switched off and there's general silence, and we hear from the left, up front, at about 10 o'clock, a gun firing. Everyone immediately looks in that direction, from where black smoke is now rising: T-34 to the left! So since last night, when we were still defending near Luoke, the Russians have advanced at least 60 kilometres... I quickly estimate the distance to the forest edge where the T-34 is positioned. It is at least 1,400 metres, so there's no point in shooting. At that range, we would achieve nothing against a T-34's armour. Our AP rounds are only effective against this type of enemy tank at less than 800 metres. The T-34 fires again and again, and a good 1200 metres down the Rollbahn there is now a black cloud – he's hit something, vehicles are burning. But then there's one of our yellow tracers going left. A hit! The T-34 immediately starts to burn. It was alone, no more are nearby.[12] ❞

the situation was even worse, as the T-34s had superior performance over soft terrain.

Despite their advantages, however, T-34s were wasted in huge numbers through amateurish tactics and poor mechanical care in the early years of the war. Furthermore, German armor and anti-tank weapons improved in quality and distribution, meaning that T-34s were ultimately destroyed in their thousands. And yet, the tank was configured for rapid production, and so however many the Germans destroyed, there were always more to come. Nor did T-34 design stand still. It went through numerous variants, including the T-34/85, which had an 85mm gun capable of taking on any of the new generation of German tanks, such as the Panther and the Tiger. In 1944 alone, 11,000 of these tanks were produced.

No single weapon won the war, but the T-34 certainly tipped the armored battle in the Soviet Union's favor. At Kursk in July and August 1943, for example, the Soviets were able to field more than 5,000 tanks, as opposed to nearly 3,000 for the Germans. The Soviet victory in that battle alone put paid to any remaining German offensive ambitions on the Eastern Front. The quality of the T-34 also meant that many of them soldiered on into the Cold War era, its principles of gunnery, armor, and suspension continuing to influence military vehicle designers to the present day.

OPPOSITE: On the attack – a T-34/76 unit advances on the Eastern Front. (Courtesy of the Central Museum of the Armed Forces Moscow)

BELOW: A war-winning tank. A propaganda photo shows the liberation of a Ukranian village by a T-34 unit. (Courtesy of the Central Museum of the Armed Forces Moscow)

TIGER I

THE PZKPFW VI TIGER I TANK IS AN ARGUABLE inclusion in a book containing some of history's greatest weapons. Appropriately used, and when it was working, it was probably the most powerful armored vehicle in-theater, capable of destroying any armored opponent it faced and invulnerable to almost all shell and shot. Yet mechanical problems and its huge weight could make it nothing more than a massive burden on crews, a liability rather than an asset.

OPPOSITE: A tank crew refueling a Tiger I. Note the men in the background taking the opportunity to re-arm the tank with ammunition. (Bundesarchiv, Bild 146-1978-107-06)

OPPOSITE, FAR RIGHT: This Tiger tank commander has a good view of the battlefield from the turret, March 1943. (Bundesarchiv, Bild 183-J05741 / Ernst Schwahn)

DOMINANT PRESENCE

The Tiger actually began its development journey prior to the war, when the German high command began to think about a heavier, more powerful replacement for its PzKpfw IIIs and IVs. A long development process began involving Krupp, Porsche, and Henschel, the latter's design winning through to become the basis of the PzKpfw VI Tiger Ausf E, which went into production in August 1942.

BELOW: Images from the so-called *Tigerfibel*, the principal field service regulations for all Tiger crews. Unlike other German service regulations which were rather dry, this book used jokes and cartoons.

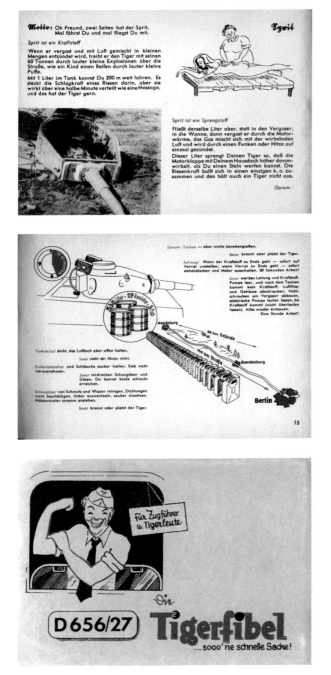

The Tiger was, quite simply, the most potent tank on the battlefield. It weighed a colossal 61 short tons (55 tonnes), and had a width of 12ft 3in (3.73m). Its armor was extremely resilient, reaching a maximum depth of 4.33in (110mm), although the boxy configuration of the hull somewhat reduced its efficacy. The Tiger's gun was an armored vehicle adaptation of the 88mm Flak, a proven tank-killer.

Yet there were issues, never entirely resolved. The sheer scale of the tank made it slow – maximum road speed was 24mph (38km/h) – and there were few bridges that could support its weight. It had to swap tracks for on-road and off-road use, a time-consuming business for support crews, and a dangerous one in combat conditions. Mechanically, it hadn't been tested thoroughly – Hitler was eager to get the Tigers into battle, hence they were thrown into the cauldron of the Eastern Front in the high summer of 1942, and thereafter served in North Africa, Italy, and Northern Europe.

FAILED EXPECTATIONS

The Tiger's experience in combat sent mixed messages. When everything was working well, the Tiger was a terrifying beast to fight, its accurate, powerful gun dispatching Allied tanks in disproportionate numbers. In one incident in 1944, following the Normandy landings, one Tiger tank destroyed 25 Allied tanks before it was finally overcome, holding up an entire

ABOVE: A Tiger fires during the battle for Kursk on the Eastern Front, 1943. (Bundesarchiv, Bild 101III-Groenert-019-23A / Grönert)

divisional advance in the process. Similar, if not greater, devastation was repeated on numerous occasions on the Eastern Front, the Tiger's crews taking advantage of Soviet tactical failures. Matters became even worse for the Allies with the later introduction of the Tiger II, which had an even more powerful 88mm gun and much thicker, sloped armor.

Yet ultimately, the Tigers fell short of expectations. Their sheer size meant they had no battlefield agility, and were limited in their abilities to cross soft terrain and keep up with more mobile formations. Mechanical breakdown was a serious issue, the tank's weight resulting in overstressed engines, brakes, and transmissions. On the Eastern Front, mud and snow would be trapped in the overlapping wheels and freeze overnight in winter, rendering the vehicles immobile by the morning. The tanks also had a voracious appetite for fuel – during the Ardennes offensive, many tanks had to be abandoned as the Wehrmacht's supplies of fuel began to run dry.

So in balance, the Tiger was arguably more of a drain on German resources than was warranted. Nevertheless, in open combat most Allied tanks were at a serious disadvantage if they faced a Tiger.

PZKPFW VI TIGER I – SPECIFICATIONS

Crew: 5

Powerplant: Maybach HL 230 P 45 V-12 water-cooled petrol engine, developing 700bhp (522kW) at 3,000rpm

Armor: 1.02–4.33in (26mm–110mm)

Length: 27ft (8.25m)

Width: 12ft 6in (3.73m)

Height: 9ft 4in (2.85m)

Weight: 61 short tons (55 tonnes)

Road speed: 24mph (38km/h)

Cross-country speed: 12mph (20km/h)

Range: 62 miles (100km)

Vertical obstacle: 2ft 7in (0.8m)

Trench crossing: 5ft 11in (1.8m)

Gradient: 35°

Fording depth: 4ft (1.2m)

Armament: 1 x 88mm KwK L/56 gun; 2 x 7.92mm MG34 machine-guns (one co-axial, and one in hull)

LEFT: The turret is lowered into place during the later stages of Tiger I production in Germany, 1944. (Bundesarchiv, Bild 101I-635-3965-05 / Hebenstreit)

M1 "BAZOOKA"

EXPERIMENTS IN RECOILLESS WEAPONS IN THE UNITED States began during World War I. The first example was produced by Dr Robert Goddard, who designed a recoilless rocket launcher in November 1918 and demonstrated it to the US Army. The Armistice a few days later, however, did not help his cause, and the project largely withered through lack of interest. In 1941, by contrast, the situation was dramatically different. Apart from anti-tank artillery, the US Army had no dedicated infantry weapons for taking on German or Japanese armor. Shaped-charge warheads were the answer – warheads designed to focus the force of an explosion onto a concentrated point. What was needed was a delivery system.

SIMPLE DESIGN

The M1 "Bazooka" was the brainchild of Captain Leslie Skinner and Lieutenant David E. Uhl, who were commissioned to devise a hand-held weapon capable of knocking out a tank. The design was unveiled in May 1942, and the "Launcher, Rocket, 2.36in, Anti-tank, M1" was accepted for service after trials at Aberdeen Proving Ground. General Electric was commissioned to manufacture 5,000 of the weapons, which incredibly it did in less than 30 days.

The "bazooka," as the weapon became famously known, was essentially a shoulder-mounted smoothbore tube, which electrically fired an M6 shaped-charge rocket with a warhead capable of punching through 4.5in (112mm), with a maximum range of 400yds (366m). Early problems with both ammunition and launcher resulted in an improved version, the M1A1 with M6A1 rocket, being produced from late 1942.

OPPOSITE: Here the portable size of the bakooka is clearly visible. (US Army Signal Corps)

OPPOSITE, FAR RIGHT: In this posed photograph a bazooka crew illustrate how they could potentially tackle a German Panther tank. In fact, it would have been unlikely that a bazooka crew would aim towards the Panther's thick frontal armor, but would instead search for weak points. (US Military)

ABOVE: The beauty of the bazooka was that it was so simple to use that specialist crews were not required. Instead individuals within a rifle patrol were trained to operate them. (US Military)

TANK KILLER

It took a lot of refinement to get the bazooka right, and serious problems included rockets sticking in the tubes and detonating, or the weapon malfunctioning in very hot or very cold conditions. Nevertheless, improvements were made to various models such as the M9 and M9A1, and the bazooka became a serviceable and useful weapon in US hands. Although its light warhead could be defeated by the heaviest tank armor, it was still capable of destroying or disabling lighter armored vehicles – the M9 could penetrate 5in (126mm) of armor – but was also useful for tackling enemy pillboxes, bunkers, or other positions. White phosphorus and incendiary warheads were introduced, giving the weapon a broader anti-personnel and anti-materiel effect.

ABOVE: The German equivalent to the bazooka – the *Panzerfaust*. The tube was marked in red with the words *Vorsicht! Starker Feurstrahl!* ("Danger! Intense Fire Flash!"). (US Military)

Bazookas needed courage and intelligence to be used properly. They created a large backblast, and the cloud of dust would serve as a magnet for return fire from enemy tanks and infantry. To be sure of hitting his target, furthermore, a soldier would often have to get very close, which required nerve and steady hands. Yet the recoilless anti-tank gun weapon became a real danger to armor in the late years of World War II. The Germans in particular developed fine rocket weapons such as the 88mm *Panzerschreck* (largely a copy of the bazooka, after Lend-Lease versions were captured on the Eastern Front) and the infamous *Panzerfaust* (see feature box). The bazooka soldiered on after the war in Korea and later, with a 3.5in M20 "Superbazooka" being used as late as the Vietnam War. A simple design had proved to be an enduring one.

PANZERFAUST

The *Panzerfaust* was a German series of recoilless anti-tank weapons put into mass production from October 1943. In basic description, the *Panzerfaust* was a steel tube fitted with a venturi nozzle at the rear end (this concentrated the rocket blast to balance out the rearward recoil) and which accepted a bulbous, flexible-fin shaped-charge missile at the front. When fired, it threw the bomb via a propelling charge rather than a rocket, so range had to be close – in the Panzerfaust 60 model, the simple aperture sight was graduated 30, 60, and 80m. Yet in urban fighting such were typical combat ranges, and with an armor penetration of 7.8in (200mm) it inflicted serious casualties on British, American, and Soviet tanks towards the end of the war.

MP40

THE MP40 WAS NO BETTER, AND IN SOME WAYS WORSE, than many other submachine-guns produced during World War II. Yet such judgments are missing the point. For the MP40 represents the successful meeting of close-quarters firepower with the wartime needs of mass production, something that all combatant nations eventually tried to achieve.

FIREPOWER EXPANSION

Lessons from the Spanish Civil War convinced the German Army of the need for a new submachine-gun to boost its infantry squad firepower. Bolt-action rifles were fine for long-range, accurate fire, and machine-guns for heavy attrition, but for close-quarters combat the submachine-gun was ideal. The new design, created by Ermawerke based on a design by Heinrich Vollmer, was the Maschinenpistole 38 (MP38).

The MP38 was different from any other submachine-gun to date. Most strikingly, it was an all-metal construction, featuring a folding metal stock consisting of nothing more than two brace arms and a shoulder plate. It was a simple

OPPOSITE: German soldiers on the Eastern Front searching for Allied troops hiding in the village of Gatnoje, August 1941. (Topfoto)

9mm blowback weapon, firing in automatic mode only at a rate of 500rpm, and was fed from a single-column 32-round box magazine. It included intelligent features such as a metal bar and hook beneath the barrel, so that the gun could be fired through armored vehicle ports without risking damaging the barrel itself.

The MP38 went into action with the German Army in 1939, at least one man of a ten-man infantry squad being armed with the weapon, dramatically increasing squad firepower. (From late 1943, squad sizes were reduced to nine men, but two of those would have submachine-guns.) It did decent service, its main problem being a poor magazine design. A greater issue, however, was that it was expensive and slow to produce. If it was to meet wartime conditions for cost and distribution, it had to be rationalized.

CHEAP WEAPONRY

The MP38 was indeed redesigned, and two years into the war the MP40 arrived. This was largely the same weapon, but using cheaper production methods and materials, suited to the varying abilities of subcontractors. The result was a huge surge in submachine-gun output, with about one million MP40 units produced during the war. As well as squad and platoon leaders, paratroopers and armored vehicle crews

ABOVE: A demonstration of the US Army's equivalent to the MP40 – the M3 "Grease Gun." (NARA via Tom Laemlein)

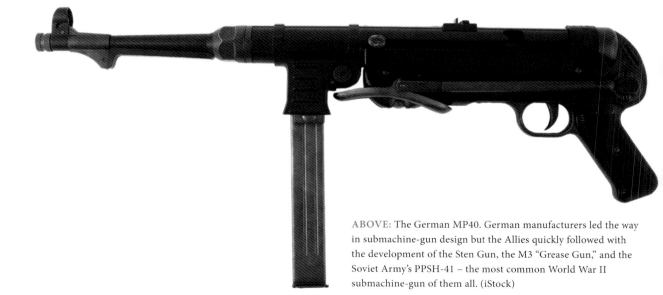

ABOVE: The German MP40. German manufacturers led the way in submachine-gun design but the Allies quickly followed with the development of the Sten Gun, the M3 "Grease Gun," and the Soviet Army's PPSH-41 – the most common World War II submachine-gun of them all. (iStock)

ABOVE: An SS soldier armed with a MP40 stands alongside his Kar 98k-armed comrades. At least two men per nine-man squad were armed with submachine-guns in the final two years of the war. (Bundesarchiv, Bild 183-97906 / Schremmer)

came to appreciate the MP40's availability and firepower, with its rate of fire compensating for its inaccuracy at ranges much in excess of 100yds (91m).

What is important about guns such as the MP40, is that they illustrate two key tactical principles. First, volume of fire is critical to achieve dominance in a combat situation. Second, it is better to have larger numbers of cheap weapons than fewer numbers of expensive weapons. It should be noted that all combatants were coming to the same conclusion. The British, for example, produced four million Sten guns between 1941 and 1945. A cruder gun is hard to find, but it meant that millions of Allied soldiers had extra firepower in their hands. Similarly, the United States rationalized the design of the Thompson submachine-gun, but also made 700,000 M3 "Grease Guns," principally made from stampings and pressings. All that was asked of such guns was that they worked, and killed enemy soldiers.

PPSH-41

The classic Soviet submachine-gun of the war was the PPSh-41, rapidly designed by Georgi Shpagin in response to Soviet experience of Finnish submachine-guns in the "Winter War" of 1939–40 and major losses of weaponry during the same campaign. Shpagin's gun was a masterpiece of reliability, simplicity, and firepower. It fired 7.62mm rounds at 900rpm from either a 35-round box magazine or a 71-round drum, making it a devastating close-quarters weapon, and it was extremely simple to maintain and strip in field conditions. It rarely malfunctioned, even in the dirtiest of conditions. The Soviets were more wedded to the idea of submachine-guns than other nations. A Red Army infantry section would typically contain three or four submachine-guns, and entire units up to battalion size were equipped with the weapons. This was made possible by the fact that five million PPSh-41s were manufactured by 1945.

P-51 MUSTANG

THE STORY OF THE NORTH AMERICAN P-51 MUSTANG is one of how a change in engine transformed the aircraft from being an average fighter to being an outstanding fighter. Furthermore, its late-war role as long-range escort altered the very nature of the strategic air campaign against Germany.

POWERPLANT REVOLUTION

The P-51 originated in a British approach to North American in April 1940, asking the American manufacturer to build P-40 fighters for the beleaguered RAF. Instead, North American built an entirely new fighter, the Mustang. With a top speed of 382mph (615km/h) – aided by an excellent laminar flow wing design – long range, and good maneuverability, the Mustang impressed the British, who took 620 as the Mustang Mk IA and Mustang Mk II. The United States took none of the fighters until after it entered the war, but ordered 310 P-51As in 1942 and increasing numbers thereafter.

The P-51's powerplant – the Allison engine – was its weakest feature. The best version of the Allison installed in the Mustang was the V-1710-81, which developed 1,200hp (895kW) and pushed the top speed to 390mph (627km/h). Such performance was excellent, but only deliverable below 15,000ft (4,572m). Consequently, the Mustang was a good low-level fighter and ground-attack aircraft, but it wasn't suited to high-altitude escort roles, which became far more important for the Allied strategic bombing campaign after 1942.

OPPOSITE: Captain Don Gentile of the 4th Fighter Group watches his crew chief, Sergeant John Ferrar, update his victory tally on his personal P-51B nicknamed "Shangri-La." Gentile claimed 21 kills between August 1942 and April 1944. (USAF)

The solution, first implemented by the British in October 1942 and then adopted by the Americans, was to re-engine the Mustang with the Rolls-Royce Merlin engine. In consequence, the Mustang's performance was completely transformed. Its level max speed immediately went up to 441mph (709km/h), as did its high-altitude performance – the later P-51H could fly at 487mph (784km/h) at 25,000ft (7,620m). Now it was ready to show its true potential.

LONG-RANGE FIGHTER

The P-51 was a fighter pilot's dream. It could turn, dive, and race with the best of the German fighters, and its six 0.5in machine-guns in the wings could smash up anything that fell under the aircraft's sights. The introduction of the "bubble canopy" in the P-51D (the model that first had six rather than four machine-guns) improved the pilot's visibility for dogfighting, and provision

ABOVE: Mustangs that had already seen extensive service undergo a refit before returning to the frontline. (Courtesy of David Mayor)

RIGHT: Mustangs return from a bomber escort mission on July 11, 1944. (Courtesy of Steve Gotts)

ABOVE: Mustangs of the 352nd Fighter Group lined up in late 1944. (Courtesy of Bill Espie)

BELOW: From the spring of 1944 onwards, Mustangs were fitted with the K-14 gunsight. Instead of the typical crosshairs one might expect, the K-14 projected a center dot of yellow light surrounded by six diamond-shaped dots. It was a gyro computing gunsight, and the pilot could preset it with the wingspan of a target. Manuals were given to pilots to explain how to use the gunsight and where the targets should be placed.

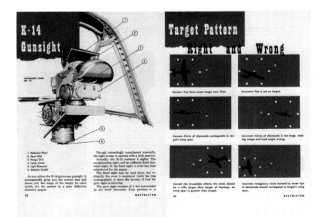

FIGHTER TACTICS

In 1943 and 1944, the Luftwaffe altered its fighter tactics to cope with the increase in US escort presence. Initially, the fighters would make a fast, head-on run at the enemy formations, blasting their targets with fire as they passed through and escaping before the escorts had time to respond. Necessary increases in the weight of German fighter armament (20mm and 30mm cannon became standard in many fighters), however, slowed aircraft performance – single-seat fighters needed to be upgunned to destroy the bombers, as the well-armed two-engine Me 110s could no longer survive in the new fighter environment. Consequently the *Sturmgruppe* tactic was adopted by some units. Cannon-armed Focke-Wulf Fw 190s would attack enemy bombers in a concentrated and coordinated group, while numbers of lighter Bf 109G fighters took on the escorts. The tactics had considerable success on occasions, but eventually the sheer weight of Allied fighter numbers overwhelmed even this intelligent tactic.

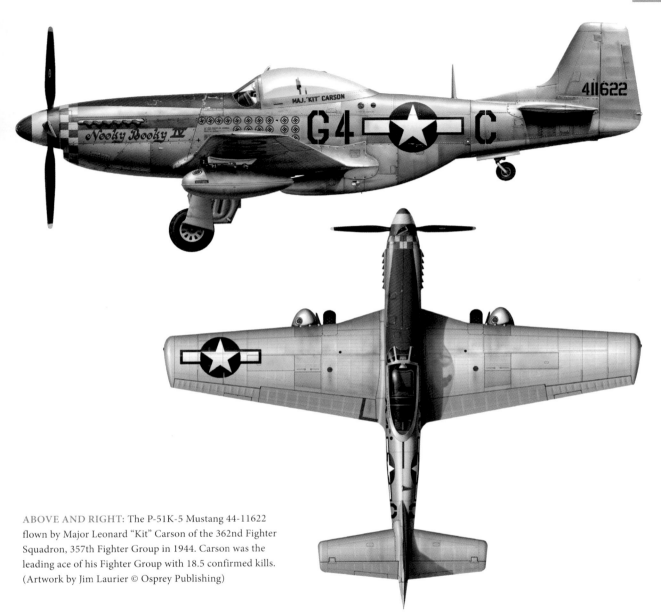

ABOVE AND RIGHT: The P-51K-5 Mustang 44-11622
flown by Major Leonard "Kit" Carson of the 362nd Fighter
Squadron, 357th Fighter Group in 1944. Carson was the
leading ace of his Fighter Group with 18.5 confirmed kills.
(Artwork by Jim Laurier © Osprey Publishing)

for underwing bombs and rockets also made the aircraft a
scourge of enemy ground forces and airfields.

In support of the Allied strategic bombing campaign, the
Mustang at first did not have sufficient range to escort
bombers all the way to their targets and back. The problem
was progressively solved from late 1943 by the introduction
of 75-gal underwing drop fuel tanks, which took the
operational range of a P-51D up to 1,300 miles (2,092km),

enough to escort a bomber all the way to Berlin and back from
southern England. Now the German fighters were no longer
able to give the bombers their undivided attention – instead,
they now had to fight for their lives against the US escorts.

The P-51 was a true workhorse fighter, and despite initial
US hesitation over adopting the aircraft, eventually 15,586
were produced. Together these aircraft changed the balance
of fighter power over the skies of the Reich.

MG42

THE CONDITIONS OF THE VERSAILLES TREATY prohibited, amongst many other things, Germany's development of sustained-fire automatic weapons. This restriction was easily circumvented by pushing machine-gun development over the border into Switzerland. This led to the 7.92mm Solothurn Modell 30 (the German company Rheinmetall-Borsig had control of the Swiss Solothurn concern), which in turn informed production of the MG15 in 1932. The MG15 was primarily an aircraft gun, but it had many innovative features, such as its 75-round saddle-drum magazine, a "straight-in-line" design, a rotating-bolt recoil operating system, and a quick-change barrel facility.

OPPOSITE: German soldiers readying their MG34 – the world's first true "general purpose machine-gun," *c.* 1939. (Courtesy of Stephen Bull)

OPPOSITE PAGE, TOP: The MG34 could also be placed on a sustained fire tripod as shown in this illustration. The MG34 was the direct forerunner of the MG42. From Weber's *Unterrichtsbuch Für Soldaten* (1938). (Courtesy of Stephen Bull)

MASS PRODUCTION

The MG15 inspired a later weapon, the great MG34. The MG34 incorporated numerous improvements over its predecessor, most significant of which was its ability to fire from a 250-round belt as well as the 75-shot saddle drum. Combined with a 900rpm rate of fire, this meant that the MG34 brought in the age of the "general-purpose machine-gun." In essence, the gun could change roles depending on its mount and sighting arrangements. Set on a tripod with long-range sights, for example, it could act in a "heavy" sustained-fire role, or as an anti-aircraft weapon. On its bipod, by contrast, the MG34 was a "light" assault machine-gun (being air-cooled, it was light enough to be carried by one man), providing intensive offensive or defensive fire support to troop maneuvers.

The MG34 served with German frontline units throughout the war. Its problem was that it was very expensive and slow to produce, being made from high-quality machining

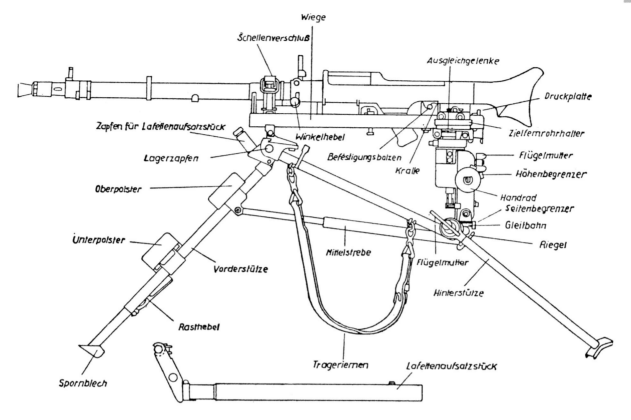

Wiege

Schellenverschluß

Ausgleichgelenke

Druckplatte

Zielfemrohrhalter

Zapfen für Lafettenaufsatzstück

Winkelhebel

Befestigungsbolzen

Kralle

Flügelmutter

Höhenbegrenzer

Lagerzapfen

Handrad

Seitenbegrenzer

Oberpolster

Gleitbahn

Riegel

Unterpolster

Mittelstrebe

Flügelmutter

Vorderstütze

Hinterstütze

Rasthebel

Spornblech

Tragerriemen

Lafettenaufsatzstück

processes. What was needed was a weapon with the same power, but was far cheaper to produce and could be turned out in larger numbers.

DEVASTATING EFFECT

The MG42 was that gun. Produced by Mauser-Werke, the MG42 utilized inexpensive, simpler manufacturing processes of pressing, stamping, and welding, plus used a new roller-locked operating mechanism which gave a blistering rate of fire – 1,200rpm. Furthermore, it was actually more reliable than the MG34, while fulfilling all of that gun's roles. Barrel change could be performed in a matter of seconds.

German infantry tactics placed machine-guns in a more central role compared to the Allies, and those who faced the MG42 gave it total respect. The ripping sound of the gun firing brought it nicknames such as "Hitler's buzzsaw" and the "linoleum ripper," and single guns were capable of holding

BELOW: The German MG42, which saw active service with the Wehrmacht until the end of the war. (akg-images)

back entire companies. Those attacking often either had to bring in mortar or artillery support to suppress the gun, or make an assault in the brief barrel-change window. For the German operators, the biggest challenge of the MG42 was controlling its ammunition consumption, which was extremely high. The gunner had to limit the amount of rounds fired in individual bursts, but even a one- or two-second burst was capable of almost tearing a man apart.

The MG42 was produced in large numbers – 750,000 – and it killed and wounded thousands of men on all European fronts. Such was the gun's quality that it was essentially put into production again in the 1950s in 7.62mm NATO caliber as the standard machine-gun of the Bundeswehr, and adaptations of the MG42 still serve in armies today.

BELOW: A German MG42 crew in the Ardennes in early 1945. (akg-images/ullstein bild)

EXPERIENCING THE MG42

British Army officer Captain Alastair Borthwick of the 5th Seaforth Highlanders, here remembers what it was like to face the MG42. Note that "Spandau" was the name frequently given to the gun by British soldiers:

“ There was something much too personal about a Spandau. It did not aim at an area: it aimed at you, and its rate of fire was prodigious. It had a vindictive sound. Each burst began with an odd hiccup before getting into its stride, so that the crack of the first round was distinct and all the others ran together like the sound of tearing calico. Their pup-turrrr, put turrr was the most distinctive noise on any battlefield...[13] ”

ME 262

THE ME 262 JET FIGHTER WAS AN AUGUR OF FUTURE air warfare. Its evolution began in design terms in 1938, although the development of effective jet engines stretched out development over four years. Powered by two Junkers 109-004A-0 turbojets, the aircraft first flew on July 18, 1942. Hitler's personal interference in the project (he primarily wanted the Me 262 developed as a bomber), plus the numerous competing demands on the German war industry, meant that the aircraft did not go into production and service as a fighter until 1944. With Allied bombers hammering Germany's towns and cities on an almost daily basis, it was hoped that this revolutionary fighter would tip the balance of the air war in Germany's favor.

FAST PREDATOR

For the times, the Me 262 was an astonishing aircraft. It had a sleek airframe, with a jet engine underslung beneath each wing. Performance characteristics were well beyond any Allied fighter of the time. It had a maximum speed of 541mph (870km/h) – more than 100mph (62km/h) faster than a Mustang – and it could climb to 30,000ft (9,144m) in about seven minutes. In its basic fighter configuration it had four Mk 108 30mm cannon in its nose, and some later versions also carried 24 R4M high-velocity air-to-air rockets, which were ripple-fired at enemy bomber formations. Hitler's bomber vision persisted, and the Me 262A-2a *Sturmvogel* (Stormy Petrel) could also carry 1,100lb (500kg) of bombs. The main deficiencies of the aircraft were a short operating time of around an hour, plus a much poorer performance at low speed. The jets were also prone to flameout, contributing to a high accident rate.

JET TACTICS

The Me 262 appeared in combat in mid 1944, and as its numbers grew – a total of 1,430 were produced – alarm spread

OPPOSITE: An Me 262 photographed in 1944, with the cannon apertures clearly visible in the nose cone. (akg-images)

ABOVE: Rapidly advancing American troops discover an Me 262 in perfect condition and even loaded with belts of bullets, April 17, 1945. (Getty Images)

through the Allied air crews. For interception missions, the Me 262 pilots' main tactic was to make a fast dive from about 6,000ft (1,828m) above the bomber formation, screaming through the enemy aircraft, with cannon blazing, at speeds beyond anything gunners or escort fighters could handle. (Electric gun turrets couldn't even track the fighter.) In fact, thus deployed the Me 262 was actually *too* fast – the pilot didn't have time to properly sight his guns – so the tactic was modified. The jet would dive through the bombers, then throttle back and climb up underneath the targets, burning off excess speed to deliver a devastating attack beginning at about 650yds (594m) range.

Thus deployed, Me 262s could be unnerving opponents. In one action alone, on March 18, 1945, Me 262s shot down 12 US bombers and one fighter. Me 262 aces began to appear, such as Hauptmann Franz Schall, who downed 17 aircraft in the jet, including ten US P-51 fighters.

In high-speed combat, there was little that the Allied fighter pilots could do against the Me 262. When it was returning to base or sat on the ground, however, was another matter, and dozens of the jets were destroyed by Allied ground-attack sorties. At low-level, the Me 262 was also vulnerable to heavy anti-aircraft fire like any other aircraft, as was evidenced in the heavy losses of jets during Operation *Bodenplatte* in January 1945, when the Luftwaffe unleashed an major offensive against Allied air bases in the Low Countries. Dozens of Allied aircraft were destroyed, but the point was the industrial might of the Allies could endure such losses. Like all other German jet projects, the Me 262 came too late to make a difference to the war. What it achieved, however, was to demonstrate that the jet was the true future of air warfare.

DOWNING AN ME 262

Although Allied fighters were outperformed by the Me 262, some pilots still managed to down jets in open combat. One was Soviet ace Ivan Kozhedub, who here describes an encounter with an Me 262 over the Oder in February 1945:

" Quickly whipping around, I give my fighter full throttle and head off in pursuit of the enemy. I approach his tail, getting to within 500 meters of the jet. A successful maneuver, agility and speed have allowed me to approach my quarry.

But what's this? Tracers fly at him – it is clear that my wingman was over-eager! I angrily curse Titarenko under my breath, for I am certain that my plan of action has now been irretrievably ruined. But his tracers unexpectedly help me, as the German pilot begins to turn to the left – in my direction. The distance sharply narrows and I close with the enemy. With uncontrolled agitation, I open fire, and the Messerschmitt 262 literally falls apart and pieces tumble earthwards.[14] "

ABOVE: To prevent destruction by Allied bombers the Me 262 was frequently constructed underground, in this instance in an underground workshop in the moutainous region of Thüringia. (Bundesarchiv, Bild 141-2738)

V-WEAPONS

As the war began to turn against Hitler, he became increasingly focused on the development of *Vergeltungswaffen* (retaliation weapons), technologies that would give Germany back the tactical and strategic advantage. Several weapons were conceived under this category, but the most famous and influential were the V-1 flying bomb and the V-2 ballistic missile.

VENGEANCE WEAPONS

The V-1 was the first to appear, which went into production in 1943. In summary, the V-1 was a pilotless aircraft powered by a top-mounted pulse-jet engine, with a large warhead in its nose. It had an operational range of just 150 miles (240km), and was launched from either a ramp or dropped by a specially modified bomber. Launched in the direction of the objective, the V-1 was "guided" towards its target by gyroscopic means. An odometer determined when the V-1 had reached the target, at which point it put the bomb into a steep dive to the impact point.

Between June 13, 1944, and the end of the war more than 10,000 V-1s were fired at England, although only 3,531 of these actually struck home – the rest suffered from either mechanical failure or were shot down by British fighters or anti-aircraft defenses. In total, they killed 6,184 people and injured nearly 18,000. Combined with their relative cheapness, and the fact that they had tied down significant numbers of British fighter

OPPOSITE: V-2s were often constructed in tunnels to keep them hidden from the Allies. Here a V-2 is under construction in Mittlewerk tunnel. (NARA)

aircraft, they can be classed as reasonably effective, although their results paled into insignificance when compared with the Allied strategic bombing campaign.

BALLISTIC MISSILE

The V-2 weapon was radically different to the V-1. A towering missile measuring 46ft 1in (14.04m) high, it was fired in a long ballistic trajectory to a maximum velocity of 3,600mph (5,750km/h) and an altitude that took it to the edge of space. It carried a massive 2,150lb (975kg) warhead to a maximum range of 200 miles (320km).

On paper, the V-2 had much to recommend it. There was simply no defense against a V-2, which would plunge to earth in complete silence at well beyond the speed of sound. It was powered by alcohol and liquid oxygen, the rockets burning for just over a minute, with gyroscopes and accelerometers again providing guidance. At a pre-set height, the engines would cut out, and the V-2 would continue to the target in ballistic free fall.

ABOVE: A V-2 missile ready for launch. (NARA)

BELOW: The devastation caused by one of the first V-1 rockets to hit London. Kentish Town, June 19, 1944. (Mirrorpix)

" *It was a cigar-shaped thing with a fin and a flame belching out of the back and a terrible humming noise.* "

John Brasier, V-1 attack eyewitness

Production of the V-2 began in earnest in May 1944, and England received its first strike on September 8, 1944. Thereafter, more than 3,000 V-2s were fired at the UK and other Western European targets, particularly Antwerp, although it should be noted that there was about a 10 percent mechanical failure rate. A total of 2,754 Londoners were killed by the missiles, and 6,523 wounded.

The V-2 program cost far more time and money than Germany could actually afford at that stage of the war, and in the big picture that investment did not bring significant strategic dividends. What the V-weapons did achieve,

ABOVE: A V-1 flying bomb on its way to London during the "Little Blitz" of 1944. (NARA)

RIGHT: A V-1 with only partial damage discovered by the USAAF Ninth Air Force in northern France. (Military History Institute)

FI-103A-1 V-1 FLYING BOMB – SPECIFICATIONS

Length: 25ft 4in (7.73m)
Wingspan: 17ft 6in (5.33m)
Warhead: 1,870lbs (850kg) Amatol high explosive
Maximum cruising speed: 415mph at 4,500ft
    (7,670km/hr at 1,375m)
Maximum range: 125–130 miles (200–210km)

GUARDS CHAPEL INCIDENT

On Sunday June 18, 1944, a large congregation of civilian and military worshippers had gathered at the Guards Chapel, Wellington Barracks, near Buckingham Palace in London for morning worship. At 11.20am, the chapel was hit largely without warning by a V-1 flying bomb, which in a matter of seconds reduced the building to a massive pile of rubble. Emergency rescue teams rushed to the scene, and started to pull or dig people from the rubble, a process that took 48 hours to complete. The final casualty list was 121 people killed and 141 seriously injured. Incidents such as this reinforced the British government's commitment to devoting significant air resources to the V-weapon threat.

however, was to reveal to the world the potential for the conduct of future warfare via long-range missiles. A total of 127 German engineers involved in the V-weapons programs moved to the United States, where they helped the Americans develop the PGM-11 Redstone nuclear-armed ballistic missile, which was descended from the V-2 and went into service in 1958. The Soviets also acquired V-2 engineers and examples, and indeed manufactured two types of ballistic missile – the R1 and R2 – based directly on the V-2 design. The V-1 also informed postwar missile technology, providing a conceptual start for surface-to-surface tactical cruise missiles such as the US MGM-1 Matador cruiser and MGM-13 Mace. The V-weapons had not affected the outcome of the world war, but they did shape the nature of the Cold War.

V-2 BALLISTIC MISSILE – SPECIFICATIONS

Length: 45.9ft (14m)

Warhead: 2,150lb (975kg) blast warhead with impact fusing with 1,609lb (730kg) cast 60/40 Amatol high explosive filling

Maximum speed: 171 miles/sec (275km/sec) at engine cut-off; 132 miles/sec (212km/sec) at apogee; 184 miles/sec (296km/sec) at re-entry; 129 miles/sec (207km/sec) at impact; 330 seconds flight time

Maximum range: 195 miles (314km)

ATOMIC BOMB

THEORETICAL INVESTIGATIONS INTO THE POSSIBILITIES of releasing energy from atoms began in the early 1900s. Yet although this theory was taken to an advanced level in Europe, it would be the United States who would pick up the theory and transform it into weaponry. Once that occurred, the political and strategic history of the world would never be the same again.

MANHATTAN PROJECT

The race to build an atomic bomb began in earnest in 1939. In August that year, the world's greatest physicist, Albert Einstein, warned the US President, Franklin D. Roosevelt that Germany was actively pursuing the development of atomic weaponry, and that the first country that succeeded would effectively become the world's dominant power. The message, brought to Einstein by scientists Leo Szilard, Eugene Wigner, and Edward Teller, galvanized the US administration into action.

In 1942, the innocuously titled "Manhattan Engineer Project" was created. This would be one of the largest and most costly industrial projects in history, whose sole purpose was to create the world's first atomic weapon. Under the overall control of ruthlessly efficient military engineer Colonel Leslie R. Groves, the project brought together the greatest scientific minds from across Europe and the United States. The challenges not only included creating a working bomb – a project of breathtaking complexity in itself – but also how to produce enough suitable uranium and plutonium to achieve the "critical mass" necessary for an explosion.

OPPOSITE: A replica of "Little Boy" on display at the National Museum of the US Air Force at Wright Patterson AFB, Dayton, Ohio. "Little Boy" was a gun-type fission weapon, which used explosive charges to fire a sub-critical uranium bullet onto a sub-critical cylinder, the sudden combination of the two resulting in critical mass and an atomic explosion. (Alamy Ltd.)

ABOVE: The air and ground crews of the B-29 *Enola Gay*, which dropped the world's first atomic bomb. (Photograph by George E. Staley/National Air & Space Museum Archives/Smithsonian Images)

Unlike many postwar nuclear weapons, the first atomic bombs were fission devices, which worked by splitting an atom of uranium-235 and plutonium-239 with a single neutron. The splitting of the atom released neutrons, which in turn bombarded more nuclei, creating a chain reaction that released enormous amounts of energy. The culmination of the Manhattan Project's work came on July 16, 1945, in the New Mexico desert, when a test plutonium device was detonated with the force of 22,000 short tons (22 kilotons) of TNT.

DROPPING THE BOMB

The inauguration of atomic warfare came on August 6, 1945, when the uranium bomb "Little Boy," dropped by the B-29 *Enola Gay*, detonated about 1,900ft (580m) above the Japanese city of Hiroshima. With a fireball hotter than the sun, and a blast of 13 kilotons yield, the bomb killed 70,000 people in one searing instant and utterly destroyed 4.7 square miles

(12km²) of the city. Tens of thousands more people would die over the coming months, from burn injuries and a key after-effect of atomic weaponry – radiation poisoning. Three days later, Nagasaki suffered a similar fate from a plutonium bomb, "Fat Man." For the US, the bombings had the intended effect, forcing the unconditional surrender of Japan.

Postwar international politics was dominated by atomic and nuclear weaponry, the latter using atomic fusion rather than fission to release energy, and in so doing creating weapons with yields measured in megatons rather than kilotons. Military commanders argued over the applications of atomic weaponry, particularly as more nations detonated their first atomic test devices – the Soviet Union in 1949, Great Britain in 1952, France in 1960, China in 1964, and India in 1974 – and entered the nuclear club. Nuclear weapons were developed for both strategic and tactical use, as well as having anti-ship and anti-submarine applications, some early commanders seeing such devices as nothing more than extensions of the regular military arsenal. The US came close to using atomic bombs again during the Korean War (1950–53), but thereafter nuclear weapons became part of the massive Cold War stand-off, each side having vast arsenals of missile-launched warheads capable of laying waste to entire continents. Thankfully for humanity, the Soviet Union and the West never went to war in this context, but the threat of nuclear conflict, possible in terrorist hands or through "rogue states" such as North Korea and Iran, has never gone away.

LEFT: A pillar of smoke after the bombing of Nagasaki on August 9, 1945. The mushroom cloud rose for 11 miles (18km) into the atmosphere. (Library of Congress)

BELOW: The devastation at Nagasaki, a full two months after "Fat Man" hit. (Alamy Ltd.)

OPPOSITE, LEFT: Nagasaki and Hiroshima pointed to the future. Testing at Bikini Atoll, July 1946. (Library of Congress)

OPPOSITE, RIGHT: Colonel Paul Tibbets, the pilot of the *Enola Gay*, waves to photographers as he prepares to take-off on August 6, 1945. (Alamy Ltd.)

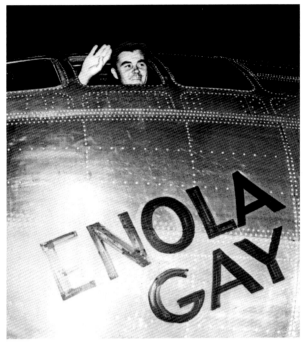

ATOMIC EFFECTS

The following is part of a US report entitled *Strategic Bombing Survey* published on July 1, 1946, for the US government. Here it describes the experience of the Hiroshima bomb from the ground:

" Eyewitness accounts of the explosion all describe similar pictures. The bombs exploded with a tremendous flash of blue-white light, like a giant magnesium flare. The flash was of short duration and accompanied by intense glare and heat. It was followed by a tremendous pressure wave and the rumbling sound of the explosion. This sound is not clearly recollected by those who survived near the center of the explosion, although it was clearly heard by others as much as fifteen miles away. A huge snow-white cloud shot rapidly into the sky and the scene on the ground was obscured first by a bluish haze and then by a purple-brown cloud of dust and smoke...

The duration of the flash was only a fraction of a second, but it was sufficiently intense to cause third degree burns to exposed human skin up to a distance of a mile. Clothing ignited, though it could be quickly beaten out, telephone poles charred, thatchroofed houses caught fire. Black or other dark-colored surfaces of combustible material absorbed the heat and immediately charred or burst into flames; white or light-colored surfaces reflected a substantial portion of the rays and were not consumed. Heavy black clay tiles which are an almost universal feature of the roofs of Japanese houses bubbled at distances up to a mile. Test of samples of this tile by the National Bureau of Standards in Washington indicates that temperatures in excess of 1,800°C must have been generated in the surface of the tile to produce such an effect. The surfaces of granite blocks exposed to the flash scarred and spalled at distances up to almost a mile. In the immediate area of ground zero (the point on the ground immediately below the explosion), the heat charred corpses beyond recognition. "

MODERN WARFARE
1945–PRESENT

AK47

THE AK47 IS ARGUABLY THE MOST INFLUENTIAL weapon in history. It is certainly the most widely distributed, with more than 80 million AKs and variants sold or issued around the world since the gun was first introduced in 1947.

OPPOSITE: The AK47 is so simple to use even children wield it. Here an Acehnese boy carries his AK47 during military training in the jungles of the Pidie district, Aceh, Indonesia. A weapon designed to service the needs of the Red Army has become the weapon of choice for armies and insurgents throughout the Third World. (AFP/Getty Images)

ASSAULT RIFLE

In the early 1940s, German gun designers created a radical new type of infantry weapon – the "assault rifle." Up until this point, there were essentially two types of standard infantry firearm. Rifles fired full-power rifle cartridges, which gave ranges in excess of 1,000yds (914m), but with a powerful recoil unsuited to hand-held automatic fire. Submachine-guns, by contrast,

delivered controllable full-auto fire through using pistol ammunition, but had a short effective range up to about 100yds (91m). A German study of actual combat conditions, however, concluded that fighting ranges rarely exceeded a few hundred yards – beyond such distances it was difficult for a soldier to see the target, let alone shoot it.

For this reason, the Germans developed a new "intermediate" cartridge – the 7.92 x 33mm *Kurz* (short) – which gave rifle-like performance over practical ranges, but with low enough recoil for full-auto fire. Several weapons were produced for the cartridge, including the famous Sturmgewehr MP44, which bore a passing resemblance to the future design ascribed to Mikhail Kalashnikov.

SIMPLE MASTERPIECE

The traditional story of the creation of the AK47 is centered squarely upon the figure of Kalashnikov. It states that while he was recovering from injuries received during the battle of Bryansk in October 1941, this Red Army sergeant began the conceptual journey to design an assault rifle based around a new

AK47 – SPECIFICATIONS

Caliber: 7.62 x 39mm
Operation: Gas
Length (stock extended): 34.25in (870mm)
Barrel: 16.37in (416mm)
Weight (empty): 8.59lb (3.90kg)
Magazine: 30 rounds
Cyclic rate: 600rpm
Muzzle velocity: 2,300ft/sec (710m/sec)

intermediate Soviet cartridge, the 7.62 x 39mm M1943. In January 1948, this rifle – the AK47 – won the design contest to become the Red Army's new standard infantry rifle. Recent research by historians such as C.J. Chivers, however, has

BELOW: In what is possibly a staged photograph, North Vietnamese Army troops are shown assaulting a South Vietnamese military position. The AK was a mainstay of the north throughout the Vietnam War. (Tom Laemlein)

ABOVE: A cutaway illustration of the 7.62mm AKM assault rifle showing the detail of the 30-round magazine as well as the bolt and firing pin. The AKM was a simplified, lighter version of the AK47 developed in the early 1950s. (Artwork by Alan Gilliland © Osprey Publishing Ltd.)

BELOW: The AK47 has been developed into a myriad of different varieties and is still in use the world over. Here a Kalahnikov-type rifle fitted with a grenade-launcher is used in a house-clearing exercise (those are only role-players in the background) in Iraq. (Tom Laemlein)

revealed the creation of the AK47 more as a collective Soviet state enterprise. Whatever the origins, however, there was no doubting the significance of what finally emerged.

The AK47 is actually a very basic weapon. It is gas-operated, with a rotating-bolt mechanism. Full-auto rate of fire from a curved 30-round box magazine is 600rpm. Its one sophistication is a chromium lined bore, to better withstand wear. The AKM version issued from 1959, simplified the production process, and later included an angular muzzle compensator. Accurate range is short – about 274yds (300m). Nothing is particularly impressive about these statistics.

ULTIMATE RELIABILITY

Alan James, a young officer serving with the Rhodesian African Rifles during the brutal bush war in Rhodesia in the late 1970s/early 1980s, recounts the following incident, a stunning testimony to the AK's reliability:

“ On the Zambezi River, they [the ZAPU insurgents] had a river crossing from Zambia. They came across in dinghies, and we had a contact with them as they hit the shoreline. Lots of them went into the water with their packs and all the rest of it, most of them couldn't swim … but once the contact was over anything that was lost in the river obviously you couldn't see it or retrieve it. Six months later we were coming along that same stretch of river – remember it was the dry season – and we saw the butt of an AK47 sticking out of the sand … still in the water. We pulled it out and the magazine was still in it. It was on fire and was actually on automatic. We got the magazine out, but we couldn't clear the breech [i.e. pull back the cocking handle to empty the round in the chamber]. We tried to kick it … we kicked it several times but it was solid. So we put the magazine back in and pulled the trigger and it fired all 30 rounds. ”

ABOVE: A member of the Popular Front for the Liberation of Palestine reassembles a Kalashnikov assault rifle in Jordan in early 1969. (Library of Congress/*Look* Magazine Photograph Collection)

Where the AK excels, however, is its awesome reliability. Unlike most other assault rifles, the AK can be severely contaminated by dirt, snow, water, and all manner of debris, and it will keep working. It is simple to strip and maintain, and its fire over its practical range is devastating. In short, here is a gun to inspire confidence.

The virtues of the AK, as noted, mean that it has been made and distributed in greater numbers than any other weapon in history. Just in an official capacity, more than 60 countries have adopted the weapon, while illegal distribution has ensured its status as the number one terrorist and insurgent firearm in the world. It has spawned numerous variants and copies, including the Chinese Type 56 – a direct AKM copy also produced in the millions – and the AK74 version in 5.45 x 39mm caliber. AKs alone have made entire wars and insurgencies possible, and literally millions of postwar deaths have been dealt by the gun. Kalashnikov certainly gave the Red Army the weapon it needed. In doing so, unfortunately, he also created what is today one of the world's greatest security issues.

UZI

Few modern firearms have achieved the iconic status of the Uzi. It was designed in Israel in the late 1940s and early 1950s by Lieutenant Uziel Gal, an officer in the Israeli Army. The War of Independence of 1948 had just ended, but the Israeli military was eager to acquire a standard-issue submachine-gun, rather than rely on the hotchpotch of war surplus designs it currently had in stock.

TELESCOPING BOLT

When Gal was looking around for inspiration, he was attracted to an earlier Czech design, the CZ 23 (and its variants). The CZ 23 had two distinct innovations. First, the "telescoping" bolt was tubular at the front, wrapping around the rear end of the barrel when ready to fire. This design allowed the overall dimensions of the gun to be reduced, while keeping the barrel long enough to provide useful ballistic performance. The second feature was that the magazine slotted directly up through the hollow pistol grip, again reducing the dimensions of the gun while also giving the weapon a focused center of balance.

Gal reworked and perfected these two elements in a blowback submachine-gun that referred to his name, the Uzi. The Uzi was cheap and quick to produce, ideal for a country with a developing industrial base, as the outer body was a simple metal pressing. Ingeniously, Gal created several recesses in this body

OPPOSITE: General Chaim Bar-Lev, Chief of Staff for the Israeli Defense Force, inspects Israeli tank crewmen armed with Uzis shortly before the Yom Kippur War, 1973. (IDF Archive)

to catch sand, dirt, and debris, keeping it away from the internal workings. These features created an extremely reliable weapon for Middle Eastern warfare. (Although the gun will, like any weapon, jam if the contamination is severe enough.) The stock was either a fixed wooden or folding wire version. With the wire stock folded, the gun measured just 18.5in (470mm) long, creating a concealable, portable weapon.

HAND-HELD FIREPOWER

What really defined the Uzi, however, was its firepower. With a cyclical rate of fire of 600rpm, it could empty its 25- or 32-round magazine of 9mm Parabellum rounds in just seconds, giving it a lethal close-quarters punch. (It can also fire semi-auto.) Yet its balance around the pistol grip made such fire perfectly controllable.

ABOVE: The Brazilian armed forces are among the Latin American military users of the Uzi. Here, a visit, board, search and seizure team of the frigate Independencia rappel onto their ship during a training exercise. (US Navy)

BELOW: An Uzi submachine-gun with stock folded. (istock)

ABOVE: Israeli Defence Force soldiers on exercises in the Neguev Desert, near the Egyptian border *c.* 1997.
(© Antoine Gyori/Sygma/Corbis)

UZI – SPECIFICATIONS

Caliber: 9 x 19mm Parabellum
Operation: Blowback
Length (stock folded): 18.5in (470mm)
Length (stock extended): 25.6in (650mm)
Barrel: 10.23in (260mm), 4 groove, r/hand
Weight (empty): 8.15lb (3.7kg)
Magazine: 25- or 32-shot detachable box magazine
Cyclical rate: 600rpm
Muzzle velocity: 1,312ft/sec (400m/sec)

The Uzi was utterly convincing, and became one of the most prolific submachine-guns in postwar history. Designed in 1948, it was issued to the Israeli Army from 1951, and was first battle-tested in the 1956 Suez campaign. Thereafter it saw service in every major Israeli conflict, where it proved ideal for clearing confined enemy positions, such as those encountered on the Golan Heights during the 1967 Six-Day War. Mechanized infantry also appreciated the weapon, which was convenient to store within an armored vehicle.

Numerous other armies took on the gun, yet Uzis have also had widespread distribution to international police and security forces, from the US secret service and SWAT teams through to Sri Lankan special forces. "Mini" and "Micro" versions are available, both of reduced dimensions but increased rates of fire. The Micro-Uzi, for example, measures just 9.84in (250mm) with the stock folded and fires at 1,250rpm. Whatever the variant, the Uzi encapsulates everything a successful submachine-gun should offer – firepower, reliability, and ease of handling.

B-52 STRATOFORTRESS

Today the B-52 Stratofortress appears as a relic of another age, which in many ways it is. As the longest-serving aircraft in the US arsenal, however, it still manages to make itself relevant to conflicts very different to that for which it was conceived.

STRATEGIC BOMBER

With the atomic age still in its infancy, the Boeing B-52 Stratofortress was intended as a long-range bomber for the US Strategic Air Command (SAC). Slated as a replacement for the Convair B-36, it was pictured flying intercontinental missions into the heart of the Soviet Union, there to deploy atomic weapons against key cities and military installations.

When the first prototype flew on April 15, 1952, onlookers were treated to an astonishing sight. It was a vast aircraft standing 48ft 4in (14.7m) high, 157ft (48m) long, and powered by eight Pratt & Whitney turbojet engines. Range in the production versions could exceed 8,000 miles (12,875km). Here was air power at its most majestic.

B-52s began entering USAF service in 1954. Predictably, given its time in service, there have been a succession of variants and upgrades, as avionics, weapons systems, electronic countermeasures (ECM), and other systems have been

OPPOSITE: A B-52 leaves behind its trademark dense black smoke trails as it takes off. This particular aircraft, a B-52G-95-BW (58-0159), flew out of Jeddah, Saudi Arabia was part of the bombing campaign of Operation *Desert Storm*. (Courtesy of Jon Lake)

ABOVE: A B-52 flies over the Pacific Ocean on a routine training mission. (USAF)

BELOW: In one of the best known images of the Vietnam War a-B-52 drops a stick of 500lb Mk 82 bombs. This aircraft (B-52D-60-BO 55-0100) amassed an astonishing 5,000 combat hours during the Vietnam War alone before it was retired from active service. (Courtesy of Robert F. Dorr)

improved. The B-52G, for example, received an increased internal fuel capacity, shortened tailplane, plus was adapted to launch two North American GAM-77 (AGM-28) Hound Dog stand-off missiles, AG-69A short-range attack missiles (SRAMs), or (from 1976) AGM-86 air-launched cruise missiles (ALCMs). Like its predecessors, it featured four 0.5in machine-guns in its tail position, but these were now operated remotely by a gunner stationed up in the main crew compartment. The last version is the B-52H, which replaced the four tail guns with a single 20mm cannon.

CONVENTIONAL STRIKES

The expanding US conflict in Vietnam during the 1960s brought B-52s into the role of conventional rather than nuclear bombers. The "Big Belly" modification program from 1965 in particular gave the B-52D a truly awesome carpet-bombing capability. A B-52D with the modification could carry up to 108 500lb (252kg) bombs, but other variants also conducted heavy bombing raids. Used against

North Vietnam, Cambodia, and Laos, the B-52s left a trail of devastation, particularly in the great "Linebacker" raids of 1972 – 20,000 short tons (18,143 tonnes) of bombs were dropped on Hanoi and Haiphong alone during *Linebacker II* (December 18–29, 1972).

In Vietnam, the B-52 had demonstrated that carpet-bombing still had a place in the age of precision bombs and missiles, and in so-called "limited" conflicts. Their utility in this role has persisted. In the Gulf War of 1990–91, B-52Gs flew a total of 1,624 missions (flying from Saudi Arabia, Spain, and England) to drop 25,700 short tons (23,315 tonnes) of conventional bombs on Iraqi troop positions and industrial targets. Most recently, since 2001 B-52s have hit remote targets in both Afghanistan and Iraq.

BELOW: Few other weapons in the 20th century have seen such extensive service as the B-52. First introduced into active service in 1954, it has also been deployed on bombing missions deep within Iraq and Afghanistan over 50 years later. (Courtesy of Jon Lake)

BOMBING EFFECTS

A B-52 carpet-bombing strike can destroy almost everything within a corridor a mile long and half a mile wide. Here Sam Ryskind, a soldier who served in the Gulf War of 1990–91, remembers witnessing a B-52 raid in the distance:

“ As I sat in my foxhole, this bombardment was taking place eight to 12 miles [12–19km] away. These planes were flying over, non-stop. And from where I was, I couldn't see the bombs dropping, but I could feel the "boom, boom, boom-boom, boom," coming down. After a day or two of this – it was incessant – I was thinking, "If I can feel this here; what is it like to be right under it?" I could feel the deep explosions, the rumbling like a low-frequency vibration, making things tremble. [The sound] wasn't coming from the air; it was the whole ground that was emitting this sound. It is extremely hard to imagine how people could endure it. ”

The carpet bombing strategy is crude (although the B-52 can also drop precision-guided munitions [PGMs]), but its enormously destructive effects on men, materiel, and morale keep several hundred B-52s in service. Indeed, while the USAF currently works on its Next-Generation Bomber projects, a retirement date for the B-52H is provisionally set for 2040. Exactly how long they will remain so is unclear, but after more than a half-century of service and with several more decades of service guaranteed, their place in aviation history is assured.

ABOVE: With a white livery due to its previous role at the USAF Test Centre, this aircraft was nicknamed "Snow Bird." It then served during Operation *Desert Storm*. Here it is shown launching a test round from its bomb bay. USAF pilots will continue to train on B-52s for several years to come, with a planned retirement date currently only set for 2040. (Courtesy of Jon Lake)

USS *NAUTILUS*

As World War II ended, one of the lingering limitations on submarines was their diesel powerplant. Diesel engines require oxygen to work, so when a submarine was submerged it was driven by one or two hours of electrical power, stored in batteries. Tactically, this meant that much of a submarine's working life was spent on the surface, where it was vulnerable to air attack, and only submerged during an immediate attack run. Once submerged, furthermore, the submarine commander had to maintain a slow ship speed to avoid draining the battery too rapidly, hence it struggled to engage faster-moving warships.

NUCLEAR SOLUTION

During the last two years of World War II, the German *Kriegsmarine* tackled this problem by introducing a *Schnorkel* breathing tube on some U-boats, which provided the engines with oxygen when the submarine was at periscope depth. After the war, however, the United States took a bolder approach. The US Atomic Energy Commission, formed in 1946, and the Westinghouse Electrical Company, took on the challenge of a nuclear propulsion system for submarine use. Westinghouse produced the pressurized water-cooled S2W reactor, and the submarine to take it was commissioned.

USS *Nautilus* (SSN-571), the world's first nuclear-powered submarine, was launched on January 21, 1954. It is difficult to overstate the revolution in submarine warfare that it represented. Nuclear powerplants need no oxygen to function, and enriched uranium fuel can sustain power for periods of time measured in years, not hours. Combined with onboard air-purifying and drinking water production equipment, nuclear power meant that submarines could stay submerged almost indefinitely, and run at high speeds.

From the outset, USS *Nautilus* demonstrated this shift in capabilities. In 1955, on its inaugural cruise, *Nautilus* made a

OPPOSITE: USS *Nautilus* returns home after her stunning crossing from the Pacific to the Atlantic under the Arctic ice. She was the first submarine to successfully make this voyage, a journey that has since been repeated by countless submarines. (US Navy)

THE SINKING OF THE *BELGRANO*

On April 30, 1982, the nuclear-powered hunter-killer submarine HMS *Conqueror* was making protective patrols around the British naval task force heading to retake the Falkland Islands from the Argentines. It detected the venerable Argentine cruiser ARA *General Belgrano*, which was outside the British-imposed Total Exclusion Zone established around the islands. Despite its position, the cruiser was deemed a threat to the British ships, so the *Conqueror*'s commander, Chris Wreford-Brown, was ordered to make an attack. On May 2, therefore, the submarine fired a spread of three conventional torpedoes at the *Belgrano*, two of which struck home, one at the bow, and the next just forward of the stern. The second torpedo did the most damage, killing an estimated 275 men in the explosion. *Belgrano* began to sink, and the abandon ship order was given 20 minutes after the torpedoes struck. The total death toll was 323 sailors. This incident is the only occasion to date in which a nuclear-powered submarine has sunk another ship in a torpedo attack.

submerged voyage of nearly 1,400 miles (2,253km) in less than 90 hours, and in July–August 1958 she sailed across the entire circumference of the North Pole, traveling 1,830 miles (2,945km) under the polar ice. The submarine would stay in service until 1980, and by the time it was decommissioned it had sailed half a million miles.

STRATEGIC EFFECTS

Nautilus inspired other nations to construct their own nuclear submarines, at first the Soviet Union, France, and Britain, but later China and India. In the late 1950s, submarine-launched ballistic missiles (SLBMs) were introduced with the US *George Washington* class, each submarine carrying 16 Polaris nuclear missiles with a range of 1,200 miles (1,931km). The Soviets acquired similar capabilities during the 1960s, and since then the strategic reach of submarines has increased dramatically. The Trident-missile equipped *Lafayette* (US) and *Resolution* (UK) class vessels can hit targets at ranges of 7,500 miles (12,069km). Fast-attack submarines like the US *Los Angeles* class, by contrast, can deploy Tomahawk cruise missiles, Harpoon anti-ship missiles (ASMs), and active homing torpedoes.

BELOW: A UUM-44 SubRoc missile launches into the air from a submerged submarine. These long-range nuclear-armed anti-submarine missiles were deployed on all US nuclear submarines between 1965 and 1989, and gave the United States a critical first-strike and counter-response capability against enemy submarines. (US Navy)

ABOVE: A fast attack nuclear submarine on the surface. The fast attack sub was used for surveillance and reconnaissance, primarily during the Cold War to watch for a break out of the Soviet Navy. (US Navy)

OPPOSITE PAGE (TOP): *Nautilus* in a dry dock being overhauled. (US Navy)

BELOW: USS *Nautilus* (SSN-571). (Artwork by Tony Bryan © Osprey Publishing Ltd.)

Nuclear submarines have changed the balance of world power. As a result of their formidable underwater endurance – with appropriate food supplies, the latest subs can stay underwater for up to six months. They patrol the world unseen, ready to deliver nuclear-tipped or powerful conventional strikes at a moment's notice. By sitting deep underwater, they also stay beyond the reach of all but the most specialist detection technologies. Whether such vessels have made the world a safer place remains to be seen.

UH-1 HUEY

ROTARY-WING FLIGHT TOOK ITS FIRST TOTTERING STEPS in the early years of the 20th century, and by the last years of World War II military helicopters were making a limited appearance from the likes of Sikorsky and Hiller. The end of what had been an almost entirely fixed-wing war, however, galvanized interest in helicopter. Helicopters offered numerous potential tactical advantages, particularly in the realms of infantry assault, medevac, cargo lift, or shipboard deployment. Helicopters such as the Vought-Sikorsky R-4, R-5, R-6, S-55, and S-56, the Piasecki H-21 and HUP Retriever, the Hiller H-23, and the Bell Model 47, all piston-engined designs, gave the United States its first rotary-winged capability. Yet it was Bell's UH-1 that truly established the age of combat helicopters.

OPPOSITE: The US Navy made extensive use of Hueys during the so-called "Brown Water" war in the Mekong Delta during the Vietnam War. In particular, Hueys were used to interdict water-borne supply traffic and also to insert Special Forces teams deep into enemy-held territory, as shown here. (US Navy)

BIRTH OF THE "HUEY"

The Bell UH-1 evolved from a US Army contract to develop a new, turbine-powered medevac helicopter. Turbine engines offered far more power than piston engines, and were also lighter, and Bell already had some experience of turbine designs in upgrades of its Model 47. The resulting Model 204/XH-40 prototype first flew on October 22, 1956, powered by a Lycoming T53-L-1 turboshaft delivering 700shp (522kW) and lifted by a two-blade rotor. US Army impressions of this helicopter, another

evaluation aircraft (the YH-40), and pre-production models were favorable, and the first production order was for 183 Bell HU-1As – the letter designation spawned the infamous "Huey" nickname, which stuck even after redesignation to UH-1A in 1962.

The subsequent history of UH-1 variants is long and complex, with multiple versions produced for the US Army, Navy, and Marine Corps as well as dozens of export models. A major development was the Model 205 UH-1D, a stretched variant that also led to the UH-1H, with its more powerful engine. Regardless of variant, all users were won over by the spacious passenger cabin, rugged reliability, good flying characteristics, speed of around 127mph (204km/h), and decent lift capability. In the context of the Vietnam War, it also became a ground-breaking assault helicopter.

UPGUNNED

UH-1 helicopters became the US forces' workhorse during the Vietnam War. From the very outset of the conflict, US troops

ABOVE: Infantrymen disembark from a Huey, Vietnam, 1967. (Corbis)

BELOW: Experiments in 1962 showed that the helicopter could introduce a quantum leap in battlefield mobility when compared to ground-based transport, allowing men and machines to be moved with unprecedented speed. (TRH pictures)

ABOVE: Vietnam was a true helicopter war, with UH-1s helping to revolutionize American tactics through gunship conversions and rapid airborne infantry deployments. These are Hueys from the 1st Cavalry Division (Airmobile), delivering troops to a small village near Bong Son during Operation *Eagle Claw* in February 1966. (US Marine Corps)

began field fitting the helicopters with weaponry such as a door-mounted Brownings, or M60 machine-guns, or twin pods of 2.75in unguided rockets. Such weaponry proved extremely useful for, say, suppressing enemy troops around a "hot" landing zone or self-defense during a medevac operation. By fitting the helicopters so (even pure utility helicopters acquired armament), US troops in effect created the world's first helicopter gunships.

BELL UH-1H – SPECIFICATIONS

Type: Utility/assault helicopter
Powerplant: 1 x Avco Lycoming T53-L-13 turboshaft
    delivering 1,400hp (1,044kW)
Length (rotor stowed): 57ft 9.5in (17.61m)
Height: 14ft 6in (4.42m)
Main rotor diameter: 48ft (14.63m)
Maximum speed: 127mph (204km/h)
Range: 318 miles (512km)
Weight (empty): 5,210lb (2,362kg)
Weight (max take-off): 9,500lb (4,309kg)
Armament: various, but basic configuration of two
    7.62mm machine-guns

Simply bolting weapons to a helicopter, however, could reduce its performance. In response, Bell introduced the UH-1C in 1965, a dedicated gunship variant which had the power and systems to cope with the weaponry. Bell was, at this time, also about to introduce the AH-1 HueyCobra gunship, but throughout the war UH-1s continued to serve as assault and gunship helicopters, not least on account of the thousands of them deployed. Weapons mounted on UH-1s included M75 40mm automatic grenade launchers, TOW anti-tank missiles, and GE M134 six-barreled 7.62mm MiniGuns, firing at 2,000rpm.

UH-1s paid a heavy price in Vietnam – 2,591 were lost in combat or in accidents. Yet they gave US troops true air mobility, deploying and extracting troops and thereby saving them long, dangerous journeys by foot or vehicle to the combat zones. Since Vietnam, UH-1s have remained in service throughout the world, and are operated by more than 60 air forces who also recognize its qualities.

BELOW: One of the original roles envisaged for the Huey was as a medical evacuation helicopter and in that role it saved thousands of lives in Vietnam. Here, a US Army UH-1D evacuates the wounded from an armored troop carrier during the riverine campaign in the Mekong Delta. (US Army)

SA-2 "GUIDELINE"

ALTHOUGH ANTI-AIRCRAFT GUNS CLAIMED THOUSANDS of aircraft during World War II, postwar militaries looking for more precise ways in which to down enemy aircraft, particularly the new generation of fast-moving jets. During the 1950s and 1960s, therefore, emerged the first generations of operational surface-to-air missiles (SAMs).

MISSILE DEFENSE

After 1945, the Soviets were the most active nation in developing SAM systems, the first being the radar-guided S-25 Berkut (NATO reporting name: SA-1 "Guild"). Eager to protect themselves from possible atomic-tipped US air attacks, the Soviets subsequently produced a broad range of SAM types to cover all altitudes and ranges, including the low-altitude SA-3 "Goa" and long-range mobile systems such as the SA-4 "Ganef."

The S-75 Dvina – better known by its NATO reporting name SA-2 "Guideline" – fitted into this arsenal as a medium- to high-altitude SAM. It was introduced in 1958, and went on to become the core of Soviet air defense between the 1960s to the 1980s. Through major modification programs at regular intervals, however, the missile has remained on active service in small numbers in the Russian Federation, and in several other states.

The SA-2 is a big missile, 35ft 5in (10.8m) tall – hence it was nicknamed the "flying telegraph pole" by US pilots during the Vietnam War. It has a range of 31 miles (50km) and a lofty operating

OPPOSITE: Shortly after the SA-2 (referred to as the S-75 in the USSR) entering production, the Soviets looked for ways to improve its capabilities. The 17D missile shown here was developed to try to increase the range and altitude but the project was ultimately abandoned. (Courtesy of Steve Zaloga)

altitude of 92,000ft (28,000m), driven by a two-stage rocket motor. The business end of the missile contains a 429lb (195kg) high-explosive warhead, which can be contact, proximity, or command detonated, depending on the type of fuse. The blast from the warhead could destroy or damage an aircraft within a typical kill radius of 71yds (65m). SA-2s are radio guided to their targets by signals from a missile command radar, which work in tandem with early-warning systems.

IN ACTION

Typically working in batteries of six, and with a speed of Mach 3, the Soviet SA-2s were a serious air defense proposition.

ABOVE: Although most famous for their use during the Vietnam War, so-called "Red Sams" could be used at sea as well. The Soviet Navy fitted a version of the SA-2 aboard the cruiser *Dzerzhinskiy* in 1959–62. (Courtesy of Steve Zaloga)

In 1960, the United States had a shocking introduction into their reach. On May 1, a U-2 spyplane, piloted by Gary Powers, was shot down over Sverdlovsk, Russia, despite being at extremely high altitude. Another U-2 was shot down over Cuba in October 1962. Yet the United States would meet the full challenge of the SA-2 over the skies of North Vietnam, a country that thanks to Soviet supplies had built up the most sophisticated air defense system in the world. US pilots

ABOVE: A SA-2 is towed to a new location on the PR-11 transport-loader semi-trailer. (Courtesy of Steve Zaloga)

BELOW: SA-2 missiles were widely exported, not only to North Vietnam, but throughout the Middle East. This image from the 1980s shows how the "Red Sams" were deployed in the deserts of Egypt with some protection from Israeli air attacks provided by sand berms. (Department of Defense)

attacking the North faced furious barrages of SA-2s. It was actually fairly easy for US pilots to outmaneuver the missiles if they were detected early, and anti-air-defense aircraft such as the F-4G "Wild Weasel" used the SA-2's Fang Song guidance radar emissions to deliver precise missile strikes on the SAM installations. Therefore, of literally thousands of SA-2s fired, only 150 US aircraft were downed directly by the missiles. Yet by making medium- and high-altitude flight perilous, the SA-2s forced the US aircraft to fly at lower altitudes, where they suffered heavily from conventional anti-aircraft fire.

SA-2s were also used in combat in several Middle Eastern conflicts, and it is estimated that some 13,000 have been launched in action since they first came into service. In part, they represent a changed world in air defense, in which electronic warfare became as critical to survival in the air as tactical flying skills.

ABOVE: The last major variant of the SA-2 – the Avanguard 5Ya23. (Courtesy of Steve Zaloga)

BELOW: The launch of a Guideline missile. (Courtesy of Steve Zaloga)

EARLY US SAMS

The United States also adopted a variety of SAM systems during the 1950s and 1960s. Its first was the Nike Ajax, introduced in 1954. It was command guided by computer and radar and had a range of up to 30 miles (48km) at speeds of Mach 2.3. The Ajax could tackle aircraft up to 70,000ft (21,336m), but the MIM-14 Nike Hercules, which went into service in the late 1950s, had more than double the altitude and range, and could take a nuclear warhead. (Note that the SA-2 also had nuclear warhead capability.) Other early US SAMs include the RIM-8 Talos, RIM-2 Terrier, and RIM-24 Tartar – all for naval use – but also the MIM-23 Hawk, a semi-active radar homing missile that would be the mainstay US Army/Marine Corps SAM defense until it was replaced by the MIM-104 Patriot and the FIM-92 Stinger in the 1990s. Hawks were never fired by US forces, but were used with success by export customers such as Israel and Iran in Middle Eastern conflicts.

SA-2 GUIDELINE MISSILE AND LAUNCH SYSTEM – SPECIFICATIONS

System Data
System designation: SA-75M Dvina
US/NATO designation: SA-2b Guideline Mod 1
Fire control radar: RSNA-75M (Fan Song B)
System effectiveness: 80 percent probability of kill with
    3-missile salvo (theoretical)
Missile Data
Length: 35.1ft (10.762m)
Maximum speed: Mach 3
Weight: 5,040lb (2,287kg)
Warhead: 420lb (19kg) high-explosive fragmentation
Maximum effective range: 18 miles (29km)
Maximum effective altitude: 16.7 miles (27km)

AIM-9 SIDEWINDER

WHILE THE SOVIETS TOOK THE IMMEDIATE LEAD IN many aspects of postwar missile technology, the same cannot be said for guided air-to-air missiles (AAMs). In 1953 engineers at the US Naval Weapons Center built a prototype of a new AAM. Three years later that prototype entered production as the AIM-9B Sidewinder, becoming a standard AAM of the US Navy and US Air Force. Today, more than 60 years after that weapon was introduced, modern versions of the Sidewinder are still in use as primary air defense weapons, having proved themselves in combat on hundreds of occasions.

OPPOSITE: A close-up of AIM-9J missiles beneath the wing of an F-4 Phantom. The AIM-9J was developed between 1968 and 1970, and began to replace AIM-9Es in 1972. The type saw only limited service in the Vietnam War, being credited with just three MiG kills.

HEAT-SEEKER

The Sidewinder is a heat-seeking missile, honing in on infrared radiation emitted by an aircraft's engine exhaust heat. It was purposely a short-range weapon, for use in the twists and turns of an aerial dogfight. The AIM-9B, therefore, had a range of just 1.2 miles (2km) – not dramatically different from long-range cannon fire – but this distance has steadily improved over time. The modern AIM-9X variant, for example, can engage targets up to 6 miles (10km) away.

Range is just one of the many features improved over the Sidewinder's long period in service. A critical juncture was the introduction of the AIM-9L in 1976. In previous versions, a launch aircraft had to be behind the target for the missile to acquire adequate lock-on to the jet's heat signature. The AIM-9L ushered in an enhanced infrared guidance system that could achieve lock-on even when fired to the side or front of the target aircraft. It was also fitted with an active laser proximity fuse, detonating the high-explosive/fragmentation warhead automatically when close to the enemy aircraft.

ABOVE: An F-15 strike fighter equipped with a combination of Sparrow and Sidewinders AAMs during Operation *Desert Storm*, 1991. (USAF)

Continuous upgrade programs have ensured that the AIM-9 stays relevant to modern warfare conditions. In its modern AIM-9X format, the Sidewinder includes such features as the ability to discriminate between decoy flares and aircraft exhausts (actually introduced with the AIM-9M), improved detection of low-signature targets (such as helicopters), and hi-tech interface with helmet-mounted control systems (the pilot can achieve missile lock-on simply by looking at the target).

EVOLUTION IN WAR

More than 200,000 Sidewinder missiles have been produced to date, and the system has been sold to or made under licence by at least 50 countries. Such longevity and popularity would not be possible had the AIM-9 not been thoroughly tested in combat. Yet its early use in the Vietnam War proved somewhat disappointing. Tactical inexperience with AAMs (early AAMs were intended more for intercepting bombers rather than dogfighting with MiGs), plus the poor state of some contemporary electronics, led to kills rates of about 16 percent – 175 missiles were launched between 1965 and 1968, but killed only 28 MiGs.

Refinements in the AIM-9's technology and tactics dramatically improved its kill rates during the 1970s and early 1980s, particularly with the introduction of the AIM-9. In the Falklands War in 1982, Royal Navy Sea Harriers had an 80 percent kill rate with AIM-9Ls against Argentine aircraft, and similar figures were achieved by the Israeli Air

ABOVE: An AIM-9 is fitted to an F-15C Strike Eagle during a standard NATO exercise. (USAF)

Force (IAF) in action against Syrian fighters over the Lebanon. The 1991 Gulf War saw 11 Iraqi fighters downed with Sidewinders.

The Sidewinder is undoubtedly the most influential AAM missile since 1945. Its upgrade programs have ensured that the skies remain a dangerous space for those facing this ground-breaking weapon.

AIM-9L – SPECIFICATIONS

Length: 9ft 5in (2.87m)
Body diameter: 5in (127mm)
Wingspan: 2ft 1in (0.64m)
Launch weight: 191.4lb (87kg)
Warhead: 20.9lb (9.5kg) high-explosive/fragmentation
Fuse: Active laser
Guidance system: Infrared
Propulsion: Solid propellant
Range: 5 miles (8km)

F-4 PHANTOM

SUPERLATIVES CLUSTER EASILY AROUND THE McDonnel F-4 Phantom. It was in US service for nearly 40 years, longer with some other air forces, in which time it broke numerous aviation records and excelled in combat time and time again, particularly over the skies of Vietnam in the 1960s and 1970s.

ALL-MISSILE JET

The Phantom began as a successful attempt by McDonnell (which became McDonnell Douglas in 1967, following a merger with Douglas Aircraft) to meet a US Navy requirement for a new and innovative type of aircraft – a multi-role, all-weather fighter-bomber, capable of establishing air superiority, operating as a fast interceptor, and conducting a variety of ground-attack and strike missions. From this demanding brief emerged the F-4 Phantom, the YF4H-1 prototype first flying on May 27, 1958, with the original production version for the US Navy being designated the F-4A.

The F-4 was an arresting aircraft. A two-seater aircraft with a strong, hunkering appearance, it had 12° dihedral angle in the outer wings and tailplane with 23° of anhedral, this configuration giving the aircraft maneuverability and stability. An AN/APQ-72 radar was mounted in the nose to provide an all-weather capability, and the aircraft was powered by two potent J79-GE-2 and -2A engines, each having 1,610lbf (71kN) of afterburning thrust. Most eyebrow-raising was the armament – in a complete break from tradition, the early F-4s had no cannon armament, its air-to-air capability coming purely from four Sparrow AAMs.

The Phantom was an astonishing aircraft for the time, and quickly broke 16 aviation records. In 1961, for example, it

OPPOSITE: A US Navy F-4J complete with a "MiG-killer" emblem. US Navy Phantom pilots successfully downed 17 MiGs during Operations *Linebacker I* and *II* of the Vietnam War during 1972–73. (Courtesy of Brad Elward)

BELOW: A recreation of the Phantom II that was flown by Captain Steve Richie and his navigator Captain Chuck DeBellevue during the Vietnam War. This is probably the most famous Phantom in existence as it was responsible for shooting down five MiG-21s and one MiG-19. This feat garnered "ace" status for Richie and also made the F-4 the highest-scoring US combat aircraft since the Korean War, 1950–53. (Artwork by Tom Tullis © Osprey Publishing Ltd.)

smashed the world absolute speed record when an F-4 flew at 1,606.342mph (2,585.086km/h), and in 1962 it also set numerous climb records, with figures such as 114.548 seconds to reach 49,000ft (15,000m). The performance characteristics of the Phantom were irresistible, and the US Air Force adopted the aircraft as the F-4C, taking deliveries from 1963.

COMBAT WORKHORSE

The Phantom was soon the premier aircraft of the US Navy, US Marine Corps, and US Air Force. During the 1960s and 70s, Australia, Egypt, Germany, Greece, Iran, Israel, Japan,

South Korea, Spain, Turkey, and the United Kingdom also became Phantom users. The aircraft itself went through a bewildering number of variants, both in the United States and abroad. These included the major production variant – the F-4E – plus specialist aircraft such as F-4G "Wild Weasel," used to suppress enemy air defenses.

OPPOSITE: An F-4J Phantom II shown in the typical USAF camouflage livery of the Vietnam War. (Artwork by Mark Postlethwaite © Osprey Publishing Ltd.)

MARK POSTLETHWAITE GAVA.

ABOVE: A Navy Phantom fires one of its AIM-7 Sparrow missiles.

BOTTOM RIGHT: An F-4D Phantom in flight armed with an AIM-4D Falcon missile as its secondary armament. During the Vietnam War, many US pilots lamented the absence of cannon armament in the early F-4 variants, and this was reintroduced during the 1960s.

Because of its longevity and widespread distribution, the F-4 saw combat in dozens of conflicts. Its proving ground was the Vietnam War, where it provided heavy ground-attack capability – the F-4E could carry up to 12,980lb (5,888kg) of ordnance – and also locked horns with North Vietnamese MiG fighters. The US Air Force alone downed more than 100 MiGs, and the Navy killed 40 aircraft for the loss of only seven Phantoms in air-to-air combat. Nearly 700 Phantoms were lost during the conflict, the aircraft's biggest killers being anti-aircraft fire and SAMs. The experience of war, however, led to the reintroduction of cannon armament with the F-4E as many pilots felt kill opportunities had been lost because of the lack of cannon.

As well as Vietnam, F-4s saw action in conflicts such as the 1973 Yom Kippur War, the Iran–Iraq War (1980–88), and with Coalition forces in Operation *Desert Storm* in 1991. By that time, the Phantom had largely been replaced in US service by a new generation of combat aircraft such as the F-14 Tomcat and F-15 Eagle. Yet for a long slice of postwar history, the Phantom was the most formidable combat presence in the skies.

PHANTOM F-4E – SPECIFICATIONS

Crew: 2
Engines: 2 x 17,900lb (8,119kg) thrust afterburning
　　General Electric J79-GE-17 turbojets
Weight (empty): 29,535lb (13,425kg)
Weight (max take-off): 61,651lb (28,023kg)
Wing Span: 38ft 5in (11.7m)
Length: 63ft (19.2m)
Height: 16ft 6in (4.96m)
Maximum speed: 1,485mph (2,390km/h)
Service ceiling: 62,250ft (18,975m)
Range: 1,750 miles (2,817km)
Armament: 1 x 20mm M61A1 rotary cannon;
　　4 x AIM-7 Sparrow missiles or 3,020lb (1,373kg) of
　　weapons under fuselage; up to 12,980lb (5,900kg)
　　of ordnance on underwing pylons

M16

THE M16, LIKE THE AK47, CHANGED THE NATURE OF infantry small-arms through a radical shift in cartridge type. It was created by Eugene Stoner, one of the most innovative of postwar firearms designers, in the mid 1950s, and was phased into service with US forces during the 1960s, replacing the 7.62 x 51mm NATO M14 rifle. The difference between the M16 and the gun it replaced created arguments that have not died down to this day.

HIGH VELOCITY

The M16 was a definite step into modernity. Plastics featured significantly in its construction, which combined with its compact dimensions brought down its empty weight to 6.3lb (2.86kg), compared to the M14's 8.55lb (3.88kg). It was a gas-operated, rotating-bolt firearm, and its high front sight, and aperture rear sight built into a carrying handle, gave it an almost futuristic appearance compared to previous rifles.

OPPOSITE: US riflemen cross a river somewhere in Vietnam armed with their M16s. Designed to help win the Cold War for the United States, the M16 is one of the most recognizable assault rifles in the world and one of the defining American weapons of the 20th century. (US Army)

ABOVE: A US soldier takes aim with his M16. The rifle is accurate and lethal over a range of about 650yds (600m), but the performance of the round quickly drops off over long ranges. (US Army)

BELOW: The M16 was first adopted by US Special Forces and airborne troops in 1962 before it was issued to all Army and Marine units serving in Vietnam. Its use spread in subsequent decades, and to date over 10 million M16s and variants have been produced. (US Army)

Its real revolution, however, was its cartridge. It fired a 5.56 x 45mm round, the diminutive caliber about the same as a .22 air rifle but with a powder charge that pushed the bullet out at ultra-high velocity – 3,280ft/sec (1,000m/sec), as opposed to the 7.62mm's 2,800ft/sec (853m/sec). Experiments suggested that the high velocity generated huge wounds through imparting devastating shock waves as the bullet passed through tissue. Soldiers first using the weapon in Vietnam indeed gave harrowing reports of M16 rounds making gaping holes in enemy soldiers, or even removing entire limbs. Over time, the mythologies of the high-velocity, small-caliber round have steadily been exposed. The devastating effects of the M16 round often had more to do with the bullet fragmenting as it struck the human target at high-velocities; at lower velocities the round often left a clean, straight hole.

PRACTICAL WEAPON

Aside from the ballistic arguments, the fact remained that the M16 brought some definite benefits for the soldier. The round gave more manageable recoil, making full-auto fire realistic. Lighter recoil also meant that it was easier to train people to shoot accurately, particularly those with light physical frames. Smaller cartridges could be carried in greater volume than larger cartridges, increasing a soldier's firepower. For these reasons, the 5.56mm round has become a standard across NATO and in many other countries, fired from weapons such as Britain's SA80A2 and Israel's Galil.

The M16's early combat debut was not promising. Problems with inappropriate propellants plus poor maintenance advice led to the gun gaining a terrible reputation for jamming in combat. These problems were steadily overcome, however, and the M16 became the standard US Army rifle in 1967.

ABOVE: Private Leon Caffie holds aloft his M16, colloquially known to the troops as "the black rifle." Caffie went on to serve for 40 years in the US Army reserves before eventually retiring in 2010 as the Command Sergeant Major of the US Army Reserve. With deployments to Iraq and Afghanistan his career was almost as lengthy as that of the M16. (US Army)

BELOW: Sergeant Karen Antonyan qualifies at night with his M16A2 rifle on the last day of the 2005 Department of the Army NCO and Soldier of the Year Competition at Fort Lee, Virginia. (US Army)

The updated M16A2 took over in 1983, introducing a heavier barrel, improved sight system, a combined flash suppressor/muzzle compensator, and a three-round burst facility instead of the M16's full-auto. The Colt M4 carbine, a compact version of the M16A2, has also become a popular weapon in the US military. More than 40 countries have used or adopted M16-type weapons to date.

Meanwhile, the arguments about caliber rage on. At the time of writing, there is some impetus towards switching back to a heavier round, such as 6.8 x 43mm cartridge. While these debates are arcane to some, for serving members of the military who might face combat, they are utterly relevant.

ABOVE: A US rifleman search a bunker in Vietnam armed with his M16. (US Marine Corps)

M16 – SPECIFICATIONS

Caliber: 5.56 x 45mm
Operation: Gas, rotating bolt
Length: 39in (990mm)
Barrel: 20in (508mm), 6 grooves, r/hand
Weight (empty): 6.3lb (2.86kg)
Magazine: 30-round detachable box
Rate of fire: 800rpm
Muzzle velocity: 3,280ft/sec (1,000m/sec)

SCUD MISSILE

The SS-1 SCUD missile provides a good example of how an individual weapon system can drift in and out of public consciousness, according to its influence in a particular war or campaign. Known as the R-11 in Soviet terminology, the SS-1 tactical ballistic missile entered the Soviet arsenal in the late 1950s.

TACTICAL WEAPON

In its first major variant, the SS-1b, the SCUD had a range of just 80 miles (130km), but subsequent models extended that capability dramatically. The SS-1d, which entered service in 1965, could reach up to 373 miles (600km), although the trade-off was poor accuracy – its circular error probable (CEP) was in the region of 2,952ft (900m), although this was a big improvement over the SS-1b, which Western sources calculated as having a CEP of 2.5 miles (4km). (Being a ballistic missile, the missile was only powered during the

OPPOSITE: A Soviet R-11 missile. The SCUD missile was initially developed as the centerpiece of Soviet plans to fight nuclear war in the heart of Europe. However, it was never used in its intended role and has instead become a symbol of the changing nature of war in the aftermath of the Cold War thanks to the use by Iraqi forces during the 1991 Gulf War. (US Military)

ABOVE: An image of the devastation caused to Tel Aviv, the Israeli capital, by SCUD missiles during the Gulf War. Saddam Hussein's Iraqi forces were almost helpless in the face of the Coalition; the only effective long-range weapon in the Iraqi arsenal was their collection of SCUD missiles. (Time & Life Pictures/Getty Images)

LEFT: In response to the SCUD attacks of 1991, Israel developed the Arrow anti-ballistic missile system, here seen test firing in 2003. (Getty Images)

initial 80-second climb phase of its flight, gyroscopes providing the primary guidance information.) The SCUD could compensate for such inaccuracy by delivering nuclear warheads, although in actual use its warhead has tended to be 2,205lb (1,000kg) of high-explosives.

A key virtue of the SS-1 was that it could operate entirely from a mobile transporter, erector, launcher (TEL) vehicle. The SCUD crew could therefore hope to evade the attentions of enemy aircraft and ground forces, firing from concealed positions then moving on before air assets could home in on the launch. Initially SCUDs were deployed on converted

JS-III heavy tank chassis, but later moved to the MAZ-543 (8 x 8) truck, with a wheeled configuration that gave far better cross-country mobility.

DISTANT STRIKES

As with many postwar Soviet weapons systems, the SCUD was widely distributed, both to Warsaw Pact countries and Middle Eastern export clients. First combat use came in the Arab–Israeli Yom Kippur War of 1973, when Egypt ineffectually fired an unknown number of FROG-7 and SS-1c missiles at Israeli cities. During the Iran–Iraq War in the 1980s, however, nearly 700 SCUDs were exchanged in the so-called "War of the Cities," both sides having acquired the missile. (Iraq's SCUDs included al-Hussein missiles – essentially SCUDs modified for extended range by reducing the warhead and increasing fuel space.) Soviet forces also fired nearly 2,000 SCUDs during their war in Afghanistan, using them to target remote *Mujahideen* positions.

ABOVE: US Patriot missiles streak into the night sky to intercept Iraqi SCUD missiles launched against Tel Aviv. (Getty Images)

PATRIOT WARS

During the Gulf War, the United States deployed MIM-104 Patriot air defense missile systems to defend Israel and Saudi Arabia from the SCUD attacks. Upgrades to the system in the late 1980s supposedly gave it the ability to intercept and kill incoming ballistic missiles. The Patriots were soon streaking up into the skies over places such as Tel Aviv and Riyadh, and the results were apparently impressive – the US Army claimed an 80 percent interception rate over Saudi Arabia and a 50 percent rate over Israel, later revised to 70 percent and 40 percent respectively. Yet post-conflict analysis revealed the actual hit rate to be lower than 10 percent. One of the problems was that the Scud-Bs used by Iraq had been modified to achieve greater speed, but the result was that they frequently broke apart during re-entry. This would cause a loss of Patriot lock-on, and the SCUD's warhead section would frequently tumble to the ground.

However, it was the 1991 Gulf War that made the SCUD a household name. In an attempt to expand the conflict, Saddam Hussein ordered SCUD-type missiles to be fired at Israel and Saudi Arabia. In total, around 90 such missiles were launched, generating a huge Coaltion "SCUD hunting" effort by strike aircraft and Special Forces units. Many SCUDs were destroyed by the Coalition, but the TEL mobility and the Iraqi use of night launches and decoy vehicles made the missiles hard targets to find, track, and destroy. One noteworthy statistic is that 42 SCUD launches were actually seen by Coalition air strikes, but only eight of the TELs were visually acquired for bombing.

During the 1980s, an improved generation of SCUD – the SS-1e – was produced in the Soviet Union. By using active terminal radar homing its CEP is about 164ft (50m), and it can take fuel-air explosives, anti-personnel bomblets, and runway-cratering munitions, as well as high-explosive and nuclear warheads. The fact that former Soviet technology has been readily copied by many other states, means that such missiles may make an appearance in future conflicts.

MIG-21

THE SOVIET UNION'S JET AGE BEGAN IN EARNEST on April 24, 1946, when a prototype aircraft designated as I-300, powered by two BMW 003 turbojets, made its first flight. This in turn evolved into the MiG-9 jet fighter, of which about 550 were built. Yet it was Artem I. Mikoyan and Mikhail I. Gurevich's next design, the MiG-15, that would transform Soviet air power.

NIMBLE OPPONENTS

The MiG-15 first flew in December 1947 and began equipping Soviet air units the following year. For its day, it was an excellent fighter, and it gave US F-86 Sabre jets an equal opponent during the Korean War (1950–53). The MiG had dizzying maneuverability, a decent maximum speed of 684mph (1,100km/h), and three nose-mounted cannon to provide air-to-air punch.

Some 18,000 MiG-15s would be built either in the Soviet Union or under licence in communist countries. MiG's reputation for producing basic but respected fighters continued with the MiG-17 "Fresco" and the "MiG-19 "Farmer," the latter being the first standard Soviet jet that could break the sound barrier in level flight. Yet in 1959, a new MiG fighter began to enter service, and it altered the stakes in international air power.

OPPOSITE: A Soviet Air Force pilot inspects the air-to-air missiles mounted on the wings of his MiG-21 fighter.

The MiG-21 "Fishbed" was a true supersonic fighter-interceptor. A delta wing, slender fuselage, and a powerful R11 afterburning turbojet gave the MiG-21 the ability to reach and hold Mach 2. In its very first configuration, it was armed only with two 30mm cannon, but in the MiG-21F Fishbed-C it could also take two K-13 Atoll infrared homing AAMs.

To chart the history of the MiG-21's development to date would take a book in itself. More than a dozen variants have been built in the Soviet Union/Commonwealth of Independent States (CIS) alone, in addition to licence-built versions from China, India, and Czechoslovakia. Over time, steady improvements have moved the MiG-21 from being a second- to a third-generation fighter. Aircraft such as the MiG-21-97 and MiG-21-2000 (both upgrade packages, the latter being an export aircraft developed by Israel Aircraft Industries) include features such as beyond-visual-range missile engagement, integration with head-up display (HUD)

ABOVE: A MiG-21 in Israeli Air Force markings flies over the Middle East. The Israelis acquired an Arab MiG-21 in 1966, following the airborne defection of a Syrian pilot.

BELOW: A MiG-21 taxis along an airstrip. Note the highly swept delta wings, providing both speed and maneuverability.

ABOVE: Egyptian MiG-21s proved vulnerable to Israeli Mirages, particularly those in the hands of skilled pilots. These dramatic stills from a gunsight camera show the moment a MiG-21 is destroyed during a sortie in 1966. The secondary frame in the final image is probably the start of the ejection seat sequence.

helmets, sophisticated electronic aviation management, electronic countermeasures (ECM) suites, and other capabilities that make it a respected comparison to even the latest Western jets.

PROLIFIC FIGHTER

More than 11,000 MiG-21 jets have been built, equipping the air forces of over 30 countries. The type has been heavily battle tested. In the Vietnam War, it became the United States' most threatening air opponent, fast-moving groups of MiGs being vectored by ground control units to intercept low-level US ground-attack missions. In fact, such were the US losses against MiGs that the US Navy and US Air Force both developed new fighter schools to teach advanced dogfighting

SIX-DAY WAR AIR STRIKE

The opening phase of the Six-Day War of 1967, fought between Israel and the Arab nations of Egypt, Syria, and Jordan, was a stunning and brutal demonstration of modern air power. A top priority of the Israeli Air Force (IAF) was to neutralize opposing air assets quickly to allow Israeli ground forces to operate under friendly air superiority. The IAF's primary target was the Egyptian Air Force, which had 450 combat aircraft, 350 of which were MiG fighters, compared to the IAF's 350 aircraft (250 fighters). Beginning at 0845hrs on June 5, IAF jets began pounding Egyptian airfields, approaching very low to stay beneath radar and SA-2 SAM capabilities. The Israeli aircraft wrecked dozens of aircraft on the ground with cannon fire and bombs, or in air combat, where the Israeli Dassault Mirage III proved superior to many Arab jets. By the end of the first day, Egypt had lost 300 of its aircraft. The small air forces of Jordan and Syria were similarly decimated. Israel lost just 19 aircraft delivering a blow from which the Arab states never recovered.

ABOVE: A recreation of a MiG-21F-13 – one of the last to be delivered to Egypt prior to the start of the 1967 Six-Day War. The jet survived the destruction of June 5, 1967. This variant of the MiG-21 carried a 490-liter auxiliary fuel tank beneath its fuselage and R-3S missiles beneath each wing. (Artwork by Jim Laurier © Osprey Publishing)

skills. MiG-21s have also featured very heavily in Middle Eastern conflicts (Arab nations being a major export market), although poor levels of training and inadvisable tactics led to extremely heavy losses of the type in conflicts such as the 1967 Six-Day War and the 1973 Yom Kippur War.

In the hands of skilled pilots, however, the MiG-21 remains a powerful fighting aircraft. Such are the numbers produced, and the continuing application of upgrade packages, that it will remain in frontline use well into the 20th century.

MIG-21F-13 – SPECIFICATIONS

Wingspan: 23ft 5.5in (7.1m)
Weight (empty): 10,979lb (4,980kg)
Loaded (air combat): 19,014lb (8,624kg)
Maximum speed: 1,350mph at 42,650ft (2,172km/h at 13,000m)
Range: 808 miles (1,300km)
Climb: 23,622ft (7,200m) per minute
Armament: 1 x NR-30 cannon, 1 x R-3S missiles

RPG-7

THE ROCKET PROPELLED GRENADE-7 HAS A SIMILAR significance to that of the AK47. Both are simple weapons with extremely wide distribution, and like the AK the RPG-7 has had a critically destabilizing effect on world security.

DESTRUCTIVE FORCE

Throughout World War II, the Red Army had suffered from a lack of a shoulder-launched anti-tank weapon equivalent to the American bazooka and the German *Panzerfaust*, and it looked to correct this deficit in the postwar era. The RPG-7 comprehensively filled the gap, being adopted into Soviet and Warsaw Pact service in 1961.

In design, the RPG-7 consists of a recoilless launcher tube, fitted with pistol-grip trigger unit, and a rear stabilizing grip. Iron sights are fitted as standard, but the weapon can also take a PGO-7 optical sight. To load the weapon, one of several types of high-explosive anti-tank (HEAT) missiles is inserted into the front of the launcher, the large bulbous warhead remaining outside the unit. The gunner then shoulders the launcher, takes off the safety, aims at the target, and pulls the trigger.

OPPOSITE: Although often associated with insurgent armies, the RPG-7 also played a critical role in the 1973 Yom Kippur War. Syrian teams armed with RPG-7s infiltrated Israeli lines on the Golan Heights to launch close-range surprise attacks on Israeli armor. These Syrian troops pose with their RPGs on a hillside facing Israeli positions. (Courtesy of Gordon Rottman)

OPPOSITE PAGE: An Afghan National Army soldier carries an RPG-7 and for good measure two extra rounds. (© Ed Darack/Science Faction/Corbis)

On launch, the missile is first blown from the tube by a booster charge, then at a distance of 12yds (11m) a rocket motor in the stabilizing pipe ignites, pushing the missile to a velocity of 965ft/sec (294m/sec). At the same time, fins extend from the rear of the missile, giving it a degree of spin stabilization in flight. Maximum range, depending on the projectile used, is about 164yds (150m), and the PG-7M HEAT warhead – the most common in use today – can penetrate an impressive 11.8in (300mm) of armor.

DEADLY PRESENCE

The RPG-7, and its numerous variants and copies, is today used by more than 50 countries, and has become a staple of insurgencies worldwide. Its popularity is easy to understand.

BELOW: An Afghan National Army soldier fires an RPG-7. Perhaps due to its familiarity with many Afghans, it has continued to be a popular standard weapon in the new national army. (US Army/Spc Daniel Love)

Not only is it widely available – millions of units have been produced – but it is extremely simple to use and is just as effective against bunkers, buildings, and other static positions as it is against armored vehicles. The 93mm PG-7L warhead, for example, can penetrate 3ft 7in (1.1m) of reinforced concrete, 4ft 11in (1.5m) of brick, and 8ft 2in (2.5m) of logs and earth. Improvements in warhead design have also kept pace with armor enhancements; the PG-7R warhead, designed to defeat explosive reactive armor (ERA), can punch through 23.6in (600mm) of armor.

The RPG-7 was first used in combat by the Egyptians against the Israelis during the 1967 Arab–Israeli War. Since then it has gone on to destroy thousands of vehicles, kill probably tens of thousands of people, and even bring down helicopters (as was the case in the infamous "Black Hawk Down" incident in Mogadishu in 1993). Conventional armies have particularly suffered from the RPG-7's availability to insurgents. In the Vietnam War, communist troops would

ARMOR STRIKE

A US Vietnam veteran here explains the power of the RPG-7's warhead on an armored vehicle:

" A concussion is incredible, and the shrapnel is very effective, stunning the victims to a point of being completely disabled for several seconds if not minutes, depending on the severity of the hit. The jet of flame in the HEAT round is extraordinarily long. I took a hit in the left rear corner of my M113A1 ACAV [Armored Cavalry Assault Vehicle] at about two-thirds up from the lower edge of the side ... and the flame actually cut through the rear ramp exit door slicing it as if it had been cut with a torch. This slice was well over 18in long. If you happen to be unlucky enough to be standing in the path of this lightning bolt when it hits the side of the armor, you can well imagine the carnage.[15] "

hit US firebase bunkers and tanks with multiple RPGs in coordinated ambushes. Soviet forces in Afghanistan in 1979–89 found their RPG-7s turned against them by the Afghan *Mujahideen*, who proved adept at using them in close-range attacks on Russian armor. In more recent times, US, British, and Coalition troops in Iraq and Afghanistan have been plagued by near constant RPG ambushes – RPGs are second only to IEDs in the number of casualties inflicted on US forces in Iraq. It is ironic that while Western armies have invested much money and effort into combating sophisticated guided weapons, the unguided RPG-7 has actually proved far more of a threat.

BELOW: An RPG-7 fitted with an image intensifier night vision sight, giving the user an effective viewing range of *c.* 1,300ft (400m). Below is the PG-7 HEAT (High-Explosive Anti-Tank) projectile. (Beryl Barnett)

HARRIER

In 1957, the British Hawker Siddeley aircraft company explored a new concept in aviation design. Its P.1127 demonstrator utilized vertical/short take-off and landing (V/STOL) capabilities through thrust vectoring – rotating engine exhaust nozzles allowed the pilot to direct thrust through a full 90-degree angle. The result was an aircraft that had similar take-off and landing properties to a helicopter, but with near supersonic-level flight speeds.

BRITISH HARRIERS

The P.1127 began a long evolution that led to the British Harrier GR. Mk I, powered by a Bristol Pegasus 101 turbofan. As we shall see, British development of the Harrier is only one side of the aircraft's story, but it proved to be a highly successful one. The GR.1 entered RAF service on April 1, 1969, as a single-seat close-support and reconnaissance fighter, and was steadily improved in terms of performance, combat capability, and electronics.

Harriers cannot take off vertically with a full weapons load (although they can land with the same), but require only a short runway strip to get airborne, giving them wide tactical flexibility. Diverse weapons options also ensure the Harrier has a true multi-role capability; the GR.3 model, for example, can take 5,000lb (2,268kg) of ordnance, including unguided or precision-guided bombs, 2in rocket pods, cluster bomb dispensers, and, for air-to-air combat, Sidewinder missiles.

Convinced of its capabilities, the Royal Navy also adopted and adapted the Harrier, the BAe Sea Harrier going into service aboard *Invincible*-class aircraft carriers in the late 1970s. The

OPPOSITE: A Harrier coming into land on the flight deck of an aircraft carrier, demonstrating its V/STOL capabilities. (Getty Images)

ABOVE: A Harrier jet of 1(F) Joint Force Squadron hovers as it comes in to land on the flight deck of HMS *Ark Royal* during a training exercise on July 14, 2010. (Getty Images)

LEFT: A British Harrier based at RAF Cottesmore dropping a Paveway II laser-guided bomb. (JACK PRITCHARD/AFP/ Getty Images)

Sea Harrier had improved avionics and the Blue Fox airborne interception radar, and the later FA.2 upgrade also gave it the ability to launch AIM-120 AMRAAM (Advanced Medium Range Air-to-Air Missile) beyond-visual-range missiles.

Being a subsonic aircraft in a supersonic age, the Harrier had plenty of detractors. They were silenced in 1982, when Harriers gave a compelling performance during the Falklands War. Just 28 Sea Harriers managed to fly 1,190 sorties while retaining 95 percent serviceability. Utilizing their stunning maneuverability, they shot down 20 faster Argentine jets for no air-to-air losses, while also proving invaluable in a ground-attack role.

US HARRIERS

The United States has also been a major user and developer of Harriers. The GR.1 was modified and taken into US Marine Corps service as the BAe AV-8A, deliveries beginning in 1971. The AV-8A was deployed in both land-based and carrier-based contexts, and was eventually upgraded to the AV-8C variant with new avionics, plus some features from another Harrier variant, the AV-8B Harrier II.

This aircraft was a joint McDonnell Douglas/BAe venture, the US company having purchased development rights when the Marine Corps bought the AV-8A. Entering service in the early 1980s, the AV-8B was a substantial redesign, with an improved wing, lighter composite fuselage, high-visibility cockpit, a more powerful engine, and the ability to carry a weapons load of 17,000lb (7,711kg). Further additions to the AV-8B have included forward-looking infrared (FLIR) systems.

TOP LEFT: The second generation of the Harrier jump jet – the Harrier AV-8B Harrier II – has been used extensively by the US Marine Corps. (US Army)

BOTTOM LEFT: Two US Marines AV-8B Harrier jets are shown launching from the aircraft carrier USS *Bon Homme Richard* on April 5, 2003, in the Persian Gulf. Harrier jets carried out bombing missions throughout Operation *Iraqi Freedom*, providing close air support to troops on the ground as Coalition forces moved towards Baghdad. (Photo by Justin Sullivan/Getty Images)

Note that the US/British Harrier also went into service with the British as the Harrier II. Unlike the US aircraft, the British equivalent does not have a nose-mounted radar, but the latest GR.9 and GR.9A versions include advanced avionics and weapons systems.

As with the British aircraft, the US Harriers have justified their existence through excellent close-support combat service, particularly in the 1991 Gulf War plus operations in Iraq and Afghanistan. Defense reviews continue to threaten the Harrier's existence, but the lessons of recent history argue for its value.

BATTLE OVER THE FALKLANDS

Harrier pilot Lieutenant-Commander Mike Blisset remembers an engagement with Argentine Skyhawks over Goose Green during the Falklands War:

❝ The Skyhawks were in a long echelon, spread out over about a mile, I locked a Sidewinder on one of the guys in the middle and fired. My first impression was that the missile was going to strike the ground as it fell away – I was only about 200 feet above the ground. But suddenly it started to climb and rocketed towards the target. At that moment my attention was distracted somewhat as a Sidewinder came steaming past my left shoulder – Neil [his wingman] had fired past me, which I found very disconcerting at the time!... Then I glanced back to the right and saw my missile impact on the Skyhawk I had aimed at. Suddenly, about 800 yards in front of me, there was a huge fireball as the aircraft blew up in the air; there was debris flying everywhere.[16] ❞

EXOCET

ANTI-SHIP MISSILES (ASMS) FIRST MADE THEIR appearance during World War II, the Germans leading the way with the Henschel Hs 293 and the Ruhrstahl/Kramer X-1, the latter better known as the "Fritz-X." The Hs 293 was essentially an SC 500 bomb fitted with a tailplane, short wings, and a rocket booster motor. Once the bomb was dropped from an aircraft, the booster took it up to a speed of around 559mph (900km/h), and it was guided to its target by the bomb-aimer, who controlled the bomb using a radio-linked joystick. (A flare on the rear of the missile enabled him to track it visually.) The Fritz-X worked on similar principles, but unlike the Hs 293 was a free-fall glide bomb – it had no external power source.

Both types of weapon were deployed in limited numbers during World War II. In ideal conditions they were both accurate and destructive, and they damaged or sank dozens of vessels in the Mediterranean, including the Italian battleship *Roma* and the British battleship *Warspite*. Growing Allied air superiority meant that the German guided bombs would have limited effect during the war itself, but in the postwar period missiles soon replaced gunfire and bombs as the greatest danger to shipping.

BEYOND VISUAL RANGE

The Soviets were pioneers of both air- and surface-launched ASMs. The AS-1 Kennel was their first, being a turbojet-powered cruise missile with a range of up to 107 miles (172km), guided by a combination of autopilot, radar beam rider, and semi-active homing radar. It was followed soon after by the SS-N-2 Styx, which used radio-command and terminal active radar homing. It became the first postwar ASM to be deployed in combat, when Egyptian missile boats sank the Israeli destroyer *Eilat* in 1967.

OPPOSITE: The Pakistan Navy test-fires an Exocet missile in 2001. (AFP/Getty Images)

By this time, the rest of the world had caught up with the Soviets. Ever more sophisticated ASMs were produced by NATO countries, including the Exocet. The Exocet is a French weapon that entered service with the French Navy in 1975. Its immediate strength is its versatility – by 1979 it could be launched from land, sea, or air (in the AM39 version), and had a range of 31 miles (50km). Typical of many modern ASMs, the Exocet approaches its target at a "sea-skimming" altitude, reducing the chances of enemy radar detection. An active radar seeker guides it to its target in the last 7.5–9.3 miles (12–15km) of the attack – during this phase the altitude drops to as low as 10ft (3m). A 363lb (165kg) high-explosive/fragmentation warhead provides the destructive effect, with a delayed-action impact fuse allowing the missile to penetrate the warship before detonation.

FALKLANDS WAR

The shocking proof of the Exocet's effectiveness came in 1982, when the British deployed a huge naval Task Force to reclaim the Falkland Islands from an Argentine invasion. On May 4, the Type 42 destroyer HMS *Sheffield* was struck by an Exocet launched from an Argentine Super Etendard aircraft. The missile punched through *Sheffield* just above the waterline amidships. Even though the warhead didn't detonate, the attack killed 20 people and set the ship ablaze – it eventually sank on May 10. Two weeks later, on May 25,

BELOW: HMS *Sheffield*, damaged by an Exocet missile attack during the Falklands War, May 1982. Twenty people lost their lives in the incident and the ship later sank in the South Atlantic. (Photo by Martin Cleaver/Pool/Getty Images)

USS *STARK*

On the late afternoon of May 17, 1987, an Iraqi Mirage F1 aircraft locked its Cyrano-IV fire-control radar onto a distant target in the Persian Gulf. That target was the USS *Stark*, a guided-missile frigate conducting patrols in the contested region. Although the destroyer's defense systems recognized the threat, no immediate action was taken, and the Mirage launched two Exocet missiles, the first at a closing range of 22 miles (35km). Both missiles tracked in and struck the *Stark*, hitting near the port bridge wing. A total of 29 US sailors were killed immediately, with another eight men dying later. The reasons for the attack are still unclear but it provided many lessons for the US Navy about defense in potentially hostile waters.

ABOVE: USS *Stark* listing to port after being struck by an Iraqi-launched Exocet missile. (Corbis)

LEFT: USS *Stark* with a hole blown in her hull after being hit by Exocet missile in the Persian Gulf. Of the two missiles launched by the Iraqi Mirage fighter jet, one failed to explode, otherwise the damage would have been far worse. (Photo by Francois Lochon//Time Life Pictures/Getty Images)

two Exocets struck the container ship *Atlantic Conveyor*, packed with vital helicopters and vehicles for the land campaign, the ship sinking five days later.

Only international restrictions on the sale of Exocets to Argentina prevented more British ships being targeted by these lethal systems. More than 100 Exocets were fired in combat during the 1980s, mostly by Iraq against Iranian ships and oil platforms during the Iran–Iraq War, but two also damaged the USS *Stark* in 1987 (see feature box). The Exocet has consequently become one of the most tried and tested ASMs of the postwar period, and it demonstrates how a few missiles can change the fate of an entire naval campaign.

USS *NIMITZ*

Nothing today represents American power projection better than a US Navy *Nimitz*-class carrier. In the previous chapter, we have seen how aircraft carriers altered the very nature of naval warfare in the 20th century. The *Nimitz* carriers are the ultimate expression of that change.

NUCLEAR CARRIERS

An important day in the history of postwar US naval aviation was September 24, 1960, with the launch of the USS *Enterprise*, the US Navy's first nuclear-powered aircraft carrier, which was powered by eight Westinghouse A2W pressurized water-cooled reactors. The introduction of nuclear power was nearly as

OPPOSITE: F/A-18C Hornets and F-14 Tomcats adorn the flight deck of USS *Nimitz* during the 1990s. (US Navy)

significant for carriers as it was for submarines (see entry on USS *Nautilus*, pp.291–293). Not only did nuclear energy give the *Enterprise* almost unlimited range, but it freed up huge amounts of space compared to conventionally powered tankers – gone was the need for fuel oil storage tanks, smokestacks, and fume ducts – which could now be devoted to aircraft, ammunition, and other systems.

The *Enterprise* laid the foundations for the greatest series of US carriers in history, the *Nimitz* class. In total, ten carriers of this class were constructed between 1968 and 2006, these vessels being: *Nimitz, Dwight D. Eisenhower, Carl Vinson, Theodore Roosevelt, Abraham Lincoln, John C. Stennis, Harry S. Truman, Ronald Reagan,* and *George H.W. Bush.*

MASTERS OF THE SEA

A run through of a few technical specifications of *Nimitz* class carriers gives some impression of their military muscle. The carriers have a typical displacement of approximately

ABOVE: USS *Enterprise*, which immediately preceded USS *Nimitz*, was the world's first nuclear-powered aircraft carrier. It is here seen underway in the Atlantic in 2004. (US Navy, Rob Gaston)

BELOW: A catapult crew member directs an F-14B Tomcat onto one of the four steam-powered catapults aboard USS *George Washington.* (US Navy, Michael D. Blackwell II)

ABOVE: The *Nimitz*-class aircraft carrier is the ultimate symbol of the United States' superpower status. (US Navy)

BELOW: Steam can be seen along the catapult run as two F/A-18C Hornets prepare to launch from USS *Theodore Roosevelt*. As befitting their status as the most valuable assets of the US Navy, nearly all the carriers in the *Nimitz* class are named after former American presidents. (US Navy, Javier Capella)

87,997 tonnes (97,000 US tons) at full load, and an overall length of 1,092ft (332.85m). The flight deck is 252ft (76.8m) wide and has an area of 4.5 acres (1.8 hectares). Two nuclear reactors drive eight steam turbines and four shafts, which in turn push the huge vessel to speeds of 30+ knots (55.5+ km/h). Total population of each ship amounts to a ship's company of 3,200 personnel, and an air wing complement of 2,480.

In terms of aircraft, a *Nimitz* carrier holds up to 82 aircraft, usually composed of 12 F/A-18E/F Super Hornets, 36 F/A-18 Hornets, four E-2C Hawkeyes, and four EA-6B Prowlers, plus four SH-60F and two HH-60H Seahawk helicopters. Together, this air wing can cover any type of air mission, from fighter interceptions through to submarine hunting. Four steam-driven catapults on the flight deck enable the carrier to launch one aircraft every 20 seconds. The carrier also bristles with defensive equipment, including Sea Sparrow SAMs, 20mm Phalanx six-barreled air defense cannon, and advanced ECM systems.

ABOVE: USS *Theodore Roosevelt* test-fires a RIM-7 Sea Sparrow missile. (US Navy, Nathan Laird)

Given such impressive force, it is little wonder that the *Nimitz* class carriers have been at the forefront of many major US military campaigns since the 1970s. The carriers' main war zone has been the Middle East, fulfilling support and combat roles during the 1991 Gulf War, Operation *Southern Watch* (during which the *Harry S. Truman*'s air wing flew 869 combat missions), and in Operation *Iraqi Freedom*. Further deployments include flying patrols over the former Yugoslavia during and after its breakup and delivering humanitarian aid to New Orleans following Hurricane Katrina in 2005. Just the presence of a carrier group in a region can have a profound influence on shaping regional policy. With each ship having a 50-year design life, *Nimitz*-class carriers remain integral to US strategic interests.

CARRIER STRIKE GROUP

Modern US carriers rarely deploy alone, instead forming the core of a Carrier Strike Group (CVSG). (This terms replaces the previous "Carrier Battle Groups.") A CVSG includes a number of ships dedicated to providing defense, additional capabilities, and support to the carrier, plus a number of other functions, such as facilitating amphibious operations. CSVGs are not a permanent establishment, and are formed to meet specific needs. A typical CVSG might consist of the carrier and its air wing, two Tomahawk-equipped guided-missile cruisers, a guided-missile destroyer (with air defense capabilities), a destroyer and a frigate with anti-submarine systems, two attack submarines, and a supply vessel.

A-10 THUNDERBOLT

FEW PEOPLE WHO HAVE HEARD OR SEEN THE A-10 Thunderbolt fight can forget the experience. Designed as a powerful close-support aircraft in the late 1960s and early 1970s, it has kept itself relevant despite being surrounded by aircraft far more advanced and flexible in terms of warfighting technologies.

SURVIVABILITY

The A-10 Thunderbolt – affectionately nicknamed the "Warthog" on account of its awkward appearance – first flew in 1972, and was selected the following year for production. Based on its experience in Vietnam, the US Air Force wanted an aircraft capable of delivering crushing ground-attack missions, but one that also had a high level of survivability in hostile anti-aircraft environments.

The A-10 ticked all the boxes. A subsonic aircraft with high maneuverability, the A-10 had two General Electric TF34-GE-100 turbofans mounted so that they exhausted over the top of the twin-boom tailplane, thus reducing the risk of heat-seeking missiles achieving lock-on. The pilot sat beneath a high-visibility cockpit in a titanium armored "bathtub," capable of withstanding a 57mm cannon strike, while much of the airframe can survive 23mm cannon fire. Fuel tanks are self-sealing, and protected by fire-retardant foam, and even with the landing gear retracted, the wheels partially emerge from the fuselage, increasing the

OPPOSITE: A close-up view of the Thunderbolt's armored cockpit, which affords the pilots extra protection particularly during ground-attack missions under enemy fire. (USAF)

likelihood of surviving gear-up emergency landings. The pilot can also manually retain control of the aircraft when hydraulic power is lost.

FLYING GUN

The A-10's defining feature, however, is its central weapon – a 30mm seven-barrel rotary cannon. Firing its shells at rates of up to 4,200rpm, a one-second burst from the cannon is enough to destroy almost any main battle tank (MBT). In addition to this awesome firepower, the A-10 can also carry 16,000lb (7,258kg) of other ordnance, including conventional and guided bombs (including JDAMs), Maverick guided anti-tank missiles, cluster munitions, and 2.75in rocket pods.

GENERAL ELECTRIC GAU-8/A AVENGER 30MM CANNON

The A-10's cannon is a weapon of unusual destructive force. Weighing 4,029lb (1,828kg) with a maximum ammunition load and measuring 19ft 5.5in (5.93m), it is a seven-barrel rotary weapon powered by a large electrical motor. At first, the cannon was configured to fire at two optional rates – 2,100 or 4,200rpm – although it has now been standardized to one rate of 3,900rpm. Firing from a distance of around 1,300yds (1,188m), the aircraft can put 80 percent of its rounds into a 40ft (12.4m) circle. The standard ammunition types are armor-piercing incendiary and high-explosive incendiary, usually in a four-to-one mix. Depleted uranium is used as the core of the anti-tank rounds, giving the shells deep armor penetration.

TOP LEFT AND BELOW: Dropping ordnance during a live-fire exercise. The Thunderbolt is an awesome killing machine, armed not only with a 4,200rpm cannon but also guided bombs. (USAF)

ABOVE: A pair of A-10s in flight over Afghanistan. They have made a significant contribution to International Security Assistance Force (ISAF) operations in the region. (USAF)

OPPOSITE TOP: An A-10 deploys flares over Afghanistan in 2008. Despite already seeing four decades of service, the aircraft is unlikely to be retired from frontline duties until 2028, proving that the so-called "Warthog" is in fact the true workhorse of the USAF. (USAF)

OPPOSITE BOTTOM: An A-10 Thunderbolt awaiting refueling. (USAF)

The A-10 was first unleashed during the 1991 Gulf War, and its performance was chilling. A-10 sorties destroyed an estimated 3,000 Iraqi vehicles, including 900 tanks. In one day alone, on February 23, 1991, two A-10s destroyed a total of 23 MBTs. A-10s also performed hundreds of other attacks on troop positions and artillery emplacements. Such was the aircraft's reliability and killing efficiency, that the US Air Force abandoned an idea to replace it with a close-support version of the F-16.

Through computer system upgrades and various other modifications, the A-10 still serves in the 21st century. Coalition troops in both Afghanistan and Iraq have enjoyed the security of calling in A-10 strikes against insurgents in hardened or inaccessible positions, and the aircraft fired 311,597 rounds of 30mm ammunition during Operation *Iraqi Freedom* alone. A-10s are periodically threatened with replacement by more sophisticated craft. Yet its combination of survivability and firepower is hard to find in any other aircraft, and its utility in low-intensity warfare is proven.

PRECISION-GUIDED MUNITIONS

ALTHOUGH BASIC GUIDED BOMBS WERE FIRST USED during World War II (see "Exocet," pp.327–329), modern PGMs emerged during the Vietnam War. In 1967, for example, US jets began dropping AGM-62 television-guided glide bombs – once dropped, the bomb sent television images of the target to the pilot in the cockpit, who then designated an aim point. Once that point was marked, the bomb would then fly itself into the target.

OPPOSITE: Row upon row of JDAMs ready to be transported to the flight deck of USS *Harry S. Truman* while the aircraft carrier was on deployment in the Mediterranean Sea in 2003. Shortly after this photo was taken it was deployed on active service in Operation *Iraqi Freedom*. (Getty Images)

LASER GUIDANCE

Walleyes were used with some success, but the true breakthrough in PGMs came in 1972. US Air Force and US Navy attack jets had made many futile sorties against targets like the Thanh Hoa Bridge, on North Vietnam's Song Ma River.

ABOVE: A precision-guided munition in flight. Despite the extreme costs of PGMs, the higher degree of accuracy and reduced risk of collatoral damage have justified the expense time and time again. (USAF)

Hundreds of general-purpose bombs, and even some AGM-62s, had failed to destroy the bridge. On October 6, 1972, however, a group of F-4 Phantom II jets launched 24 Paveway laser-guided bombs, bringing down the western span of the bridge in an attack that also destroyed a series of valuable highway and railroad river crossings. The laser-guided weapons used seekers (an optical sensor at the front end of the bomb) to sense the direction and intensity of reflected laser light, the target "painted" with a laser from either an aircraft or a ground-based laser designator unit. The seeker then sent electrical signals to the bomb's control surfaces, which adjusted the weapon's flight to its target.

This new generation of PGMs had unprecedented accuracy, hitting within a few feet of their target. By 1975, the United States had launched more than 28,000 laser-guided bombs in Southeast Asia, with a 61 percent hit rate. During *Desert Storm* in 1991, the technology had advanced to such a state that the public was shown video footage of bombs flying through designated windows or doors in buildings, or down ventilation ducts of bunkers. PGMs also acquired the ability to penetrate and destroy underground and "hardened" targets, such as reinforced concrete and deeply buried bunkers. The GBU-82, for example, can skewer through 100ft (32m) of earth or 20ft (6m) of concrete before detonating.

GPS GUIDANCE

Like any human-designed system, there are imperfections in PGM technology. Laser guidance, for example, is vulnerable to interference from inclement weather and dense smoke. Following the Gulf War, therefore, with its smoky infernos of vandalized Kuwaiti oil fields, the US Navy and US Air Force jointly developed a new guidance system, which would be impervious to weather and smoke. The result was the Joint Direct Attack Munition (JDAM), which is a general-purpose dumb bomb fitted with a new tail section containing smart

ABOVE: Preparing to load a JDAM. (USAF)

guidance electronics and, crucially, a Global Positioning Satellite (GPS)-aided inertial navigation unit. JDAM tail kits have been developed for many classes of general-purpose ordnance, including for 2,000lb (907kg), 1,000lb (454kg), and 500lb (227kg) bombs. Once the target coordinates are fed into the bomb's computer, it will use the GPS network to fly the bomb onto the target, with an accuracy of about 32ft (10m). JDAMs have been used heavily in Iraq and Afghanistan, and in their latest manifestation they have been fitted with additional laser guidance units to enable them to tackle moving targets.

PGMs are very expensive when compared to "dumb" bombs. Yet the need to reduce "collateral damage," and accurately pinpoint high-value targets, dominates modern air warfare, and the PGMs, used appropriately, can be a highly effective solution to these problems.

INTELLIGENCE ERRORS

PGMs, provided they have no technical flaws, will reliably hit their targets or aim points. Yet human error in intelligence or system operation can have catastrophic consequences. In the "kill chain" – finding, fixing, tracking, targeting, engaging, and assessing – there are multiple opportunities for mistakes. For example, during Operation *Allied Force* (1999), NATO jets accidentally attacked the Chinese embassy in Belgrade, killing three and wounding 20. In that case, the targeting process had included not only several layers of the defense establishment, but also the bureaucracy of the NATO alliance, according to Pentagon officials. In Afghanistan on December 5, 2001, a JDAM dropped from a B-52 killed three US troops, five allied Afghan troops, and injured 40 other people. The failure was tracked down to a GPS receiver's battery being changed in the middle of the action. Such incidents, and many more, show that there are always human limits to precision in warfare.

F-15 EAGLE

In 1991, the United States led Coalition forces in Operation *Desert Storm*, to eject Saddam Hussein's Iraqi Army from Kuwait. The operation saw the largest air campaign in post-Vietnam War history, one of the outcomes of which was the complete destruction or suppression of the Iraqi Air Force. Of the 37 air-to-air victories won by the US Air Force, 34 kills were delivered by one of the finest all-round fighter aircraft of the 20th century – the F-15 Strike Eagle.

OPPOSITE: With a kill ratio that exceeds 105:0, the F-15 Eagle has never lost an air-to-air dogfight and is undoubtedly one of the most successful aircraft of all time. Here an F-15A demonstrates in dramatic fashion the zoom climb, supposedly the best way to intercept high-flying Soviet aircraft. (USAF)

SPEED AND MANEUVERABILITY

Although the F-15 would go on to fulfill many roles, it was designed in the late 1960s as an air-superiority fighter. Its creators at McDonnell Douglas had to meet the challenges of some of the fast, agile Soviet aircraft then in widespread service.

ABOVE: Four F-15Cs take to the skies in the mid-1980s where they served as part of the NATO force in Europe. (USAF)

BELOW: Half of an F-15 Eagle's payload on display. The missiles complement each other in terms of range – the Sidewinder is used for close-range targets, while the Sparrow is suited to medium-range targets. (USAF)

These included fighters such as the MiG-23 "Flogger" and the superb MiG-25 "Foxbat," which had a top speed of 2,115mph (3,400km/h), and in demonstrations had climbed to 114,829ft (35,000m) in just four minutes 11 seconds.

McDonnell Douglas took a different approach. The MiG-25 was primarily a high-altitude interceptor, but the F-15 was designed as the ultimate close-in dogfighting aircraft. By giving the aircraft a low wing loading (the ratio of aircraft weight to its wing area) but two very powerful Pratt & Whitney turbofan engines, it generated an exceptional blend of speed and maneuverability that no other fighter could match.

HI-TECH HUNTER

The first versions of the F-15 to enter service were the F-15A (single seat) and F-15B (dual seat) in the early 1970s. The main single-seat production version was the F-15C from 1979, alongside the F-15D two-seater (primarily used as a trainer). A big change in concept, however, came in 1989, with the introduction of the advanced F-15E Strike Eagle, which had a ground-attack capability added to its fighter role, with the electronics and hardware points to deploy PGMs, "dumb" bombs, and bomblet dispensers.

Regardless of the model, the Eagle is a state-of-the-art aircraft. The pilot, sat under a high-visibility bubble canopy, receives key tactical, weapon, and flight information directly on his HUD helmet screen, and the HOTAS (hands on throttle and stick) system means he can access most important combat functions quickly via the flight control stick. The APG-63 X-band pulse doppler radar enables the F-15 to engage and destroy enemy aircraft at beyond visual range, using AIM-7M Sparrow and AIM-120 AMRAAMs, while in close combat the AIM-9L/M Sidewinder and a 20mm M16A1 rotary-barrel cannon come into play. The Strike Eagle also includes the Tactical Electronic Warfare System (TEWS), an ECM system that jams enemy radar systems and triggers systems such as chaff and flare dispensers.

F-15s have served with Israel, Saudi Arabia, and Japan as well as the US Air Force. Indeed, the first air-to-air F-15 kills came in the late 1970s and early 1980s, when Israeli F-15s

BELOW: A glimpse of the improved heat-seeking missile provided for the new generation F-15 – the AIM-9L known as "Mike." (USAF)

FAR BELOW: A more detailed view of the AIM-9L. The AIM-9L is an "all-aspect ratio" air-to-air missile, meaning that it can engage enemy aircraft from all directions, including head on. It ensured that if a pilot targeted one enemy aircraft with his "Sparrow," and then acquired another target visually, then he could use his AIM-9L. (USAF)

MIG KILLS

Captain Rhory R. Draeger, a USAF F-15C pilot, here describes the shooting down of two MiG-29s with AIM-7 missiles during the Gulf War:

" Because of the environmental conditions, I saw it all – even though we didn't have them visually when we first fired. Very shortly after firing, I picked them up. They descended. They were 13,000. Now they're at 500ft... They're at low altitude, flying in echelon formation about a mile between them. And I see the missiles go right into impact. I call, "Splash two." This means, we got two fireballs out there and the two MiGs are dead that we were going after. There were no Iraqi shoots. Our missiles had them head on and they just rocked out of the sky. Real small fireballs because they were real low on gas. From what we could tell, they never locked us up [acquire the F-15s with their missile lock-on systems]. They might have been attempting to, but we didn't get any indications that they had.[17] "

ABOVE: An F-15C test fires the AIM-120 Advanced Medium-Range Air-to-Air Missile, or AMRAAM, known by the nickname "the Slammer." (USAF)

shot down numerous Syrian fighters – including MiG-21 "Fishbeds" and MiG-25s – for no combat losses. During the 1991 Gulf War, F-15s helped the Coalition achieve complete air supremacy in only three days. They also destroyed dozens of Iraqi armored vehicles, bunkers, and troop positions, utilizing the LANTIRN (Low Altitude Navigation and Targeting Infrared for Night) navigation and targeting pod system for after-dark ops.

By 2008, F-15s had killed 104 enemy aircraft for zero losses, proving its worth in the role for which it was conceived. The Eagle will of course, be replaced, and is already being so in some areas of US service by the F-22 Raptor. Its successors, however, will have a hard act to follow.

AH-64 APACHE

By the end of the Vietnam War in 1975, most militarily developed nations had either built or acquired attack helicopters – helicopters specifically designed to deliver heavy firepower rather than perform utility or assault roles. The United States had the HueyCobra, the Soviets the Mil Mi-8 Hind, the French had armed versions of the Aérospatiale Gazelle, and the British the Westland Lynx. In 1984, however, the US Army took delivery of its first AH-64 Apache helicopters, which took rotary-winged combat capabilities to new levels.

NEW LETHALITY

The first Apache model, the AH-64A, caused a stir amongst the international defense community, which saw immense potential in the new aircraft. With a predatory, insect-like appearance, the AH-64A was powered by two General Electric T700-700 turboshafts that could push the helicopter to a maximum speed of 192mph (306km/h). The helicopter was also fitted with infrared-suppressing exhaust systems to reduce its heat signature to infrared homing missiles. Its body featured armor capable of resisting strikes by 23mm cannon shells, and the AH-64A could also fly and hunt in almost all weathers, and at night.

What was really surprising, however, was its lethality. Standard armament was a 30mm chain gun and stub hardpoints that could take 16 Hellfire guided anti-tank missiles or pods of 2.75in rockets. These weapons were linked by computer targeting systems through to the crew's Integrated Helmet and Display Sighting System (IHADSS), which enabled the pilot and co-pilot to acquire targets simply by looking at them.

OPPOSITE: An Apache conducts a live-fire exercise on the Korean border. (JUNG YEON-JE/AFP/Getty Images)

ABOVE: Apaches are designed as tank-busters, a role which they expertly performed during the 1991 Gulf War. They also deploy in close support roles alongside friendly armor, in this case US M2 Abrams. (Department of Defense)

BELOW: Apaches are designed to fly at extremely low altitudes using the terrain and vegetation to hide from enemy eyes and radar. (Department of Defense)

The Gulf War of 1991 showed the fearsome power of the AH-64A. A total of 277 of the helicopters were involved, and between them they destroyed more than 500 Iraqi vehicles. A single Apache could hover up from behind cover, and acquire and kill a tank, armored personnel carrier (APC), or other vehicle every few seconds, from ranges of 5 miles (8km). In the 100-day war, the AH-64 had more than justified its existence.

AH-64D LONGBOW

Later in the 1990s, a new version of the Apache arrived in service – the AH-64D Longbow. It was immediately distinguishable from its predecessor by the large, mushroom-shaped dome containing the AN/APG-78 Longbow millimeter-wave Fire Control Radar (FCR) target acquisition system. The FCR transformed the Apache's already formidable fighting power. Allied to a new Longbow Hellfire "fire-and-forget" missile, the FCR automatically detects, classifies,

ABOVE: An Apache is off-loaded to take part in a field exercise in Alaska. (Department of Defense)

BELOW: Soldiers perform maintenance on an AH-64 Apache attack helicopter at Forward Operating Base Speicher in Iraq during Operation *Iraqi Freedom*. (Department of Defense)

AH-64D – SPECIFICATIONS

Crew: 2

Powerplant: 2 x T700-GE-701Cs turboshafts

Length: 58ft 2in (17.73m)

Height: 13ft 3in (4.05 m)

Rotor diameter: 17ft 2in (5.23m)

Weight (operational): 15,075lb (6,838kg)

Maximum speed: 171.5mph (276km/h)

Maximum hover altitude: 15,895ft (4,845m)

Maximum range: 1,180 miles (1,900km) with internal and external fuel

Armament: M230 33mm Gun; 2.75in Hydra-70 Folding-Fin Aerial Rockets; AGM-114 Hellfire anti-tank missiles; AGM-122 Sidearm anti-radar missile; AIM-9 Sidewinder air-to-air missiles

ABOVE: Before its deployment in Operation *Desert Storm*, it was alleged that the AH-64 would not be able to handle desert conditions, in spite of the fact that it had been tested on exercise in Egypt and had coped with the all-pervading sand. But it proved to be highly effective in the Gulf and later in Afghanistan. (Department of Defense)

and prioritizes multiple ground and air targets, while also enhancing the pilot's battlefield awareness and coordinating fire with other AH-64Ds. Apache weapons systems can now include air-to-air missiles such as the AIM-9 Sidewinder. Similarly dramatic changes in avionics and ECM equipment have further increased the helicopter's survivability.

The AH-64D has been combat tested in both Iraq and Afghanistan since 2001. Furthermore, export sales to countries such as the UK, Israel, and Saudi Arabia have seen the Apache fight in other contexts. Israeli AH-64s, for example, have delivered precision strikes to take out leading Hamas or Hezbollah figures in Lebanon, and in May 2001 an AH-64 even used a Hellfire to shoot down a Lebanese Cessna aircraft that was in Israeli airspace. AH-64s are not invulnerable, and have suffered most of their losses from opportunistic anti-aircraft fire, but used sensibly they give their operators a versatile command of the battlespace.

In the words of leading Apache authority Chris Bishop:

Like an infantryman the Apache uses a combination of stealth, agility, and speed of movement to enhance its fighting prowess. It can hide, duck, rise, and fight in a fluid, fast-changing environment. It combines the capabilities of an infantry squad with that of the tank and artillery, using fire-and-maneuver tactics at close quarters while at the same time being able to reach out and destroy targets at ranges of several miles with its advanced and highly accurate weaponry.

Indeed, the Apache was designed as a mainstay weapon for the US Army and it now occupies a role as important as anti-tank guns or field artillery enjoyed during World War II.

F-117 NIGHTHAWK

THE F-117 NIGHTHAWK, WHEN IT ENTERED production in the late 1970s, was at the absolute cutting edge of combat aviation, and was shrouded in the deepest levels of secrecy. Exploration of "low observables" technology began as a joint pursuit of the Defense Advanced Research Projects Agency (DARPA) and the US Air Force earlier in the decade, and by 1977 Lockheed and Northrop were in the running to produce a new aircraft using the advanced research. Lockheed won out with what would become the F-117A Nighthawk.

STRATEGIC CAPABILITIES

The F-117 has been described as a fighter, but it is actually more of a strategic strike aircraft, designed to penetrate enemy air defenses and hit protected targets of critical importance, such as nuclear missile silos or command-and-control posts. Compared to conventional aircraft, the F-117 was (and remains) bizarre to behold. Its wedge-shaped airframe was composed of entirely flat surfaces with angular joins, the configuration being computer designed to diffuse radar returns. Radar-absorbent materials also covered the entire outer skin, and to reduce heat emissions detectable from the ground, the engine exhaust was set over the aft fuselage. Equipped primarily with laser- or GPS-guided bombs, the Nighthawk could slip into hostile airspace at subsonic speed, deliver its ordnance, and escape while producing only intermittent and flickering patterns on enemy radar.

First combat testing for the F-117A came during Operation *Just Cause* – the US invasion of Panama in 1989 – when two aircraft attacked the Rio Hato barracks. The aircraft was then

OPPOSITE: This top view of an F-117 Stealth fighter shows the strange angularity of its design, which along with its material construction gives it a negligible radar signature. The F-117 Nighthawk, along with the B-2 bomber, provided the USAF wiht stealth capabilities. (USAF)

ABOVE: A B-2 drops 32 inert 500lb GBU-38 JDAMs on the Utah Testing and Training Range. The B-2 was first deployed in conflict during the war in Kosovo where it was reportedly responsible for destroying almost a third of all NATO targets. (USAF)

BELOW: A B-2 leads two F-117s in flight. Although the F-117 has now been phased out in favor of its successor the F-22 Raptor, the B-2 continues to serve on the frontline in Afghanistan. (USAF)

used heavily in the 1991 Gulf War, hitting hardened and sensitive targets throughout Iraq, and delivering 1,271 combat sorties with no losses.

Such records seemed to show that the F-117 did what it was intended to do, and upgrade programs further enhanced its avionics and combat computers. Yet it was not invulnerable. On March 27, 1999, during the Kosovo War, an F-117 was shot down over Serbia by a Yugoslav copy of the SA-3 "Goa" SAM system. Nevertheless, F-117s went on to serve successfully during the air campaigns of Operation *Iraqi Freedom* in 2003. Since then, the F-117 has been phased out in favor of more modern stealth aircraft such as the F-22 Raptor.

STEALTH BOMBER

The F-117 is really only one half of the United States' stealth story. In 1987, the US Air Force revealed the existence of another low observable aircraft, this time a long-range bomber – the Northrop B-2 Spirit. The B-2 was designed with a similar

F-117 MISSION

Lieutenant-Colonel Barry E. Horne remembers piloting an F-117 against an Iraqi ammunition bunker during the 1991 Gulf War air campaign:

" I approached from south to north, and used only one weapon. Right after release, I detected that the thumb tracker was overly sensitive. That caused me considerable difficulty late in the delivery. At one point, the tracker caused the sight-line to move, or rather jump, approximately 100 ft south of the target. I regained control and manage to steer the weapon to final impact. The bomb hit precisely in the middle of the double bunker, striking the wall that separated them. The explosion was absolutely brilliant. It seemed to engulf the sky all around me. For a moment I was afraid that it might even reach up and grab me.[18] "

ABOVE: A 2,000lb GBU-27 training round is positioned for loading into the bomb-bay of an F-117 during pre-war training shortly before the outbreak of the 1991 Gulf War. (Denny Lombard/Lockheed Martin)

ABOVE: The air campaign for F-117 pilots during the First Gulf War came to an end on February 28, 1991. This brought 43 continuous nights of service for the air crews to a conclusion. (Courtesy of Rose Reynolds)

strategic purpose to the F-117, but with the ability to deliver much heavier payloads, including nuclear weapons. The same stealth technologies were applied, but on a larger scale, and the capabilities are impressive – a range of more than 6,000 miles (9,656km) and the capacity to deploy ordnance ranging from 80 500lb (227kg) bombs to 16 B-61 or B-63 nuclear weapons. The B-2 was used heavily as a conventional bomber in the Kosovo war and in both Afghanistan and Iraq since 2001. Its survivability is impressive, but the huge cost of maintaining its low observable qualities have raised a question mark over its value for money. Nevertheless, aircraft like the F-117 and the B-2 have established the principles of stealth strike capability.

M1 ABRAMS

Main battle tanks (MBTs) offer land forces two main virtues: firepower and survivability. In the modern world, no armored vehicle represents these qualities better than the US Abrams. Its first variant, the M1, went into production in 1980 and was state-of-the-art at every level.

SURVIVABILITY

The M1 was wrapped in composite armor based on the resilient British Chobham type, and no US tank before or since has imparted such a degree of armored protection to a crew. It was powered by a Lycoming gas turbine, which could push the 63-short-ton (57.2-tonne) vehicle to a maximum road speed of 45mph (72km/h). A 105mm fully stabilized gun, with advanced fire-control, was supplied with 55 rounds. During the 1980s and 1990s, improved versions appeared. The M1A1 replaced the 105mm rifled gun with a superior 120mm smoothbore weapon, plus upgraded NBC (nuclear, biological, chemical) systems, while the M1A2 introduced more advanced navigation, fire-control, and surveillance systems.

The Abrams has more than proved itself in combat. During the 1991 Gulf War, Iraqi T-72s were completely outclassed by

OPPOSITE: An M1 Abrams photographed during the final tank battle of Operation *Desert Storm* on March 2, 1991. When the Iraqi Hammurabi Armored Division attempted to evade the formal ceasefire on Saddam Hussein's orders, their plan became unhinged when they ran into the US 24th Infantry Division. The Iraqi column was quickly overrun by Abrams and Bradleys while being fired upon by Apache helicopters from above. In just a couple of hours the Iraqis lost 187 armored vehicles, 34 artillery vehicles and 400 trucks – all for the loss of just one Abrams. (US Army)

ABOVE: The gun barrel of an M1 Abrams complete with an optical sensor to help assess and engage targets. (GDLS)

BELOW: The 2nd Armored Division, Fort Hood, Texas on exercise with their newly received M1 Abrams tanks, c. 1983. (Courtesy of Steve Zaloga)

the M1A1's night-fighting systems, fire-control, and crew training. Abrams would often engage and destroy T-72s beyond the Soviet tank's main gun range – the last thing the Iraqi tank crews would see were the flashes of the guns on the horizon. In the later 2003 invasion of Iraq, one incident saw a single company of Abrams destroy seven T-72s at point-blank range in only five minutes during the battle of Mahmudiyah, with no US losses.

FIREPOWER

Such superior firepower needs exploring further. The Abrams tank is fitted with the smoothbore M256A1 120mm gun. The gun's ideal range is around 3,280yds (3,000m), but with the latest fire-control systems some gunners can engage targets out past 4,374yds (4,000m).

The velocity of the round – which flies faster than an assault rifle bullet – translates into truly devastating target impact (see feature box). Of course, visually acquiring a

DEPLETED-URANIUM AMMUNITION

The Abram's main tank-killer round is the M829A1 Armor-Piercing Fin-Stabilized Discarding-Sabot Tracer (APFSDS-T). This consists of a slim sub-caliber depleted uranium (DU) dart encased in an aluminum sabot that fits the bore of the gun. Once the shell is fired, the sabot peels away, leaving the dart – made from one of the hardest substances known – to fly onwards at incredible velocity, with fins acting like the flights on an arrow. Note that there is no explosive content whatsoever – the APFSDS-T does all its damage by kinetic energy alone, slamming through the target with the force of an 11-ton truck hitting a wall at 70mph (43km/h), but with the impact concentrated over an area of less than an inch square. Having punched through a tank's armor, the heat transfer of the round can ignite fuel and ammunition. Pieces of fragmented armor and other objects violently fly around the tank interior (lethal detritus such as this is called "spall," and can occur from shockwaves alone, even if the rod has not penetrated). Occupants can be literally vaporized.

BELOW: The size of the dust cloud gives some indication of the speeds that the Abrams is capable of – 60mph (96km/h) although limited to 45mph (72km/h) to ensure that crews do not sustain injuries when traveling cross-country. (Department of Defense)

> *The spectacular and catastrophic explosions often lifted the turrets 30–40ft in the air and tore the vehicles apart.*
>
> **Captain Mark Gerges, Commander of Bravo Company, 2–70 Armor, at the battle of Medina Ridge, 1991.**

ABOVE: An Abrams fitted with a mine rake. (Courtesy of Steve Zaloga)

M1 ABRAMS – SPECIFICATIONS

Crew: 4
Length: 32.3ft (9.8m)
Width: 12ft (3.6m)
Height: 9.5ft (2.8m) (to top of machine-gun)
Engine: 1,500hp Avxo-Lycoming gas turbine
Fuel capacity: 505gal (2,295 litres)
Maximum road speed: 41mph (66km/h)
Main armament: 120mm M256 smoothbore gun
Main gun rate of fire: 6rpm
Secondary armament: M240 7.62mm co-axial
    machine-gun

target far from ensures a hit, and it is here that the Abrams' onboard digital fire-control computer does much of the work. A laser range-finder precisely calculates the distance to the target, and the computer makes automatic adjustments to the barrel angle based on factors such as round drop, air resistance, air temperature, gravity, windspeed, ammunition type, propellant temperature, tube wear, and relative motion. The rapid calculations made by the fire-control system, combined with a fully stabilized gun system, mean that the Abrams can shoot accurately even when crashing up and down rough terrain.

In service in Iraq, Abrams have proved vulnerable to IEDs like all armored vehicles, although the vehicle's impressive protection means actual crew losses have been kept low. Some experts predict the demise of heavy armor in the near future, but it will take a persuasive alternative to replace a tank such as the Abrams.

M2/M3 BRADLEY

THE IDEA OF USING ARMORED VEHICLES TO TRANSPORT infantry into battle took hold firmly during World War II, as evidenced in a broad range of half-tracks and carriers amongst the combatants. The postwar era, however, rendered such vehicles largely obsolete. In an age of fast maneuver warfare and more lethal and varied weapons systems, infantry carriers required better survivability and firepower if they were to hold their own alongside MBTs.

OPPOSITE: The British equivalent of the Bradley is the FV510 Warrior, although the British Army still relies on the 1960s vintage FV432 armored personnel carrier. Here an FV 432 of the 7th Brigade Royal Scots, 1st United Kingdom Armored Division, crosses into Kuwait from southern Iraq during Operation *Desert Storm*. (Department of Defense)

FROM APCS TO IFVS

During the 1940s and 1950s, the United States developed a new range of armored personnel carriers (APCs). These were fully tracked box-bodied designs, and sufficiently armored to withstand all small-arms fire and some cannon rounds. The first version, the M44, was a little too unwieldy – it could carry up to 27 men – but subsequent models such as the M75 and M59 reduced passenger numbers to about a dozen, giving them better speed and maneuverability. The greatest of the US APCs – the M113 – used aluminum armor, making it light enough to be air transportable. To date, more that 80,000 M113-type vehicles have been produced, and they still serve in the US Army, albeit in rear-echelon support duties.

Other countries were also forging ahead with APC designs. The British brought out the FV432 from 1963, with space for ten troops and fitted with an NBC protection system, while the Soviets produced the BTR-50 from 1954, based on the PT-76

light tank. All these vehicles were armed to some degree, typically with one or two machine-guns, but in the late 1960s the Soviets changed the game with the BMP-1 infantry fighting vehicle (IFV). The BMP-1 was as much about combat as transportation. Troops inside could fire their weapons through gun ports, while the vehicle also had a 73mm cannon and wire-guided anti-tank missiles. It was largely in response to the BMP-1's appearance, and to that of subsequent BMPs with even greater firepower, that the Bradley IFV was developed.

FORCE MULTIPLIER

The Bradley came into service in the early 1980s, and fell into two designations – the M2 IFV and the M3 CFV (Cavalry Fighting Vehicle), reflecting differences in tactical use rather than major differences in design. The M2 has a three-man crew plus space in the back for seven fully equipped soldiers (the M3, being a scout vehicle, has three crew plus two scouts).

It is fully armored with aluminum and spaced laminate armor, which combined with an NBC system makes it highly survivable. A two-man turret mounts the heavy weaponry – a 25mm Bushmaster chain-gun firing armor-piercing rounds; a co-axial 7.62mm machine-gun; and twin TOW anti-tank missile launcher on the left side. (The M3 also carries Dragon or Javelin anti-tank systems.)

With its firepower, protection, and excellent cross-country capabilities, the Bradley steadily began to replace the M113 in frontline use. The Bradley came into its own during the 1991 Gulf War. Their performance during this conflict won high praise, particuarly for its speed as it could easily keep pace with the charging M1A1 Abrams while the M113 could not.

BELOW: A Bradley rolls through the range during the 3rd Advise and Assist Brigade, 4th Infantry Division's gunnery training at Camp Buehring, Kuwait. (US Army)

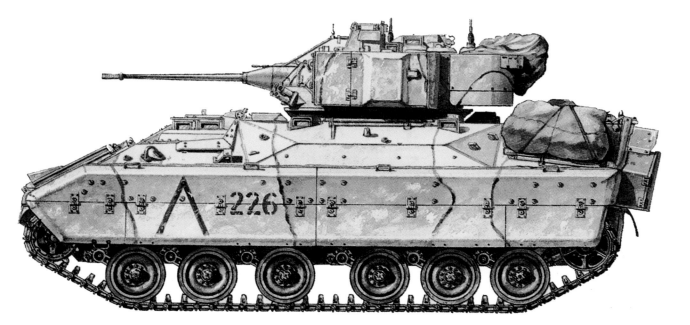

ABOVE: M3A1 Bradley Cavalry Fighting vehicle, 24th Infantry Division (Mech), February 1991. Unique to the Division, the 2nd Squadron used a simple camouflage pattern instead of the monotone CARC Tan found on other vehicles. (Artwork by Peter Sarson © Osprey Publishing Ltd.)

Standard tactics were for the tanks to take the lead due to their superior armor with the Bradleys acting as protective screens. But once the enemy defenses were reached the Bradleys would move forward to add their very effective firepower to the fray. Indeed, more enemy armored vehicles were destroyed by Bradleys than by Abrams MBTs, and only three out of the 2,200 deployed were knocked out in combat. In Iraq and Afghanistan, Bradleys have given superb troop protection, particularly in urban combat scenarios where troops need safe transportation through the streets, but also heavy close-quarters firepower when needed. The latest versions of the Bradley are fitted with features such as advanced tactical navigation systems and improved fire control. At the time of writing, however, possible replacements are under development.

TOW MISSILE

The Hughes BGM-71 TOW (Tube-launched, Optically tracked, Wire-guided) anti-tank missile is, in its latest configurations, still in frontline service more than 50 years after it was introduced, and with more than 45 armed forces. It has been adapted for use from armored vehicles and helicopters as well as by infantry. The basic TOW has a range of 4,100yds (3,750m) and an armor penetration of 23.6in (600mm). Guidance is via two command wires, connected to the missile, that spool out from the launcher unit after firing – the operator simply keeps the sight on the target to fly the missile to impact. The TOW II introduced a "flyover shoot-down" capability, in which the missile actually fires two explosively formed penetrator (EFP) slugs down onto the target's more vulnerable top areas, while the new TOW-ER has moved over to wireless command guidance.

BGM-109 TOMAHAWK

DURING THE 1991 GULF WAR, THE WORLD'S MEDIA broadcast many astonishing sights. Not least of them was the image of BGM-109 Tomahawk "cruise missiles" literally racing down streets at treetop level, going on to slam into high-value targets with astonishing precision. Such weapons were a sobering illustration of how lethal long-distance warfare had become.

OPPOSITE: A US ship-launched BGM-109 Tomahawk climbs into the sky from the guided missile cruiser USS *Winston Churchill* in 2003. The launch was from the eastern Mediterranean, in support of Operation *Iraqi Freedom*. (US Navy)

TRACKING TO TARGET

The BGM-109 Tomahawk Land Attack Missile (TLAM) was a product of US interest in cruise missiles during the 1970s and 1980s. Cruise missiles offered the ability to deliver nuclear or conventional warheads onto far-distant targets with unprecedented accuracy, and with the advantage of making the flight to target at low-level and with a small radar signal, improving its prospects of evading the enemy air defenses.

ABOVE: The destroyer USS *Preble* conducts a Tomahawk missile launch. (US Navy)

RIGHT: A Tomahawk missile launched from the nuclear-powered fast-attack submarine USS *Florida*. (US Navy)

By the mid 1980s, two major cruise missile types were in service: the air-launched (from a B-52) AGM-86 and the submarine- or ship-launched TLAM. (Focusing on the TLAM gives a good general impression of the performance of the AGM-86.) Prior to the introduction of the Block III TLAM in 1993, the Tomahawk relied on a combination of inertial and terrain contour matching (TERCOM) navigation. TERCOM works by comparing a pre-recorded contour map of the terrain against information from an on-board radar altimeter. Subsequent versions, however, incorporated GPS navigation and Digital Scene Matching Area Correlation (DSMAC) technology, which compares the landscape visible to the

ABOVE: The Combat Information Center, also known as the Operations Room, onboard US Navy vessels where the decision would be taken and the launch sequence begun for firing a Tomahawk missile. (US Navy)

BELOW: A Tomahawk cruise missile flies toward Iraq after being launched from the cruiser USS San Jacinto on March 25, 2003, in the Red Sea. (Photo by Mark Wilson/Getty Images)

missile's camera with a digital image stored in its memory. The latest Block IV versions take the sophistication to even greater levels. These missiles include features such as inflight target reprogramming; the ability to loiter over target areas while feeding back information to a command center; and the means to integrate itself fully into the US forces' "netcentric warfare" system.

REMOTE ATTACKS

The outcome of all this technology is a missile that can fly 1,000 miles (1,600km) at low-level across complex terrain, and hit targets no bigger than an individual house, striking with 1,000lb (454kg) unitary conventional or W80 nuclear warheads, although it can also distribute submunitions over the target from a dispenser. TLAMs sounded the opening notes of Operation *Desert Storm*, and during the campaign 290 TLAMs were fired, of which 242 hit their targets. During Operation *Allied Force* (1999), as NATO forces moved against Serbian units in Kosovo, two TLAMs struck a Yugoslav Ministry of Interior (MUP) police headquarters building in Pristina, destroying two floors of the building with their 700lb (318kg) warheads but leaving the rest – and the other structures nearby – relatively unscathed. On March 20, 2003, at the start of Operation *Iraqi Freedom*, the cruisers USS *Cowpens* and USS *Bunker Hill*, the destroyers USS *Donald Cook* and USS *Milius*, and the SSNs USS *Cheyenne* and USS *Montpelier*, launched hundreds of TLAMs in the opening salvo of the war. In this initial action, at one point 36 TLAMs hit a single bunker complex in Baghdad simultaneously, the missiles fired in the (erroneous) belief that the bunker contained much of the Iraqi high command. TLAMs have also been used to target Taliban and al-Qaeda bases in Afghanistan.

BGM-109 TLAM – SPECIFICATIONS

Powerplant: Williams International F107 cruise turbofan engine; ARC/CSD solid-fuel booster
Length: 18ft 3in (5.56m); with booster: 20ft 6in (6.25m)
Diameter: 20.4in (51.81cm)
Wingspan: 8ft 9in (2.67m)
Weight: 2,900lb (1,315kg); with booster: 3,500lb (1,588kg)
Speed: 550mph (880km/h)

Range:	Block II TLAM-A – 1,500 miles (2,500km)
	Block III TLAM-C – 1,000 miles (1,600km)
	Block III TLAM-D – 800 miles (1,250km)
	Block IV TLAM-E – 1,000 miles (1,600 km)
Guidance System:	Block II TLAM-A – INS, TERCOM
	Block III TLAM-C, D & Block IV TLAM-E – INS, TERCOM, DSMAC, and GPS
Warhead:	Block II TLAM-N – W80 nuclear warhead
	Block III TLAM-C and Block IV TLAM-E – 1,000lb (454kg) unitary warhead
	Block III TLAM-D –submunitions dispenser

Since 1991, more than 1,100 TLAMs have been fired. Their precision attack capabilities, and their warhead versatility, means that within their operational range there are few places for an enemy to hide with safety.

FIM-92 STINGER

WE HAVE ALREADY SEEN SOMETHING OF THE EVOLUTION of SAM technology, when we previously considered the SA-2 Guideline (see pp.298–301). Yet SAMs produced a very different offshoot during the 1960s, one that would give even the humble infantryman the capability to bring down an advanced jet aircraft.

MANPADS

Serious interest in man-portable air-defense systems (MANPADS) began shortly after World War II on both sides of the Atlantic. Alongside medium- and high-altitude SAM systems, the Soviets and the Americans both commenced experiments in shoulder-launched guided missile technology, to give infantry and armored units the capability to engage low-level but fast-moving enemy jets.

FIRST GENERATION

The first generation of operational weapons to emerge came in the 1960s, with the US FIM-43 Redeye and the Soviet 9K32 Strela-2 (NATO reporting name: SA-7 "Grail"). Measuring 3ft

OPPOSITE: An FIM-92 Stinger ready for action. (USAF)

11.5in (1.2m) long and weighing just 18.3lb (8.3kg), the Redeye had an effective range of 14,800ft (4,500m) and ripped through the sky at Mach 1.7, using infrared homing to lock onto the target aircraft's exhaust. The SA-7 worked along similar lines, albeit with slightly less range than the Redeye.

These two systems were in the very early days of MANPADS, which (compared to modern missiles) was reflected in high miss rates and the requirement for missiles to be launched at the exposed exhaust of aircraft once it had flown by. Yet they worked, and found their way into actual combat use. About 50 Redeye missiles were covertly supplied to the *Mujahideen* fighters in Afghanistan in 1984, where they downed several Soviet jets and helicopters, although they were replaced shortly after by the Stinger (see below). The SA-7, by contrast, has seen action from the War of Attrition between Israel and Egypt in 1969 to the insurgency in Iraq since 2003 – in 2006, an SA-7 missile even brought down an Apache helicopter. (The missile has obviously been improved significantly over its lifetime.)

BELOW: A US Marine fires a Stinger during training in 2009. Stingers gained notoriety during the Soviet–Afghan War but they continue to be extremely useful. (USMC)

BRITISH MANPADS

Between 1975 and 1985, the main British Army MANPAD was the Blowpipe. This was a manual command to line of sight (MCLOS) system, the operator guiding the missile to target via a sight and a joystick. It was a poor performer, complex and inaccurate, and during the Falklands War had no more than a 10 percent hit rate. It was replaced with the far more convincing Javelin, which had a semi-automatic command line of sight (SACLOS) guidance system – the operator has to keep the sight fixed on the target after launch, but the missile guides itself to impact. From the Javelin came the Starburst in 1989, which replaced the Javelin's radio command SACLOS with a more accurate laser unit, one that was also more difficult to jam. In the late 1990s, however, the Starstreak HVM arrived. This fourth-generation weapon flies at Mach 3.5 and deploys three laser-beam riding submunition darts. To date it has never been tested in combat, the real proof of any military technology.

ABOVE: Extensively used by the *Mujihideen* in the 1980s when covertly supplied by the CIA, Stingers are now used by ISAF forces throughout Afghanistan. (USAF)

RIGHT: Troops undergo training with the latest generation of Stingers. (USAF)

NEW GENERATIONS

The Stinger came into service in 1981, developed as a next-generation replacement for the Redeye. Its central improvement was an infrared guidance system that allowed launches against aircraft in any aspect to the shooter, even head on. First combat testing actually came in the hands of British Special Forces soldiers in the Falklands War in 1982, who brought down two Argentine helicopters with the system, although the regular army was using a British-made MANPAD, the Blowpipe.

The most intensive use of the Stinger, however, came when the US supplied some 500 units to the *Mujahideen* in their war against the Soviet occupiers. Previously, the Afghan fighters had struggled against Soviet attack jets and Mil Mi-8 helicopter gunships with cumbersome Oerlikon cannon and small-arms. The introduction of the Stingers radically changed the situation. Although accurate kill figures are not available,

the Soviets certainly lost dozens of aircraft during the first few months in which they faced Stingers, and the weapon system made a definite contribution to the eventual Soviet expulsion from the country.

Several stages of enhancement have kept the Stinger in service. The latest missiles include features such as identification-friend-or-foe (IFF) computers, range extension to 5 miles (8km), and countermeasures systems, plus it has been developed for mounts on armored vehicles and helicopters. MANPADS have ensured that even at speed and low levels, modern aircraft still operate in a threat environment.

IMPROVISED EXPLOSIVE DEVICES

As long as there have been explosives, there have been what we now class as improvised explosive devices (IEDs). Yet the wars in Afghanistan and Iraq have tragically sharpened our awareness of these weapons – around 50 percent of US and British casualties have been caused by IEDs.

TACTICAL ADVANTAGES

IEDs come in a bewildering variety of forms, limited only by the imagination and materials of bomb-makers. Common devices include artillery or mortar shells command detonated by a mobile phone (sometimes multiple shells are "daisy-chained" together for optimum effect); propane tanks stuffed full of explosive; bombs placed in animal carcasses or drinks cans, or even in fake kerbing stones made from Plaster of Paris; vehicle bombs driven at speed towards the target; suicide bomb vests; even crude explosively formed penetrators (EFPs) – basic shaped-charge warheads, sometimes detonated by a person or vehicle breaking an infrared beam.

The tactical advantages of IEDs are easy to appreciate. They give the insurgent "standoff" distance, thereby reducing the risks of casualties from an enemy who usually has superior firepower resources in direct- or indirect-fire engagements. Large IEDs maximize the potential to inflict heavy casualties within a short window of time, and provide one of the few insurgent resources for tackling heavy armor or protected installations/buildings. The opportunities and locations for

OPPOSITE: An eight-wheeled Stryker combat light armored vehicle lies on its side after accidentally detonating an IED. All the crew survived but the vehicle required a complete factory rebuild before returning to frontline service. (US Army)

ABOVE: US troops undergo IED clearance training at Fort Irwin. (US Army)

BELOW: Fighting an unconventional war in both Iraq and Afghanistan, the US Army has been forced to improve its countermeasure efforts against the threat of IEDs. The IED Interrogation Arm has been developed by the Army Research, Development and Engineering Command to assist route clearance teams. Lightweight and easy to use, it can be attached to all military vehicles currently used in theater. (US Army)

emplacing IEDs are almost limitless, therefore target selection and timing are precisely controlled.

EFFECTS

More intangibly, but just as important, are the psychological and social effects of IEDs. The expectation of encountering IEDs, for example, breeds caution and the need for modified tactics. Vehicle convoys have to be staggered, with vehicles moving in a variable, elastic relation to each other to disrupt the timing of bombers using command detonation systems. Every suspected IED must be investigated and neutralized by explosive ordnance disposal (EOD) officers, resulting in frequent halts in convoy or troop movements. The cumulative effects of these stops deprives a force of control over operational tempo, typically one of the decisive elements of maneuver warfare. Note also that just the *suspicion* of an IED has a retarding effect, a fact that insurgents have been quick to exploit. In Northern Ireland during the "Troubles," IRA operators would weigh down the trunk of a car with blocks of concrete and park the vehicle in

IEDS AND COMBAT STRESS

IEDs have a major impact effect on the morale of affected troops. The levels of combat stress they induce are profound. Mark Lachance, a US Army Iraq veteran, here draws an analogy to illustrate the profound anxiety caused by IEDs:

> It's what they do psychologically is what makes them an effective tool. You can take your most war-hardened veteran from any country and put him in a Humvee and have him go driving down a road and just have IEDs blow up randomly and it's going to slowly start to affect him after a while. I myself was in many IED strikes, and had to blow up many IEDs that were discovered before they could be used against us... Imagine this – next time you are driving down the road and you are going to work or home, look at every guard rail, every trash can, every cement kerb and all those things could blow up at any moment ... just think about that... Everything that is there is prospectively your enemy... My Staff Sergeant said it best, "It's like playing the lottery, if you play it long enough eventually you are going to win." That's how it is with roadside bombs. No-one's protected, no amount of armor can save you. Although the first ten times you might survive, all it takes is once and you're dead.[19]

ABOVE: An IED is destroyed in a controlled detonation. This particular device had been discovered on a major road in the Yosef Khel district of Paktila province, Afghanistan by US and Afghan National Police troops. (AFP/Getty Images)

ABOVE: This photograph was taken from a US medevac helicopter on November 5, 2009. A US Army vehicle burns after it was hit by an IED. Two US soldiers were killed and two injured in the incident in southern Afghanistan. (Manpreet/Romana/AFP/Getty Images)

a suspicious location. The security forces, fearing the vehicle contained a major car bomb, would have to go through full EOD procedures, putting a drain on their finances and planning. Furthermore, the enforced stop would give the bombers plenty of time to observe EOD operations, and design countermeasures.

While this book often focuses on high-tech developments in fighting technologies, IEDs remind us that in the realms of insurgency and "low-intensity warfare," simple innovations with basic explosives can be the most effective tools of warfare.

BALLISTIC MISSILES

THE STORY OF INTERCONTINENTAL BALLISTIC MISSILES (ICBMs) is primarily that of a technological race between two superpowers, the United States and the USSR. It was a race that, on several occasions, brought the world to the brink of all-out nuclear war. Although this horror was avoided, ICBMs nevertheless became the poker chips of international politics for half a century.

STRATEGIC MISSILE

The German V-2 (see pp.270–273) introduced the world to strategic ballistic missiles, and in the developing Cold War both sides sought to develop such systems with more convincing ranges and payloads. This was exclusively a nuclear race – ballistic missiles do not have the accuracy of constantly powered cruise missiles, so compensated for their inaccuracies with city-destroying warheads. Soviet innovation initially took the lead, when in 1957 the USSR introduced the SS-6 "Sapwood" multistage nuclear ballistic missile. (Multistage rockets jettison power components during the flight, meaning that the missile becomes successively light and attains a greater velocity.) The SS-6 had a range of less than 3,500 miles (5,633km), which meant that to hit the United States it had to be stationed in the Arctic north, a posting that seriously degraded their effectiveness. One way around this was the Soviet attempt in the early 1960s to base one-megaton SS-4 intermediate-range ballistic missiles (IRBMs) on Cuba, but these were withdrawn after the Cuban Missile Crisis.

OPPOSITE: Models of US (white) and Soviet (black) intercontinental ballistic missiles from 1979. (Right–Left) MX, four under-development Soviet missiles, SS-18, SS-17, SS-19, SS-16, SS-13, SS-9, Minuteman III, SS-11, Minuteman II, SS-8, SS-7, Titan. (Time & Life Pictures/Getty Images)

By this time, however, the United States was catching up. US Thor and Jupiter IRBMs were deployed in Europe in 1958, but the following year the Atlas and Titan I, true ICBMs, became operational on the US mainland. With maximum ranges of between 6,300 and 7,500 miles (10,139 and 12,070km), they had the capability to strike deep into the Soviet heartland.

COMPETING SYSTEMS

The technological ICBM arms race through the 1950s and 1960s largely revolves around launch systems and propellants. The threat from each other's missiles meant that ICBMs were steadily moved to protected underground launch silos. Furthermore, it became imperative that missiles could be launched rapidly in response to an enemy attack, hence there was a shift from liquid propellants – which had time consuming

LEFT: America's Titan I missile on a US Air Force base in 1961. (Photo by Ralph Crane/Time Life Pictures/Getty Images)

BELOW: A Russian Topol-M intercontinental ballistic missile being driven through Red Square during the nation's Victory Day parade in Moscow on May 9, 2009, in commemoration of the end of World War II. (DMITRY KOSTYUKOV/AFP/Getty Images)

SUBMARINE-LAUNCHED BALLISTIC MISSILES

Submarines offered ideal launch platforms for ballistic missiles, being able to deploy secretly near enemy coastlines and having a high level of survivability. The first submarine-launched ballistic missile (SLBM) was the Soviet SS-N-4 Sark. Introduced in 1955, it was severely limited by a short 350-mile (563km) range. Not so the US Polaris SLBMs, the first of which was operational by 1960. The A-2 variant had a range of up to 1,700 miles (2,376km). MIRV technology entered SLBMs during the 1970s, with the US Poseidon C-3 and Trident I and the Soviet SS-N-18 "Stingray." The UK also became a major SLBM user, deploying both Polaris and Trident, and the French had their own missiles in the M-4 MIRV.

storage, loading, and operational requirements – to solid propellants. Launch times of solid fuel missiles like the US Minuteman I (operational in 1963) and the Soviet SS-13 "Savage" (1969) were taken down to a matter of minutes.

The 1970s was the decade in which multiple warheads were introduced, first in the form of multiple reentry vehicles (MRVs), such as in the Soviet SS-9 "Scarp" and US Polaris A-3. MRVs deployed multiple warheads against a single target, creating a lethal nuclear "footprint," but the United States soon went further with multiple independently targetable reentry vehicles (MIRVs), first utilized in the Minuteman III. MIRV missiles could deploy multiple warheads against entirely independent targets.

During the 1980s, the theme was accuracy, as improvements in computer guidance systems meant that nuclear warheads could now be delivered to within a few hundred feet of their aiming point. The Trident I missile, for example, could deploy eight 100-kiloton warheads on targets at 4,600 miles (7,403km).

ABOVE: A photograph of an American ground-based interceptor, which is designed to destroy ICBMs before they can enter US airspace. (US Army)

The Soviets were also fielding MIRVs by the late 1970s. Maneuvering warheads (MaRVs), introduced in the US Pershing II IRBM in 1984, allowed targeting corrections even in the terminal phase, to give warheads an accuracy approaching that of cruise missiles.

Although strategic arms negotiations have reduced global stocks of ICBMs dramatically since the 1980s, they remain in considerable numbers. New systems produced by states such as North Korea, China, and, potentially, Iran, means that the possibilities of strategic nuclear warfare are not entirely distant.

UNMANNED AERIAL VEHICLES

REMOTELY PILOTED UNMANNED AERIAL VEHICLES (UAVs) first appeared in the 1940s and 50s, and were used in highly secretive fashion by the United States during the Vietnam War, where they flew more than 3,400 reconnaissance missions. Up until the 1990s, however, UAVs were ranked well below manned aircraft in terms of their tactical importance, a situation that was set to change.

RECONNAISSANCE

UAVs offer a mixed package of advantages and disadvantages. On the plus side, the absence of a pilot – the aircraft are controlled from a remote ground or air station via radio or satellite link – means that the aircraft are (generally) cheaper to produce, can pull G-forces beyond the physical limits of a pilot, have incredible endurance (multiple ground operators can control the aircraft in shifts), and can be destroyed without the loss of valued and valuable air crew. The disadvantages are mainly tactical, and often revolve around the ability of a remote operator to make judicious decisions about weapons deployment – warfighting looks very much like a video game through the UAV's cameras. Indeed, it is worth noting that in some modern UAV operations in Afghanistan, the aircraft are actually controlled in real time by operators in the United States.

A significant milestone in the history of UAVs was the debut of the MQ-1 Predator over the Balkans in 1995. The Predator offered

OPPOSITE: The USAF RQ-4A Global Hawk has an enormous wingspan of 116.2ft (35.4m). It has a maximum endurance of 36 hours and a maximum altitude of 65,000ft (19,000m). The Global Hawk is more than just a state-of-the art reconnaissance tool; if required it can also deliver a payload of 2,000lb (910kg). Here a Global Hawk is shown en route to Edwards Air Force Base, California. (USAF)

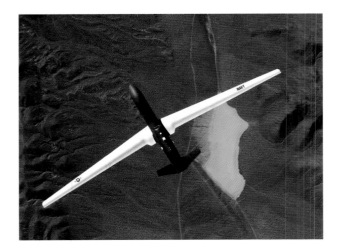

24-hour endurance, powerful surveillance technologies, and, from 2001, the ability to deploy weapons such as the AGM-114 Hellfire anti-tank and Griffen air-to-surface missiles, and other ordnance. Predators and other UAVs, such as the US Army's RQ-5 Hunter, were also used in Operation *Allied Force* over the Balkans in 1999 not only to collect intelligence, but also to identify and illuminate targets with laser target designators, for laser-guided weapons to destroy.

COMBAT DUTIES

Since that time, these drones have become major contributors to both surveillance and, increasingly, combat missions over Afghanistan and Iraq. For example, during 2001–02, Predators regularly flew over the so-called no-fly zones in sanctioned Iraq, capturing images of the Iraqi integrated air defense system. More aggressively, in Afghanistan in 2002, Predator UAVs took out suspected al-Qaeda leaders, and during the Operation *Anaconda* ground offensive they proved their mettle as a close air support asset, using missiles to provide

ABOVE: A US Navy UAV is recovered aboard USS *Wisconsin* during Operation *Desert Shield* in November 1990. Naval UAVs are usually recovered by guiding them into a net. (US Navy)

BELOW: The Global Hawk in flight, the largest and most sophisticated of the UAVs currently in use, no doubt thanks in part to their $35 million price tag. (Northrop Grumman)

BELOW: The MQ-1 Predator, the first of the hunter-killer UAVs, and the most successful, seeing extensive service in the mountainous regions of Afghanistan and Pakistan. It has even reportedly been used in a close-air support role. (USAF)

suppressing fire against Taliban militia while soldiers on the ground moved to better fighting positions.

The combat capabilities of UAVs are becoming as powerful as they are controversial. The MQ-9 Reaper, for example, was introduced into action in 2007. Fully loaded with 3,800lb (1,700kg) of ordnance, it can fly for 14 hours (28 hours in pure surveillance mode) and deliver JDAM and laser-guided bombs. From January 2009 to February 2010, Predators and Reapers between them have fired 184 missiles and dropped 77 PGMs over Afghanistan. Inevitable civilian casualties have led to criticism that UAVs encourage easy killing by operators remote from the realities of war and collateral damage.

There are now literally dozens of different types of UAVs in service with military forces around the world. Their diversity is also expanding. At one end of the scale are high-altitude UAVs, such as the RQ-4A Global Hawk, designed to fly surveillance missions of 13,800 miles (22,200km), at an altitude of 65,000ft

MG-9 REAPER – SPECIFICATIONS

Crew (remote): 2

Powerplant: Honeywell TPE331-10GD turboprop
  engine developing 900shp (671kW)

Wingspan: 66ft (20.1m)

Length: 36ft (11m)

Height: 12ft 6in (3.8m)

Weight (empty): 4,900lb (2,223kg)

Weight (max take-off): 10,500lb (4,760kg)

Payload: 3,750lb (1,701kg)

Cruise speed: *c.* 230mph (200 knots)

Range: 1,150 miles (1,850km)

Ceiling: Up to 50,000ft (15,240m)

Armament: AGM-114 Hellfire missiles; GBU-12
  Paveway II laser-guided bombs; GBU-38 JDAMs

(19,812m). At the other end are hand-held drones launched by throwing them into the air like toy planes. These are designed to provide immediate local tactical surveillance to infantry or armored units. With UAVs already replacing manned aircraft in some conventional US wings, and as they acquire some autonomous flight and targeting capabilities, there are many who predict the demise of manned combat aircraft within a generation or two.

OPPOSITE: A mini-UAV is launched in Iraq, 2006. (US Army)

BELOW: Britain is currently investigating whether a Strategic Unmanned Air Vehicle Experimental could replace the RAF's Tornado strike aircraft. BAE developed this craft as a result. (BAE)

ACKNOWLEDGMENTS

THE CREATION OF THIS BOOK HAS INVOLVED THE expertise and assistance of many people. My thanks go to them all, but some deserve a special mention. Military experts Tony Holmes, Steven Zaloga, Dr Duncan Campbell and Martin Pegler gave invaluable help and advice in putting together the definitive list of 100 weapons included here, and defense consultant and friend Hunter Keeter graciously and quickly helped fact check some of the more complex historical points (any errors, however, are my own). Sincere thanks also go to Andrew Roberts for his brilliant foreword to this edition, and to Kate Moore and Emily Holmes of Osprey, who have done a typically masterful job with picture research and overseeing design, as well as providing their editorial expertise.

My final thanks go to my ever-patient family – my wonderful wife Mia and my two effervescent daughters Charlotte and Ruby – who never fail to give me their support, humor and love.

Dr Chris McNab
January 2011

ENDNOTES

1. Julius Caesar, *De Bello Gallico*
2. Homer, *The Iliad*
3. Marcus Vitruvius Pellio, *De Architectura*
4. Marcus Vitruvius Pellio, *De Architectura*
5. George Farmer, *The Light Dragoon* (London, 1844)
6. Quoted in Tony Holmes, *Aircraft of the Aces – Legends of the Skies* (Oxford, Osprey Publishing, 2004)
7. From Bob Carruthers, *Servants of Evil* (London, André Deutsch, 2001)
8. Fraser, IWM Sound 10259
9. Unwin, IWM Sound 11544
10. From Bob Carruthers, *Servants of Evil* (London, André Deutsch, 2001)
11. Adolf Galland, *The First and the Last* (London, Methuen, 1955)
12. J. Huber, *So war es Wirklich* (self published 1994). Translated and quoted in Prit Buttar, *Battleground Prussia* (Oxford, Osprey Publishing, 2010)
13. Alistair Borthwick, *Battalion: British Infantry Unit's Action from El Alamein to the Elbe 1942–45* (London, Baton Wicks Publications, 2001)
14. From Tony Holmes, *Aircraft of the Aces – Legends of the Skies* (Oxford, Osprey Publishing, 2004)
15. Quoted in Gordon L. Rottman, *The Rocket Propelled Grenade* (Oxford, Osprey Publishing, 2010)
16. Norman Franks, *Aircraft versus Aircraft* (London, Chancellor Press, 2001)
17. Stan Morse (ed.), *Gulf Air War Debrief* (London, Aerospace Publishing, 1991)
18. Warren Thompson, *F-117 Stealth Fighter Units of Operation Desert Storm* (Oxford, Osprey Publishing, 2007)
19. Chris McNab and Hunter Keeter, *Tools of Violence* (Oxford, Osprey Publishing, 2008)

INDEX

A-10 Thunderbolts 334–337
AAMs *see* air-to-air missiles
Advanced Medium-Range Air-to-Air Missiles
   (AMRAAMs) **344**
Afghan National Army **321**, **322**
Afghanistan
   deployment of aircraft in **336**, **337**
   IEDs 367–370
Agincourt, battle of (1415) **70**, 71
AH-64 Apache helicopters 345–348
AH-64D Longbow helicopters 346, 348
AIM-9 Sidewinder missiles 302–304, **343**
air-to-air missiles (AAMs) 302–304, **344**
aircraft
   A-10 Thunderbolt 334–337
   AV-8A 325, **326**
   B-17 Flying Fortress **222**, 242–245
   B-52 Stratofortress 287–290
   F-4 Phantom 305–308
   F-4G "Wild Weasel" 300, 306
   F-14B Tomcat **331**
   F-15 Eagle 341–344
   F-117 Nighthawk 349–352
   fighter tactics 262
   Focke-Wulf Fw 190 235, 262
   Fokker D VII 205–207
   Harrier 324–326
   Hurricanes **226**, 234
   ME 262 jet fighter 9, 267–269
   Messerschmitt Bf 109 235, 237
   Messerschmitt Bf 110 262
   MiG-21 316–319
   Mirage 318
   P-51 Mustang 260–263
   RQ-4A Global Hawk **374**, **375**, 376
   seaplanes **166**
   Skyhawk 326
   Sopwith Camel 201–204
   Spitfire 234–237
   stealth 349, 350, 352

   UAVs 374–377
   WWII production statistics 7
aircraft carriers 225–227, **324**, 330–333
airships: Zeppelins 183–186
AK47 rifles 10, 280–283
Alexander the Great 27, 43
   Companion Cavalry 75
American Civil War (1861–65)
   artillery 132
   howitzers **113**
   ironclads 156–159, **156**, **158**
   land mines 208
   naval mines 141
   railways' role 11
   rifles **130**
   sabers **102**
   submarines 136–138
American Revolutionary War (1775–83)
   91, **92**, 121
ammunition *see* munitions
AMRAAMs *see* Advanced Medium-Range
   Air-to-Air Missiles
anti-ship missiles (ASMs) 327–329
anti-tank missiles 359
Antonyan, Sergeant Karen **311**
APCs *see* armored personnel carriers
Arbedo, battle of (1422) 62
archery *see* bows
Ardennes offensive (1944–45) 253, **265**
Argus, HMS 225, **226**
armor, body
   hoplites 43
   plate 53, 58, **95**
Armor-Piercing Fin-Stabilized Discarding-
   Sabot Tracers (APFSDS-Ts) 355
armored personnel carriers (APCs): M2/M3
   Bradley 357–359
Armstrong, William 145
arquebuses **62**, **86**, 87
Arrow anti-ballistic missile system **314**

artillery
   early cannons 82–84
   howitzers 111–113
   Flak 18 228, 230
   Flak 88 228–230
   French 75mm M1897 145–147
   light field 108–110
   mortars 198–200
   recoil control systems 145
   Roman bolt 31–33
   ship guns 114–117, 169–170
   see also munitions; sights and sighting
Ashubanipal, king of Assyria **17**
ASMs *see* anti-ship missiles
assault rifles 280–283
Assyrians **17**, 30
Atlantic Conveyor (container ship) 329
atomic bombs 274–277
Augeza, Captain Baron A. Odkolek von 190
AV-8A aircraft 325, **326**
axes
   Dane 54–56
   flint 14–16

B-17 Flying Fortresses **222**, 242–245
B-52 Stratofortresses 287–290
Badajoz, second siege of (1812) 112
Baker rifles 120–122
ballistae 31–32, **32**, **33**
ballistic missiles 371–373
Bang, Soren H. 231
Bannockburn, battle of (1314) 61, **63**
Bar-Lev, General Chaim **284**
Barham, HMS 241
Battle Standard of Ur **21**
Bayeux Tapestry 54, **55**, 56, 77
bayonets 7, 104–107
bazookas 254–256
Beatty, Vice Admiral Sir David 171
Belgrade, siege of (1717) 111

BGM-109 Tomahawk missiles 360–363
"Big Bertha" 113, **113**
Bikini Atoll **277**
bills 57
Birmingham, USS 225
Bishop, Chris 348
Bismarck 170, 172
Black Hawk Down incident (1993) 322
black powder 79
Blenheim, battle of (1704) 110
Blisset, Lieutenant-Commander Mike 326
Blowpipe MANPADs 365, 366
Boer Wars *see* Second Anglo-Boer War
Bon Homme Richard, USS **326**
Borthwick, Captain Alastair 266
Botha, Louis **150**
Boudicca, queen of the Iceni **23**
bows 17–19
        crossbows 72–74
        English longbows 68–71
Brandy Station, battle of (1863) **102**
Brasier, John 271
Britain
        Norman Conquest 54, **55**, 56
        Roman invasion and occupation 22, **23**
Britain, Battle of (1940) 234–235, **234**, 237
Brown Besses **93**
"Brown Water" war, Mekong Delta **294**
Browning, John Moses 152–153, 190,
        222–224, **222**
Browning M2HB machine-guns 222–224
Brunanburh, battle of (9th century) **56**
bushido 100
Bushnell, David 136, 139
Byzantines 48, **48–49**

Caesar, Julius 22
Caffie, Private Leon **311**
Cambrai, battle of (1917) 181, **182**
cannons, early 82–84
Cape Gloucester **231**
carbines **107**, 150
carpet bombing 288–290
Carrier Strike Groups (CVSGs) 333
carroballistae 33
Carson, Major Leonard "Kit" **263**
Cely, 2nd Lieutenant William: aircraft **244**
Challenger MBTs 10
chariots **17**, 20–23
Charles V, Holy Roman Emperor 87
Charles the Bold, duke of Burgundy 60
chemical weapons 194–197
Chinese rockets 79–81
Chivers, C.J. 281

chokutos 97
Christie, J. Walter 246
Churchill, Winston 238
Cohen, Samuel T. 7
Colbert, General Auguste-Marie-François
        121
Collier, Elisha 127
Colt, Samuel 11, 126, **126**, 127–128, 140
Colt M1911 pistols 151–154
Colt Navy 1851 revolvers 126–128
Conn, HMS **240**
Conqueror, HMS 292
Constantinople, fall of (1453) 83, **84**
Coombes, Flight Sub-Lieutenant Lawrence
        203
Cordelia, HMS 168
cordite 144
Corunna, retreat from (1808–09) **121**
Crécy, battle of (1346) **69**, **75**
Crimean War (1854–56) 140
crossbows 72–74
cruise missiles 360–363
Crusades 47, **65**
Cuban Missile Crisis (1962) 371
CVSGs *see* Carrier Strike Groups

daggers **60**, 98
Dane axe 54–56
Degelow, Carl 207
depleted-uranium ammunition 355
depth charges 214–217
Devastation, HMS 159
Diodorus 28, 30
Draeger, Captain Rhory R. 344
Dreadnought, HMS 170, **170**
Dreadnoughts 169–172
Dreyse, Johann Nikolaus von **123**, 124
Dreyse Needle-Gun 123–125
duels 96
Dupuy de Lome, Charles Henri 155
Dzerzhinskiy (Soviet cruiser) **299**

Eagle, HMS 225, 227
Edward I, king of England 67
Edward III, king of England **50**
Egypt: Hyksos invasion (1720 BC) 7, 19, 21
Egyptian weapons
        bows 19
        chariots **20**, 21, **22**, 23
        swords 24, **25**
Einstein, Albert 274
El Alamein, battle (1942) **228**
Enfield Pattern 1853 rifles 129–131
Enola Gay 275, **277**

Enterprise, USS 227, 330–331, **331**
Epimachus of Athens 28, 29, 30
Eskimo, HMS 217
estocs 94
Evreux, capture of (1487) **59**
Exocet missiles 327–329
explosive shells 142–144

F-4 Phantoms 305–308
F-4G "Wild Weasels" 300, 306
F-14B Tomcats **331**
F-15 Eagles 341–344
F-117 Nighthawks 349–352
Falklands War (1982) 104, 292, 303, 325,
        326, 328–329, 365
Farmer, George 103
Ferrar, Sergeant John **260**
Fiedler, Richard 176
FIM-92 Stinger SAMs 364–366
fire arrows 79–80
fire lances 81
Flak 88 guns 228–230
flamethrowers 46–49, 176–178
Flemish warriors 61
flintlocks 9, 90–93, 104, 129
Florida, USS **362**
Fly, Eugene 225
Focke-Wulf Fw 190 235, 262
Fokker, Anthony 201
Fokker D VIIs 205–207
Ford, Henry 11
Forsyth, Reverend Alexander John 129
Franco-Prussian War (1870–71) 134
François I, king of France: tomb **58**
Franks 75, 77
Fraser, Sergeant James 229
Fraser, General Simon 92, 121
Frederick the Great, king of Prussia 110
Fulton, Robert 139
fuses 144
FV432 **357**

Gal, Lieutenant Uziel 284
Galland, Adolf 244
galleys *see* triremes
Gamala **32**
Garand, John C. 231
Garros, Roland 201
gas 194–198
Gatling, Richard Jordan 135
Gatling guns 132–135
GAU-8/A Avenger 30mm Cannon 335
Gaza, siege of (332 BC) **27**
GBU-38 JDAMs **350**

General Belgrano, ARA, sinking of 292

Gentile, Captain Don **260**

George V, king of Great Britain and Ireland **180**

George Washington, USS **226**, 331

George Washington class submarines 292

Gerges, Captain Mark 356

gladiators **38**

gladius 38–40

glaives 57, **60**

La Gloire 155–156

Gobyato, Lieutenant-General Leonid Nikolaevich 198

Goddard, Dr Robert 254

Golan Heights **320**

Golden Spurs, battle of (1302) 61

Grandson, battle of (1476) 62

Greek Fire 46–49, **64**

Greek weapons

    dory spears 41–43

    triremes 34, **34**, 36, **37**

grenades

    hand 162–165, **194**

    rocket-propelled 320–323

Gribeauval, Jean-Baptiste de 110

Groves, Colonel Leslie R. 274

Guards Chapel incident (1944) 272

Gulf War (1991)

    aircraft **287**, **303**, 308, 326, 337, 341, 344, 351

    aircraft carriers 333

    APCs **357**, 358

    carpet bombing 289

    helicopters 346, **348**

    missiles 304, **314**, 315, 363

    PGMs 339

    tanks 353–354, **353**

    US dominance 10

gunpowder 84

guns

    on aircraft 267

    cartridge guns 123–124

    Dreyse Needle-Gun 123–125

    handgonnes **82**, 85

    lever-action 150

    see also machine-guns; muskets; pistols; rifles

guns/launchers 10

Gurevich, Mikhail I. 316

Gustavus Adolphus, king of Sweden 108–109, **110**

halberds 57–60

hammers 57–58

Hampton Roads, battle of (1862) 156–159, **156**, **158**

hand grenades 162–165, **194**

handgonnes **82**, 85

Harrier jets 324–326

Harrison, John 115

Harry S. Truman, USS **338**

Hastings, battle of (1066) 54, **55**, 56

HEAT missiles *see* high-explosive anti-tank (HEAT) missiles

Heldmann, Lieutenant D.R. Aloys: aircraft **206**

Helepolis **28**, **29**, 30

helicopters

    AH-64 Apache 345–348

    AH-64D Longbow 346, 348

    UH-1 Huey 294–297

Henry VIII, king of England 71, 77

    armor **95**

Henschel Hs 293 missiles 327

high-explosive anti-tank (HEAT) missiles 320

Hiroshima bombing (1945) 275, 277

Hitler, Adolf 251, 267, 270

Hittites **22**

Homer 26

Hood, HMS 170

hoplites

    phalanx formations 43

    weapons 41–43

Horne, Lieutenant-Colonel Barry E. 351

Housatonic, USS 137–138, **138**

howitzers 111–113

Huber, Johann 248

Hughes, Flight Officer Paterson: aircraft **236**

Hundred Years' War (1337–1453) **69**, **70**, 71, **75**, **83**

Hunley, CSS 136–138

Hurricane Katrina 333

Hurricanes **226**, 234

Hussite Wars (1419–34) 111–112

ICBMs *see* intercontinental ballistic missiles

improvised explosive devices (IEDs) 8, 356, 367–370

incendiary weapons 46–49, **64**, 81, 176–178

Independence, USS 227

Indian Mutiny (1857) **131**

Indonesia **280**

Innocent II, Pope 74

intercontinental ballistic missiles (ICBMs) 9, 371–373

    interceptors **373**

Invincible, HMS **172**

IRA 368, 370

Iran–Iraq War (1980–88) 308, 315, 329

Iraq War and insurgency 7, 8, 107, **282**

ironclads 155–159

Israeli Air Force **317**, 318

Israeli soldiers **284**, **286**

Jacobi, Moritz 140

Jäger rifles 120–121

James, Alan 283

Jean de Joinville 49

Joint Direct Attack Munitions (JDAMs) **338**, 339–340, **340**, **350**

Jutland, battle of (1916) 171, **172**

K-14 gunsights **262**

Kadesh, battle of (1274 BC) **22**, 23

Kai-fung-fun, battle of (1232) 80, **80**

Kalashnikov, Mikhail 281, 283

Kallanicus 46

katanas 97–100

Kentucky/Pennsylvania rifles 120–121

Kilij 101

King, 2nd Lieutenant Cecil F. **204**

Kiszely, Major John 104

Kluck, General von 174

Knightsbridge Box 229

Königgrätz, battle of (1866) **125**

Korean War (1950–53) 316

Kosovo War (1999) 350, 352, 363

Kozhedub, Ivan 269

Kriegsmarine: recruitment poster **241**

Krupp, Alfred 145

Krupp, Gustav 113

Kubinka Museum of Tank Construction 7

Kursk, battle of (1943) 249, **253**

Kurz cartridges 281

Kusunoki Masatsura **100**

Lachance, Mark 369

Lachish, siege of (701 BC) 46

Ladysmith, siege of (1899–1900) **112**

Lafayette class submarines 292

lances **63**, 75–78

land mines 210–213

Landsknecht 62

Langdon, Jesse D. 134

laser-guided weapons 338–339

Laumann, Joseph 151

Lawrence, T.E. (Lawrence of Arabia): rifle **175**

Le Marchant, John Gaspard 103

Lee, James Paris 173

Lee-Enfield short magazine rifles 107, 173–175

Lefaucheaux, Casimir 124
Leonardo da Vinci: inventions **73**
Lepanto, battle of (1571) 36
Lewis, Colonel Isaac 191, 193
Lewis guns 190–193
Lillie, Sir James 132
"Linebacker" raids (1972) 289
London
    V-1 damage **271**, 272
    Zeppelin damage **185**
longbows **60**, 68–71, 94
longswords 50–53
Loos, battle of (1915) 194–195
Los Angeles class submarines 292
Lusitania, RMS 168

M1 Abrams tanks 10, 353–356
M1 Garand rifles 231–233
M2/M3 Bradley APCs 357–359
M2 flash-hiders **233**
M3 "Grease Guns" **258**, 259
M16 rifles 309–312
M81E1 152mm gun/launcher system 10
M84 sights **233**
M551 Sheridan Armored Reconnaissance/
    Airborne Assault Vehicle 10
McLean, Samuel 191
Macgregor, Flight Sub-Lieutenant Norman:
    aircraft **202**
machine-guns
    on aircraft 201–202, **201**, 245
    Browning M2HB 222–224
    gas-operated 190–191
    Gatling guns 132–135
    invention 9
    Lewis guns 190–193
    MG15 264
    MG34 264–265, **264**
    MG42 264–266
    MP40 submachine 257–259
    Thompson submachine 218–221
    PPSh-41 submachine 259
    Uzi submachine 284–86
    Vickers Maxim 187–189
Magna Carta 74
main battle tanks (MBTs) 353–356
Malan, Adolph "Sailor" 237
Malplaquet, battle of (1709) **109**
Mannlicher, Ferdinand 151
MANPADs (man-portable air-defense
    systems) 364–366
Marignano, battle of (1515) **61**, 83–84
Marlborough, John Churchill, duke of
    109, 110, 112

Marne, first battle of the (1914) 146
Mary Rose 114
matchlocks 85–87, 90
Mauser, Peter Paul 150
Mauser C96 pistols **194**
Mauser Gewehr 98 rifles 148–150
Maxim, Hiram 9, **187**
MBTs *see* main battle tanks
ME 262 jet fighters 9, 267–269
Mesopotamians **18**
Messerschmitt Bf fighters 235, 237, 262
Metford, William 173
Mexico, US Punitive Expedition into **152**
MG15 machine-guns 264
MG34 machine-guns 264–265, **264**
MG42 machine-guns 264–266
Micro-Uzi 286
Midway, battle of (1942) 227
MiG-21 fighter aircraft 316–319
Mikoyan, Artem I. 316
Mills, William 163
mines
    land 210–213
    naval 139–141
Minié balls 130
mining 28
Minnesota, USS **158**
Mirage aircraft 318
missiles
    AIM-9 Sidewinder 302–304, **343**
    air-to-air 302–304, **344**
    anti-ship 327–329
    anti-tank 359
    BGM-109 Tomahawk 360–363
    cruise 360–363
    Exocet 327–329
    FIM-92 Stinger 364–366
    HEAT 320
    ICBMs 9, 371–373
    launched by B-52s 288
    Patriot 315, **315**
    R-11 **313**
    Redeye 364–365
    RIM-7 Sea Sparrow **333**
    SA-2 "Guideline" 298–301
    SA-7 "Grail" 364–365
    SCUD 9, 313–315
    surface-to-air 298–301, 364–366
    UUM-44 SubRoc **292**
    V-weapons 270–273
Mitchell, General Billy 226
Mitchell, R.J. 234
Mohammed II, Ottoman emperor 83
Mongols 80, **80**

Monitor, USS **155**, 156–159, **156**, **157**
Mons, battle of (1914) 174
Morat, battle of (1476) 62
Mordred **73**
mortars 198–200
MP40 submachine guns 257–259
MQ-9 Reaper UAVs 376
Mujahideen 323, 365, 366
munitions
    ammunition configurations 144
    explosive shells 142–144
    precision-guided 290, 338–340
Murphy, Audie 223
Musashi 172
muskets
    arquebuses **62**, **86**, 87
    bayonets 104–107
    Brown Besses **93**
    flintlocks 9, 90–93, 104, 129
    matchlocks 85–87, 90
    snaphance lock 91–92
    wheellocks 90

Nagasaki bombing (1945) 275, **276**
Nagashino, battle of (1575) 87
Nancy, battle of (1477) 60, 62
Napoleon Bonaparte 7
Naram-Sin, king of Mesopotamia 18
Nautilus, USS 291–293
navigation 115
neutron bombs 7
New York City **243**
Nimitz, USS 330–333
Nobel, Alfred 142, 144
Normans 54, **55**, 56, 77
Northrop B-2 Spirit bombers 350, 352
nuclear-powered aircraft carriers 330–333
nuclear-powered submarines 291–293
nuclear weapons 7, 274–277

Oda Nobunaga 87
Okinawa, battle for (1945) **220**, **224**
Operation *Allied Force* 340, 363, 375
Operation *Anaconda* 375
Operation *Bodenplatte* 268
Operation *Desert Shield* **375**
Operation *Desert Storm see* Gulf War
Operation *Eagle Claw* **296**
Operation *Iraqi Freedom* **326**, 333, 337,
    347, 350, **360**, 363
Operation *Just Cause* 349
Operation *Southern Watch* 333
Ottomans 83, **84**, 101
Owen, Wilfred 197

P-51 Mustangs 260–263
Panama 349
Panzerfaust 256, **256**
Parthian horse-archers **19**
partisans 57
Pathfinder, HMS 166
Patriot missiles 315, **315**
Pauly, Johannes 122–123
Paveway II laser-guided bombs **325**
Pavia, battle of (1525) 62, **86**, 87
Payne, Oscar 221
Pearl Harbor attack (1941) 226
Peninsular War (1808–14) 103, 112, **121**
percussion systems 129–130
Pershing, General John 222
Pétain, Marshal 147
Petropavlovsk **140**, 141
PGMs *see* precision-guided munitions
Philippine Insurrection (1899–1902) 153
Phoenicians 34, **35**
pikes 11, 61–63
pistols
    Colt M1911 151–154
    Colt Navy 1851 126–128
    Mauser C96 **194**
    revolvers vs. automatics 153
Platz, Reinhold 205, 206
Pleasanton, General Alfred 102
Plunkett, Thomas **121**
poison gas 194–198
pole-arms 57–60
    see also lances; pikes
polybolos 33
Popular Front for the Liberation of Palestine
    283
Port Arthur **140**, 141
Powers, Gary 299
PPSh-41 submachine-guns 259
Preble, USS **361**
precision-guided munitions (PGMs)
    338–340
Predator UAVs 374–375, **376**
Prussian Army 125
Puckle, James 132

Qadesh relief **20**

R-11 missiles **313**
railways 11
rapiers 94–96
Reagan, Ronald 7
"Red Sams" **299**, **300**
Reddemann, Bernhard 176
Redeye missiles 364–365

Regensburg, raids against (1943) 245
Resolution class submarines 292
revolvers *see* pistols
Rhodes, siege of (305 BC) **28**, **29**, 30
Rhodesian bush war 283
Richthofen, Manfred von 205
rifles
    AK47 10, 280–283
    assault 280–283, 309–12
    Baker 120–122
    Dreyse Needle-Gun 123–125
    Enfield Pattern 1853 129–131
    Jäger 120–121
    Kentucky/Pennsylvania 120–121
    Lee-Enfield short magazine 107, 173–175
    M1 Garand 231–233
    M16 309–312
    Mauser Gewehr 98 148–150
    Winchester 150
    see also carbines
rifling 92
RIM-7 Sea Sparrow missiles **333**
rocket launchers 254–256
rocket-propelled grenades 320–323
rockets
    Chinese 79–81
    V-weapons 10, 270–273
Roman legionary attack formations **39**, 40
Roman weapons
    artillery 31–33
    chariots **21**
    gladius 38–40
    siege towers **30**
    triremes 36, **36–37**
Rome: Circus Maximus **21**
Roosevelt, Franklin D. 274
Rough Riders **134**
Royal Oak, HMS **169**, **171**
Rozhdestvenski, Admiral Zinovi 159
RPG-7 grenades 320–323
RQ-4A Global Hawks **374**, **375**, 376
Ruhrstahl/Kramer X-1 ("Fritz-X") missiles 327
Russo-Japanese War (1904–05) 140, 141,
    159, 169, 198
Ryskind, Sam 289

SA-2 "Guideline" missiles 298–301
SA-7 "Grail" missiles 364–365
sabers 101–103
Saddam Hussein 315
saddles 75
Salamis, battle of (480 BC) 36
SAMs *see* surface-to-air missiles
samurai 87, 97–100

San Juan Hill, battle of (1898) **134**, 135
Saracens **47**, **48–49**
Sargent, John Singer: paintings by **196–197**
sarissa spears 43
Saulnier, Raymond 201
Schall, Hauptmann Franz 268
Scheer, Vizeadmiral Reinhard 171
Schilling, Pavel 140
schiltrons 61
Schmidt, Heinrich 241
Schweinfurt: raids against (1943) 245
Schwieger, Kapitänleutnant Walther 168
scorpio **31**
Scottish warriors 61, **63**
SCUD missiles 9, 313–315
Second Anglo-Boer War (1899–1902)
    112, **132**, **150**
shamshir 101
shaskas **101**, 103
Sheffield, HMS 328, **328**
shields 43, 53
Shijo-Nawate, battle of (1348) **100**
ships *see* warships
Shpagin, Georgi 259
siege weapons
    Greek Fire **48**, **49**
    Roman 31–33
    siege towers 27–30
    trebuchets 64–67
sights and sighting 146, **233**, **262**
Six-Day War (1967) 286, 318, 319, 322
Skinner, Captain Leslie 254
Skyhawks 326
smallswords 96
Smith, Sir Sidney 7
Somme, battle of the (1916) **164**, 165, 180,
    187, **187**, **195**
Somme, second battle of the (1918) **191**
Sopwith Camels 201–204
Sovereign of the Seas 114–115
Soviet Union: German invasion (1941)
    246, 247–248
Spanish–American War (1898) **134**, 135
Spanish Civil War (1936–39) 228
spears 14, **20**, **21**, **22**, 41–43
Spitfires 234–237
Spray of Blood on Kojinyama (1866) **98**
Spring Offensive (1918) **192**
Spurs, battle of (1513) **77**
Sri Lankan special forces 286
Stark, USS **329**
Starling, HMS **216**
stealth bombers 350, 352
stealth fighters 349

Stirling Castle, siege of (1304) 67
stirrups 75
Stokes, Wilfred 199
Stoner, Eugene 309
Strasser, Korvettenkapitän Peter 184
Stryker combat vehicles **367**
Stuart, General J.E.B. 102
Sturmgewehr MP44 rifles 281
submachine-guns *see* machine-guns
submarines
    ballistic missiles 373
    depth charges 214–217
    Hunley, CSS 136–138
    Nautilus, USS 291–293
    Type VII U-boats 238–241
Suez campaign (1956) 286
Sumerians **21**
surface-to-air missiles (SAMs) 298–301,
    364–366
SWAT teams 286
Swiss warriors **61**, 62
swords
    arming swords 53
    Bronze Age 24–26
    chokutos 97
    gladius 38–40
    hoplites 41
    katanas 97–100
    longswords 50–53, **60**, 94
    rapiers 94–96
    sabers 101–103
    smallswords 96
    wakizashis 99–100
Szilard, Leo 274

T-34 tanks 7, 11, 246–249
Takeda Katsuyori 87
talwar 101, **103**
tanks
    Challenger MBTs 10
    M1 Abrams 10, 353–356
    M551 Sheridan 10
    MBTs 353–356
    Mk I/IV 179–182
    T-34 7, 11, 246–249
    Tiger I 250–253
tantos 98
Tel Aviv **314**
TEL vehicles *see* transporter, erector,
    launcher (TEL) vehicles
Teller, Edward 274
Theodore Roosevelt, USS **332**, **333**
The Thin Red Line (painting) **131**
Thirty Years' War (1618–48) 108–109

Thompson, John T. 218–220
Thompson submachine-guns 218–221
Tiesenhausen, Hans-Dietrich von 241
Tiger I tanks 250–253
Titan I ICBMs **372**
Togo, Heihachiro 159
Topol-M ICBMs **372**
Torgau, battle of (1760) 110
torpedoes 166–168, **238**
tournaments **58**, **76**
TOW (Tube-launched, Optically tracked,
    Wire-guided) anti-tank missiles 359
Trabanten Guard: weapons **57**
Trafalgar, battle of (1805) **116**
transporter, erector, launcher (TEL) vehicles
    314, 315
trebuchets 64–67
triremes 34–37
Trollope, Captain John L. **204**
Tsushima, battle of (1905) 159
Turtle 136

U-boats *see* submarines
Udet, Lieutenant Ernst **207**
UH-1 Huey helicopters 294–297
Uhl, Lieutenant David E. 254
unmanned aerial vehicles (UAVs) 374–377
Unwin, Flight Sergeant George 235, 237
Urban (gunmaker) 83, 84
US Marines **151**, **232**
US Navy: recruitment posters **167**, **217**
UUM-44 SubRoc missiles **292**
Uzi submachine-guns 284–86

V-weapons 270–273
Valencia, bombardment of (1288) 80–81
Verdun, battle of (1916) 147
Vickers Maxim machine-guns 187–189
Vicksburg, passage of (1863) **158**
Victory, HMS **116**, **117**
Vielle, Paul 143–144
Vietnam War (1954–75)
    aircraft 288–289, **288**, 308
    helicopters 294–297
    missiles 299–300, **302**
    PGMs 338–339
    rifles **281**, **309**, **312**
    RPGs 322–323
Vikings 50, 54–56
Virginia, CSS 156–159, **156**, **158**
Viscount, HMS **215**
Vitruvius Pollio, Marcus 29, 32, 33
Voigländer, Werner Ritter von 217
Vollmer, Heinrich 257

wakizashis 99–100
Walker, Captain Samuel 127
Walter de Milemete 82
war-hammers 57–58
War of the Cities 315
warships
    aircraft carriers 225–227
    depth charges 214–217
    Dreadnoughts 169–172
    ironclads 155–159
    ships of the line 114–117
    triremes 34–37
    see also submarines
Wheeler, Artemus 126–127
wheellocks 90
Whitehead, Robert 166
Wiesel, Elie 7–8
Wigner, Eugene 274
Wilkins, Alan 32
Wilson, Lieutenant W.G. 179
Winchester rifles 150
Winston Churchill, USS **360**
Wisconsin, USS **375**
Wolff, Oblt Kurt 202
World War I (1914–18)
    artillery **145**, **146**, 147, **147**
    bayonets **105**, 107
    "Big Bertha" 113, **113**
    couched-lance charges 78
    explosives **144**
    land mines 210
    naval mines 141
    weapons overview 160–207
World War II (1939–45)
    aircraft carriers 225
    cavalry charges **152**
    Dreadnoughts 170–172
    flamethrowers **178**
    hand grenades 165, **165**
    katana use 100
    LMGs 193
    naval mines 141
    weapons overview 208–277
Wreford-Brown, Chris 292

Yamato 172
Yom Kippur War (1973) 308, 315,
    319, **320**
Ypres, battle of (1915) **105**
Ypres, second battle of (1915) 194

Zeppelin, Count Ferdinand von
    184
Zeppelins 183–186